# FROM MOUNTAIN FASTNESS TO COASTAL KINGDOMS

Money is central to the functioning of economies, yet for the pre-modern period, our knowledge of monetary systems is still evolving. Until recently, historians of the medieval world have conflated the use of coins with a high degree of monetization. States without coinage were considered under-monetized. It is becoming more evident, however, that some medieval states used money in complex ways without using coinage. Moneys of account supplanted coins wholly or in part. But there is an imbalance of evidence: coins survive physically, while intangible forms of money leave little trace. This has skewed our understanding.

Since coin usage has been well studied in the past, these essays flesh out our consideration of societies that used money but struck no coins. Absence or shortage of coining metals was not the causative factor: some of these societies had access to metal supplies but still remained coinless. Was this a strategic choice? Does it reflect the unique system of governance that developed in each kingdom?

It is surely time to unravel this puzzle. This book examines money use in the Bay of Bengal world, using the case of medieval Bengal as a fulcrum. Situated between mountains and the sea, this region had simultaneous access to both overland and maritime trade routes.

How did such 'cashless' economies function internally, within their regions and in the broader Indian Ocean context? This volume brings together the thoughts of a range of upcoming scholars (and a sprinkling of their elders), on these and related issues.

**John Deyell** is an independent researcher originally from the University of Wisconsin, Madison. A former visiting Professor at the Centre for Historical Studies, Jawaharlal Nehru University, New Delhi, he writes on the pre-modern monetary systems of the Indian Ocean world.

**Rila Mukherjee** is Professor in the Department of History, School of Social Science, University of Hyderabad. A former Director of the Institut de Chandernagor, she is currently Chief Editor of the *Asian Review of World Histories*, and Series Editor of Cambridge's *Pasts and Futures*.

# From Mountain Fastness to Coastal Kingdoms

*Hard Money and 'Cashless' Economies in the Medieval Bay of Bengal World*

*Edited by*
JOHN DEYELL
RILA MUKHERJEE

Routledge
Taylor & Francis Group
LONDON AND NEW YORK

MANOHAR
2019

First published 2020
by Routledge
4 Park Square, Milton Park, Abingdon, Oxon OX14 4RN
605 Third Avenue, New York, NY 10017

First issued in paperback 2023

*Routledge is an imprint of the Taylor & Francis Group, an informa business*



*British Library Cataloguing-in-Publication Data*
A catalogue record for this book is available from the British Library

*Library of Congress Cataloging-in-Publication Data*
A catalog record for this book has been requested

ISBN: 978-1-03-265426-3 (pbk)
ISBN: 978-0-367-41915-8 (hbk)
ISBN: 978-0-367-81688-9 (ebk)

DOI: 10.4324/9780367816889

Typeset in Minion Pro 11/13
by Ravi Shanker, Delhi 110 095

MANOHAR

*To*

NICHOLAS G. RHODES

(26 May 1946–7 July 2011)

# Contents

# Introduction

John Deyell and Rila Mukherjee

> Not everything that can be counted counts,
> and not everything that counts can be counted.[1]

This is the conundrum for economic historians of pre-modern Asia: some economies have used money in complex ways without using coinage, while others have used coinage while being virtually moneyless. And many states relied on monetary systems situated somewhere between these extremes, using objects such as silk, cotton textiles, or even almonds as money. The literature often fails to make the distinction, since there is an imbalance of evidence: coins survive physically, while other forms of money tend to perish. This has skewed our understanding of these historical economies. Historians have conflated the use of coins with a high degree of monetization in the economy, and vice-versa, which may be called a kind of bullionist approach. It is surely time to unravel this puzzle, which may be more apparent than real, in order to bring clarity to the broader economic and social history of the medieval period.

This book will examine money use in the eastern Indian Ocean world, using the case of medieval Bengal as a fulcrum. Since coin usage has been well studied in the past, we hope to flesh out our understanding of societies that used money but struck no coins. Moreover, some of these societies had access to metal deposits but remained coinless. How did they function internally, within their regions and in the broader Indian Ocean context? This volume brings together the thoughts of a range of upcoming scholars (and a sprinkling of their elders), on these and related issues.

## Why Focus on Bengal?

Bengal was a nodal junction for both maritime and overland communications routes. Its key position at the apex of the Bay has often been highlighted by geographers and historians. Being the point of origin of many agricultural and manufactured products, since ancient times it was also the transit entrepôt for the movement of goods, people, and ideas between the Gangetic plains, the Tibetan plateau, coastal kingdoms and sea-borne destinations alike. Situated at the cultural meeting-point of the Indian subcontinent, Central Asia and Southeast Asia, Bengal's influence was felt far beyond its political boundaries. Examining this geographic and cultural landscape in detail, Rila Mukherjee shows that the physical realities of the Bay of Bengal played a large part in setting the stage for the economic and historical dramas of the medieval South and Southeast Asian world. She also highlights the ways in which the dynamics of rulership, administration, and exchange in this landscape responded to similar stimuli with similar 'cashless' approaches to economic governance.

The history of medieval Bengal falls into two fairly clear periods: the early medieval (defined as extending from Sasanka of Gauda, *c.* 600 CE, to Lakshmana Sena, *c.* 1200) and the later or high medieval (from Bakhtiyar Khalji, about 1200 to Daud Karrani, 1576). In the earlier epoch, the economy relied on moneys of account supplemented by cowry shells. In the later era, silver coinage gradually displaced the earlier system. The dramatic change of monetary systems between the two periods provides a challenging case study for the monetary historian.

Even in the medieval world, states and economies did not exist in a vacuum. Commercial interaction with neighbours was unavoidable, especially when, as in Bengal, a kingdom lacked indigenous metal resources. Contacts further afield, both overland and maritime, were also much in evidence. Exchanges were often commercial in nature, but did not preclude religious, cultural, and diplomatic activities making use of trade caravans pulled by pack animals and ships steered by experienced navigators.

## Bengal in the Broader Context

The early medieval era was one of political consolidation, when erstwhile provinces of the former Gupta empire (corresponding to modern Bihar, West Bengal and western Bangladesh), were brought under Pala rule. It was a period of expansion of the cultivated frontier, when communities of settlers slowly tamed the great jungle-covered delta known as Vanga. It was also a period of great cultural change: Buddhism revived under royal patronage, and both Buddhism and Hinduism absorbed indigenous tantric practices. It was a dynamic period as reflected in Bengal's relations with its immediate neighbours and its more distant contacts. On its fluid western boundary, Pala Bengal bordered on the Gurjara-Pratihara realm; on its southwestern fringes it touched upon the margins of the Rashtrakuta kingdom. Over the generations, the rulers of these three proto-imperial systems competed for prestige, territory, and the allegiance of vassal kings and thrived on the trade between these empires.

On its east Pala Bengal bordered the kingdom of Harikela, which linked India with the Burmese and Buddhist lands beyond. Bengal's influence was felt throughout Southeast Asia, both via trade relations and because of the comings and goings of Buddhist pilgrims. Bengal's king Devapala was in correspondence with the Sailendra ruler of Java, Balaputradeva, undertaking arrangements on his behalf for the reception of Javanese monks at the great vihara of Nalanda. Other than maritime Buddhist circulations, it was about this time that the influence of the *Ramayana* reached its height in several Southeast Asian cultural realms, providing vivid testimony to the power of sea travel in this era. Shore temples from Somnath on the Kathiawad coast and Mamallpuram on the Tamil coast to Bali—functioning also as navigational landmarks—attest to these exchanges, which also involved a two-way flow of gifts and goods, and an exchange of money and monetary analogues.

Bengal was not the only coastal kingdom on the Bay of Bengal, as Radhika Seshan reminds us in her exploration of money use in the peninsula from Chola to Vijayanagara times. The Cholas' adroit use of religious prestige, naval power, and merchant guild commercial strength was parlayed into a period of tremendous influence throughout the eastern Indian Ocean, bringing it into alliance, and ultimately into conflict, with the empire of Srivijaya (Indonesia). The Cholas broadly relied on moneys of account in their taxation system and pattern of religious endowments. There existed in their realms, however, a range of coins, from small to large in value, that sometimes (but not always) provided the sinew for their monetary system. Seshan explores how an occasional resort to physical money under the Cholas transformed into a universal reliance on physical coinage under the successor Vijayanagara state.

Within Bengal itself, two manifestations of the Gupta gold *dinara* currency survive into the period of our study: Gupta-style gold coins (standing king/seated goddess) generally found in Radha (the tract of country along the southern course of the Ganges to Tamralipti/Saptagrama); and post-Gupta derivative gold coins of Sasanka of Gauda (Siva-Nandi/seated goddess) found generally in Varendra (northwest Bengal). Another tract in Bengal, Pundravardhana, appears to have used a different, and largely debased, gold coinage. As Suchandra Ghosh explains, to the east of Bengal the Samatata kingdom issued lighter, less pure gold coins from the Gupta period well into the seventh century. This was succeeded by the issue of silver coins by the Harikela kingdom. While these coins all show the influence of Bengal in design (imitating Kushan, Gupta, and Sasanka coins in succession), they have no pattern of dispersal west into Bengal. Neighbouring Arakan struck a silver coinage known as the early Chandra coinage. The likelihood is that Samatata/Harikela coinage did not circulate west of the Meghna River.

## Exploring Monetary Systems

Other than two unique ceremonial gold coins in the names of Dharmapala and Devapala respectively, there were no gold coin issues in Bengal from the eighth to the early thirteenth centuries. There were no silver coins of any kind issued by the Palas or Senas; epigraphic mention of silver *drammas* in the vicinity of Nalanda refer to the Pratihara *Sri Vi(gra)* coins of that denomination, found in hoards as far east as central Bihar. Not a single copper or other base metal coin attributable to the Palas or Senas has ever been recovered or identified.

It is possible that earlier Mauryan silver *karshapanas* and Gupta gold *dinaras* continued to circulate for centuries after their issue, but not likely as there are no hoards.

The issue of Bengal's monetary systems is more difficult of treatment. How did Pala Bengal function in the absence of a local coinage? It was a complex state, in which the administration was highly developed (as evidenced by the titles of officials listed in copperplate grants), where revenue was raised through a broad assessment on agricultural production, as well as through customs duties, cesses and tolls on commercial activity; where the government undertook expenditures on royalty, the aristocracy, military, navy and administration; where public works were financed; and where charitable and religious endowments and grants were made. Within this kingdom, surplus crops were harvested and goods were manufactured, to be bought and sold in markets. Luxury goods and special commodities were imported from afar. There was a significant trade in horses for the military and aristocracy. Elephants were imported and traded, often for military and work purposes. Further east, in Srihatta (Sylhet), there was a thriving trade in eunuchs east to China and west to the Abbassid domains. Many if not all these myriad transactions involved money, at the very least in the form of money of account. Money was present; but the coins were minted beyond areas under direct Pala administration.

Sayantani Pal reviews the inscriptions which record that some transactions were valued in a money of account called the *kapardika purana*. After some confusion of interpretation, it is now felt that this refers to a *value* or price of a *purana*, that is to say the ancient Mauryan silver *karshapana*, long out of circulation, which was to be *paid* or settled via the medium of cowries.

Cowries were imported into this region from the Maldives by private merchants who were also engaged in the export of rice. The trade of rice for cowries was profitable in both directions and thrived into the high medieval period.[2] The local use of cowries continued despite regular contact with regions that used metallic coins, such as the Gurjara realm and Harikela. In Orissa as well, the monetary system was based primarily on cowries, supplemented by sporadic local issues of gold coins. In fact, Orissa's reliance on cowries lasted well into the 1820s.[3] Bin Yang describes the influence of cowries from interior Yunnan into Chiang Mai; indeed it was the subject of a legal treatise of the medieval Thai kingdom. He finds that cowry values served as both money of account and a medium of exchange in mainland Southeast Asia.

Indeed, well into the colonial period, large tracts of Bengal and Orissa were known to rely exclusively on cowries as the physical medium of exchange at the village level. Can this be the whole story? Although a very efficient medium of exchange for the range of value most of the population would encounter in their daily lives, cowries were an awkward store of value; their bulkiness made them problematic for savings. However, if we are able to determine how broadly the money of account was used, we may solve this problem, since a money of account, if closely managed by accountants in the employ of government or business, can serve quite adequately as a store of value.

At this point, it is important to emphasize that Bengal did not lack coinage because of a dearth of precious metals (gold and silver), or indeed a lack of base metals (copper, lead or tin). M.N. Rajesh shows that Tibet was a conduit for silver to Bengal via Cooch Behar and other entrepôts. Bengal maintained maritime links with Pegu in Burma and Srivijaya in the Malay Straits which enabled it to maintain a relatively constant supply of silver bullion from inland sources in Yunnan and gold from the 'Suvarnadvipa' archipelago.[4] This bullion was not imported in the form of coinage, since contemporary Burma, Sumatra and Java relied on moneys of account, settled in gold or silver ingots or other commodities.[5]

The 'proof of the pudding' of course, was the establishment by the successor Bengal sultanate (*c.* 1200-1538) of a major silver coinage. Sutapa Sinha explores in some detail how the history of this later money has been painstakingly built through long careful examination of the coin hoards of Bengal. She shows that patterns of trade and revenue, both internal to the kingdom and with its neighbours, are revealed by a close examination of coin hoards.

The eventual success of this monetary transformation raises the question as to what had changed in Bengal to make such a change necessary or even desirable. It is beyond the scope of this volume to address this in detail, but recent literature suggests that the new, post-1200 regime, while maintaining revenue administration systems already in place, relied upon a large and growing class of civil and military immigrants who demanded payment in coinage.[6]

Land regimes such as Bengal were not alone in undergoing such transformations. Maritime trade underwent significant changes between the early and later medieval eras, moving from a single thin network of long-distance trade into more segmented circuits that progressively drew regional economies into oceanic circulations. K.N. Chaudhuri and Hermann Kulke discerned a 'trade revolution' in the eleventh-century Indian Ocean; Geoff Wade saw this happening even earlier, in the ninth-tenth centuries. How did traditional economies tap into oceanic circuits that linked the Persian Gulf/Red Sea region with China? John Deyell explores the contrast between the coin-using economies and the others, and traces the influence of the mercantile communities of the greater Indian Ocean world on both of these, through their accounting systems and payment preferences.

By the end of our period of study, the arrival of Portuguese empire-builders and New World silver signalled the end of the medieval economy and the commencement of the pre-modern world system. This brought to a firm close the era of co-existence of coin-using and 'cashless' economies in India and in Asia.[7]

## NOTES

1. William Bruce Cameron, *Informal Sociology: A Casual Introduction to Sociological Thinking*, New York: Random House, 1963, p. 13.
2. Ibn Battuta who visited the Maldive Islands after 1342, noted 'All transactions take place in this country by means of the cowrie. . . . They are sold to the inhabitants of Bengal for rice, because the cowries

are also current in Bengal', Mahdi Husain, tr., *The Rehla of Ibn Batuta*, Baroda: Oriental Institute, 1976, p. 201.

3. J. Heimann, 'Small Change and Ballast: Cowry Trade and Usage as an Example of India Ocean Economic History', *South Asia*, III-1, 1980, pp. 48-69, especially p. 57; H.U. Vogel, 'Cowry Trade and its Role in the Economy of Yunnan: From the Ninth to the Mid-seventeenth Century', part II, *Journal of the Economic and Social History of the Orient*, 36, 3, 1993, pp. 309-53, especially p. 342.
4. Pranab K. Chattopadhyay, 'In Search of Silver: Southeast Asian Sources for the Coinage of Bengal', in Gouriswar Bhattacharya et al. (eds.), *Kalhar: Studies in Art, Iconography, Architecture and Archaeology of India and Bangladesh,* Delhi: Kaveri Books, 2007, pp. 296-305. John S. Deyell, 'The China Connection: Problems of Silver Supply in Medieval Bengal', in *Precious Metals in the Later Medieval and Early Modern Worlds,* Durham: Carolina Academic Press, 1983, pp. 207-27, reprinted in Sanjay Subrahmanyam (ed.), *Money and the Market in India 1100-1700,* Delhi: Oxford University Press, 1994, pp. 112-36; John S. Deyell, 'Cowries and Coins: The Dual Monetary System of the Bengal Sultanate', *Indian Economic and Social History Review*, 47-1, Jan.-Mar. 2010, pp. 63-106, especially 'Sources of Silver', pp. 88-91; Bin Yang, 'The Bay of Bengal Connections to Yunnan', in Rila Mukherjee, ed., *Pelagic Passageways: The Northern Bay of Bengal Before Colonialism*, Delhi: Primus Books, 2011, pp. 317-42.
5. Kenneth Hall, 'Coinage Trade and Economy in Early South India and its Southeast Asian Neighbours', *Indian Economic and Social History Review*, 36-4, 1999, pp. 431-59, especially pp. 449-50.
6. Deyell, 'Cowries and Coins', p. 66.
7. But the issues of cashless economies by no means disappeared: see Oscar Gelderblom and Joost Jonker, 'Cashless Payments in the Early Modern Low Countries, 1500-1800', in R.J. van der Spek and Bas van Leuwen (eds.), *Money, Currency and Crisis: In Search of Trust, 2000 BC to AD 2000*, London, New York: Routledge, 2018, pp. 228-30.

## BIBLIOGRAPHY

Cameron, William Bruce, *Informal Sociology: A Casual Introduction to Sociological Thinking,* New York: Random House, 1963.

Chattopadhyay, Pranab K., 'In Search of Silver: Southeast Asian Sources for the Coinage of Bengal', in Gouriswar Bhattacharya et al. (eds.), *Kalhar – Studies in Art, Iconography, Architecture and Archaeology of India and Bangladesh,* Delhi: Kaveri Books, 2007, pp. 296-305.

Deyell, John S., 'The China Connection: Problems of Silver Supply in Medieval Bengal', in John F. Richards (ed.), *Precious Metals in the Later Medieval and Early Modern Worlds,* Durham: Carolina Academic Press, 1983, pp. 207-27, reprinted in Sanjay Subrahmanyam (ed.), *Money and the Market in India 1100-1700,* Delhi: Oxford University Press, 1994, pp. 112-36.

Deyell, John S., 'Cowries and Coins: The Dual Monetary System of the Bengal Sultanate', *Indian Economic and Social History Review*, 47-1, 2010, pp. 63-106.

Gelderblom, Oscar and Joost Jonker, 'Cashless Payments in the Early Modern Low Countries, 1500-1800', in R.J. van der Spek and Bas van Leuwen (eds.), *Money, Currency and Crisis: In Search of Trust, 2000* BC *to* AD *2000*, London, New York: Routledge, 2018, pp. 228-30.

Hall, Kenneth, 'Coinage Trade and Economy in Early South India and its Southeast Asian Neighbours', *Indian Economic and Social History Review*, 36-4, 1999, pp. 431-59.

Heimann, J., 'Small Change and Ballast: Cowry Trade and Usage as an Example of Indian Ocean Economic History', *South Asia*, III-1, 1980, pp. 48-69.

Husain, Mahdi, tr., *The Rehla of Ibn Batuta*, Baroda: Oriental Institute, 1976.

Yang, Bin, 'The Bay of Bengal Connections to Yunnan', in Rila Mukherjee, ed., *Pelagic Passageways: The Northern Bay of Bengal Before Colonialism*, Delhi: Primus Books, 2011, pp. 317-42.

Vogel, H.U., 'Cowry Trade and its Role in the Economy of Yunnan: From the Ninth to the Mid-seventeenth Century', part II, *Journal of the Economic and Social History of the Orient*, 36, 3, 1993, pp. 309-53.

1

# From Mountain Fastness to Coastal Kingdoms

## The Contours of the Medieval Bay of Bengal World

Rila Mukherjee

This volume deals with 'Bengal', 'South India', Tibet, Yunnan and Lan Na; these regions fall in the nation states of India, China, and Thailand, countries either fringing the Bay of Bengal or connecting to its uplands. Present political or geographic entities do not correspond to those with the same names that are covered in this volume; there was then no India, China or Thailand in the modern sense. The boundaries of these regions fluctuated according to cultural perceptions, conditioned by economic circumstances and determined through political exigency, being dynamic, not static spaces.

### Fuzzy Regions

From the thirteenth century onwards, the term 'Bangalah' meant eastern Bengal, corresponding to the territory of Bangladesh. Lakhnauti and Bangalah were two separate polities, integrated only in the fourteenth century into what we now call Bengal. Numerous subregions existed. From the sixth century onward a four-fold classification emerged: Vanga or lower Bengal between the Bhagirathi and the Padma-Meghna rivers; Varendra or present north Bengal in India, but also containing parts of Bangladesh;

Samatata formed of the trans-Meghna territories of the Comilla-Noakhali plain and the adjacent parts of hilly Tripura; and Harikela or the areas around Chittagong and the western part of coastal Arakan. The last two units are in Bangladesh. Other territorial units, in use earlier, were Anga, Suhma and Pundra referring to eastern Bihar, Jharkhand and northern West Bengal; northwestern Bangladesh and West Bengal; and northern Bangladesh and West Bengal, respectively.

Rarh or Radha seems to have been the oldest unit, mentioned in sixth century BC Jain texts, and comprising the present West Bengal. It was divided subsequently into north, south, east and west Rarh. The unit of Gauda, connoting a people, a region, a capital, and later an empire, was another amorphous unit, first mentioned in the third-century BC *Arthashastra*. The Haraha inscription, dated to 554, mentions the Maukhari ruler Ishanavarman defeating the Gaudas who lived near the sea. This was corroborated by Prabodhashiva's undated Gurgi inscription (*c.* eleventh century) describing the Lord of Gauda as being in the watery fort of the sea' (*jalanidhi jaladurggam Gauda rajo dhishete*). These two epigraphs reinforce the Gaudas, at least at one point of history, as a coastal people, but their empire may also have included Magadha in Bihar at an unspecified time in the late seventh-eighth centuries (as stated in Vakpati's *Gaudavaho*) perhaps with Pundravardhana also, as Kalhana's *Rajatarangini* records.

Early Bengal is now seen as an aggregate of four distinct subregions, determined largely by the prevalent hydrography: Pundravardhana (initially north Bengal, but subsequently embracing a very substantial area of early Bengal), Radha (largely to the west of the river Bhagirathi), Vanga (central deltaic Bengal, covering the present Dhaka-Vikrampur-Faridpur area in Bangladesh) and Samatata-Harikela (the southeastern-most part of Bangladesh to the east of the river Meghna, embracing Noakhali, Comilla and Chittagong and also parts of Tripura in India).

Not much is known of early Bengal's political history. It invariably centres around two polities, that of Sasanka (*c.* 600-25, if not up to 637) who first turned this region into a prominent eastern Indian entity by his hostilities with Bhaskaravarman of

Kamarupa and Harsha of Kannauj; and that of the Pala rulers, especially Dharmapala, Devapala, Mahendrapala and Mahipala I who are credited with transforming Bengal into an imperial power, a successful claimant of mastery over Kannauj vis-à-vis the Pratiharas and the Rashtrakutas. The coast is noticeably absent in this narrative.[1]

Geographic and cultural units in Bengal were dynamic; moreover, there is no sharp sea/river divide or a land/water separation, Lieberman arguing that South Asia's jagged coast and fragmented internal geography sustained a marked level of polycentrism.[2] There may have been a totally different geographic perspective whereby other coasts were closer and more familiar, either in terms of distance or in terms of circuit/trail/network.[3] Moreover, the distinctiveness of the Bengal coast lies in its funnel-like shape with its wider mouth fronting the coast—the only *asamudrahimacala* region (from the mountains to the sea) in land-locked north India. Numerous rivers here draw the uplands into its ambit.

This vision helps in redrawing the regional geography, enabling us to retrieve the new frames or paradigms with deep consequences for the overall conception of nature, environment and the cultural *milieu.* Snake/dragon legends, particularly in the foundation myths of Kathmandu in Nepal and Kunming in Yunnan point to long-standing regional associations, often centred around a waterscape. The Manjusri legend, probably transmitted from China via Khotan around the first century, saw Manjusri founding Swayambhunath in Kathmandu in the early seventh century; he apparently cleared a lake infested with *nagas*, established a Chinese style governance, and installed a Chinese king.[4] This king was renamed Dharmakara and was succeeded by Dharmapala from India, thereby reconciling Chinese and Indian influences.[5] The *Nan Zhao t'u-chuan* and other contemporary texts indicate that Buddhist authority was established around 649 with the shift of the capital from Dali to Kunming. Again a lake, menaced by a dragon, was cleared. The declaration of Kunming as the eastern capital in 880 and the changeover from the Chinese era to the Sanskrit Jaya era in 889 CE confirms a move away from China and toward India.[6]

Connectivities facilitated other associations. Tibet and Nepal forged a matrimonial alliance in the seventh century CE when Songtsen Gampo of Tibet married near Patan in the Kathmandu valley a Nepalese princess—Bhrikuti—and a Chinese princess.[7] A Nan Zhao ruler attempted marriage with a Tang princess in 881 but gained instead a K'un-lun queen, most likely a Srivijayan princess, from the Malay Peninsula.[8]

Further south, Rajendra Chola's attack of Bengal in 1024/5 in a campaign stretching all along the eastern sea-board from Coromandel to the Ganga delta is indicative of routes becoming integrated along the eastern sea board. The subsequent building of Gangaikondacholapuram shows the Chola desire to tap into the maritime linkages of these northern coasts. The *padinen-vishayam* of the Chola merchant guilds refers, in an inscription at Nagapattinam (about 1090) to 'eighteen countries', one of which was Vangam, or Bengal.[9] The Western Chalukyas, under the leadership of Vikramaditya some time prior to 1068 attacked Bengal, as did the Pandyas, successors to the Cholas, in 1265.[10] And *c.* 1290 Ganapati of Warangal passed through Bengal, claiming Gauda was his vassal.[11]

Nor was this integration restricted to the coastal tracts. A Kakatiya princess, possibly a daughter of Kakatiya Ganapati was given in marriage to crown prince Jayadityadeva of Nepal in the thirteenth century. This princess, named Viramadevi, was perhaps the sister of the famous Queen Rudrammadevi.[12]

Such alliances offer glimpses into the political world of the eastern Himalaya and highlight their interactions with Bay of Bengal economies, underscoring also the integration of the eastern seaboard with Himalayan economies. By the twelfth century, the administrative unit of Pundravardhanabhukti extended unto the Himalayan foothills while also moving south and incorporating parts of deltaic Bengal. This was a large unit, later called Mahasthan or Great Place. Its numerous waterways were important transport channels leading to Kamarupa, which in turn housed the traditional land and fluvial routes into Burma, Yunnan and China that Xuanzang used. Other units too displayed upstream-downstream linkages by reconfiguring their boundaries. Harikela, on the far side of the Ganga-Brahmaputra delta, moved upward by the thirteenth century to include landlocked Srihatta and Tripura, granting these two polities outlets to the Bay; in the case of Tripura this was through the fortified port of Meherkul or Loricoel.

What are we to make of this cultural confusion, seen in oscillating geographic units over time? This uncertainty was not, as supposed earlier, the hallmark of the medieval at least in the case of South Asia but of upheavals caused by regional integration following the breakdown of the 'classical age' from about the seventh century. This is the time that the contours of the region we call Bengal start taking shape.

Chola south India emerged later, about 985, but was spatially more coherent. There was no 'south India', but a cultural and physical area known as *tamilakam*. Its subregions grew from the localised *nadu* to the larger *periyanadu* by the thirteenth century, and then into the large *mandalams*, until the eighteenth century—Cholamandalam, Tondaimandalam, Pandimandalam, Kongumandalam and Karmandalam or Gangavadi—testifying to the immense circulation visible in the Tamil country.[13]

Mengrai's Lan Na kingdom, emerging in 1259 as a mandala of city-states and functioning as an economic hub connecting the Chao Praya, Salween, and Mekong basins, ultimately covered Chiang Mai, Chiang Rai, Chiang Saen, and northern Laos. Lan Na was a more restricted polity in terms of space and power than the subregional powers referenced in the volume, being a hinterland polity laying on the caravan route running from Yunnan to ports on the Andaman Sea and the Gulf of Thailand. It has been characterized as a cultural concept rather than a firmly connected political unit, consisting of a few large and many smaller *müang* (polities), 57 in number, connected via intricately knitted relationships with one another and with the capital. The tightness and stability of relationships depended on several factors: size of population, economic potential, geographical location, historical characteristics, and kinship relations of each individual *müang*.[14]

Lying within the Bagan cultural area for a while, and probably attacked by Kublai Khan as part of his offensive against Bagan, much of Lan Na's architecture and sculpture display Bagan's influence.[15] Actually, Lan Na shows several influences, being open to various networks of religion and war. Its early Buddhist images show the influence of Pala Bengal.[16] Its southward conquest of Lamphun (Haripunjaya) in the Ping river valley (1281 or perhaps 1292) brought Lan Na into the Mon cultural sphere, as Lamphun had been the northernmost frontier of Mon Dvaravati. The Bago expedition of 1289 and Mengrai's marriage with the Hamsavati princess Ussa brought the coast close. Lan Na's web of matrimonial ties and its commitment to a reformed Theravada Buddhism—a link with Ceylon is inferred from King Sen Mua Ma's bringing back to Chiang Mai the Ceylon Buddha *c.* 1380—ensured the kingdom lasted until the mid-sixteenth century when Portuguese arrival and the Ayutthaya-Ava contest tore it apart.[17]

Tibet and Yunnan seem left out of this game of fluctuating units. Yunnan is referenced as Nan Zhao and subsequently Dali, and continuously as Tarap or Tarup but we have little idea of its boundaries; we know only that Dali was perhaps smaller in extent than Nan Zhao. Evidence from the accounts of Tarup in the Burmese chronicles leads one to conclude that the territory of Tarup—denoting Mongols and not always a coherent polity—most likely corresponds to the region of Yunnan, at one time the autonomous polity of Nanzhao-Dali, next a polity which was directly governed by a Mongol-appointed administrator during the thirteenth and fourteenth centuries, and finally a tributary of Ming China in the fifteenth century'.[18]

## Polities

This period shows the slow centralization of some polities and the relatively flexible nature of their neighbours' polities, perhaps also states, but of a different nature with more fluid boundaries and less settled agrarian patterns. These latter, located mostly in India's northeast and also in Lan Na, evolved differently, but were nonetheless involved in the same commodity trade, participating in, and influencing actively, related economies. It is difficult to characterize such polities; this region—stretching from Bengal into Burma and northern Thailand-Laos—experienced different trajectories of state formation, political legitimation and monetization. Kulke saw state formation as a processual-integrative developmment; Frasch saw states as mandalas, Pala Bengal in his opinion showing no clear core; while Schnepel and Berkemer saw polities as 'little kingdoms'.[19] Lieberman envisioned change occurring in mostly in cycles, while Aung-Thwin perceived it occurring through spirals. The triad of time, change and linear evolution being irrelevant, growth cannot be analysed within a world systems framework of cores and peripheries here. An alternate vision of political economy linked to time and change is necessary, distinct from the conventional notion of a sequential progression from the pre-historic, classical/ancient, medieval to the modern.[20] Political organization occurred along segments, relatively centralized states and more flexible ones were closely interdependent and part of a larger unit. Was this larger unit more open-ended than the contemporary nation-state model? Were they 'protected rimlands', as Lieberman describes those polities conforming to Eurasian subcategories but lying on the margins of older civilizations?[21]

With so many rimlands, it is difficult to envisage a heartland for Bengal. Imaginary political geographies add to the confusion. The Senas called themselves kings of Gauda and Vanga, but the subsection *Desasraya* (*On Lands*) of the Sena royal anthology the *Saduktikarnamrta* points to an expanded territorial vision in its names of conquered dynasties—*Anga* (body/limb); *Kuntala* (lock of hair); *Cola* (blouse); and *Kanci* (both a major city of the Cola empire and a waist-girdle). Summarizing the political geographical imagination of the Sena kingdom, *Desasraya* claims the Senas conquered *Gauda* (North Bengal), *Kalinga* (Orissa), *Cedi* (Central India—perhaps referring to the kingdom of the Candellas), *Kamarupa* (Assam), and *Kasi* (Varanasi).[22]

## The Coast

The coast too comes into this vision. Chakravarti refers to the continuous river-deltas of the east coast of India: from the Ganga delta in the north to the deltas of the Vaigai and the Tamraparni in the deep south, intermediated by the deltas of the Mahanadi (Orissa), the Godavari, the Krishna (Andhra Pradesh) and the Kaveri (Tamil Nadu) where the deltas and the coastal tracts converge. These areas are fertile and support large agrarian settlements conducive to yielding the vital resources to the monarchical polities, essential to peninsular kingdoms that did not possess the vast agrarian tracts of the north Indian kingdoms. Political formations in the peninsula were oriented to control the *doabs* and deltas of important rivers. Moreover, the east coast deltas are dotted with ports participating in coastal and long-distance trade circuits. The navigability of many of these rivers in their respective deltas offers excellent fluvial networks between the sea-board and the interiors.[23]

The coast exerted a fascination for inland powers. Lieberman sees interior Southeast Asian polities, particularly those in Burma, Thailand, Java, Laos, Cambodia and Vietnam, making a push to their coasts to access maritime wealth but concedes that the movement was spatially and temporally inconsistent. Whitmore and Li, however, see a very firm coastal orientation in Dai Viet between the eleventh and twelfth centuries visible in increasing control over inland waterways, the establishment of royal outposts, the construction of Buddhist temples as centres of trade and the emergence of a coastal literati.[24] Wade too argued for rulers shifting their capitals from the interior towards the coast in an effort to control maritime trade and centralize patronage between 900 and 1300.[25] The coast saw increasing maritime trade and the interiors more bullion imports, as well as vigorous ties with southern China and south India. Unfortunately it also saw the introduction of new crops, disease, warfare, and arms.[26]

The northern and western sides of the Bay of Bengal seem to have experienced the coastal drive earlier, Mengrai's conquest of Lamphun with its links to coastal regions such as Thaton, are reminiscent of Aniruddha of Bagan's putative conquest of Thaton in 1057 CE. Mengrai's alliance with Bago in 1289 is even more indicative of inland Lan Na's drive toward the coast. Chakravarti sees an earlier 'pull' toward the coast in South Asia. Inscriptions of a local ruler before Sasanka—Gopachandra—

in sixth-century Bengal, show that he brought coherence to the entity known as Bengal. Gopachandra had briefly succeeded in politically integrating the different sub-regions of early Bengal: Vanga, Radha and Suhma/Dandabhukti—with the exception of Radha, regions blessed with rivers, rivulets and waterbodies. These fluvial communication networks are evident from the frequency of occurrence of names of rivers, streams, and rivulets on which stood boat-parking stations (*naubandha/naudanda*). Although the Vanga region was not exactly on the coast, administrative documents of the second half of the sixth century also recorded the presence of ship-building sites (*navataksheni*) and an awareness of the proximity of the region to the eastern sea (*praksamudra*) which becomes Vangasagara or the Sea of Vanga in a Sanskrit inscription of *c.* 971 CE.[27] While Arabs sailors called it Bahr Harkhand, a name possibly derived from Harikela, the name *Banggela hai* in a Jesuit-inspired Chinese map dated 1607 implied that the focal point remained *Vangasagara* for the Chinese.[28]

Further south, the middle Chola period of Rajaraja I (c. 1120) witnessed a remarkable expansion of Chola power from the core territory in the Kaveri basin and Kaveri delta to other intermediary zones like Tondaimandalam in the northern part of Tamilnadu and Pandyamandalam in the Tamraparni-Vaigai valleys and to peripheral zones like Kongudesa (western part of Tamilnadu bordering on Kerala) and Vengi (in the deltas of the Krishna and Godavari).[29] While the term *pattinam* distinguished 'ports' as those located primarily on sea coasts, 'ports' of the interior were further distinguished in Tamil epigraphy by the epithet *erivirapattinam*. The sea is dominant in tracing Chola-Srivijaya conflicts and in the Chola desire to establish a permanent foothold in the coastal districts of Song China.[30] The southern Bay was in Chinese perception a Chola sea; it was called the Chu-li-ye or Chu-lien coast, derived from the Tamil 'Cholamandalam'.[31]

Tibet and Yunnan were intimately connected with the Bay of Bengal economies by virtue of the horse and cowry trades, and Bengal functioned as a transhipment point. Other than evidence of Pala influence in its sculpture, upland Lan Na seems absent from these interactions.[32] Given this absence of a paramount power—

the distinctive feature of the classical age—how do we trace money use within such oscillating boundaries and fuzzy contours?

## Money

Sailing through the Bay of Bengal, the merchant Suleiman al-Tajir's account of *c.* 851 noted that despite possessing much gold and silver, Bengal's overseas trade was carried on through cowry or cypria moneta.[33] Subsequently, Minhaj Siraj in the thirteenth century, Ibn Battuta in the fourteenth, Ma Huan in the fifteenth and Tome Pires in the sixteenth centuries, travellers and diarists, noted the trajectory of cowry circulation in the Bay of Bengal.[34]

Yunnan was unarguably the epicentre of cowry usage; nevertheless silk was also a medium of exchange on many sectors of the Silk Route including Yunnan.[35] The kingdom of Nan Zhao used silk as money until the ninth century, but this practice, also prevalent in Chinese Central Asia, was gradually displaced by cowries when Chinese silk routes through Central Asia were threatened in the eighth century. This shows how political events impacted networks, and demonstrates the economy of landlocked Yunnan becoming integrated into that of the Bay of Bengal trading system.

Travelling in this landlocked region, Marco Polo remarked on three singular aspects of the region: a thriving trade in eunuchs *from* Bengal, a flourishing commerce in horses *into* Bengal, and an absence of coinage despite an abundance of gold and silver in nearby Yunnan and the Shan states.

There is an enigmatic absence of minted coinage everywhere, suggesting that large rice-based agricultural economies like the Palas, Bagan, and Khmers, all found the same monetary answer to their problem of economic organization: coinless, but by no means without currency. This was the period of powerful subregional economies in Southeast Asia, Coedès claiming that their rise usually correlated with a decline in Chinese centralized power: tenth-century Angkor; the return of Cham central power to the northern provinces; the vitality of Srivijaya; and the growth of the Khmer, Cham and Burmese kingdoms at the end of the eleventh century.[36] But these were essentially without coined money. The last Arakan coinage hoards date to the ninth-tenth centuries, as do coins from Mon sites; there were, for Gutman 'no local coins from the rest of mainland Southeast Asia after the fall of Funan and Dvaravati, their function being replaced by barter, cowry shells and standardized metal bars or lumps'.[37] Was political and economic destabilization the reason for the disappearance of coins at centres such as Bagan, Sukhotai and Angkor? Should we link an absence of coins with lack of monetization?

Evidently not. Transactions continued, rice, cereal, cloth and fairly standardized lumps of silver and gold serving as money. Lan Na paid salaries with rice, silver, cowries and attendants, although Mengrai claimed to Bagan in 1291 that he possessed an abundance of precious metals, stones, horses and elephants.[38] Despite lying in the metal corridor between South and mainland Southeast Asia, the Khen and Cachari polities have left few if any coins at all, so we have no idea of the media of circulation. The neighbouring Tripura and Ahom polities started minting coins only in the fifteenth-sixteenth centuries.

While earlier surplus wealth had been redistributed through leadership strategies to vassals, as in the case of the Pyu chiefs, these were now redistributed in Bagan through monastic and temple complexes. When repairing the monastery at Bodh Gaya in the twelfth century, although King Kyanzittha of Bagan accumulated funds through gold, silver and precious stones, there was no mention of a measure of value or a medium of exchange.[39] This changed in the next century, with rice, oil, copper and silver appearing as values. One eleventh-century inscription says Kyanzittha's wealth was 80 *koti*.[40] What precisely this quantity expressed is unknown. It may perhaps have been a weight of silver, and if so, one can speculate that metal had an exchange function in the early Bagan period.[41]

Iron seems more precious for the Bay economies in the long term. While travelling to India from Palembang, in 671, Yjing observed that iron (*loha*) was much in demand in the Nicobars (Lo-jen-kuo, Lanjabalus); ships going to and from Palembang stopped here to exchange iron against ambergris, bananas, coconuts, round chests of rattan and bamboo, and probably coir ropes to bind planks together.[42] In 1154 Srivijaya brought in iron from Sofala, probably for transhipment into China which always needed iron and other metals.[43] A drainage of metals from 1074 led to interdictions on coin export and attempts at paper money by the later Songs and by the Yuans.[44] In the fifteenth century King Tiloka of Lan Na extended his conquests into Sipsongpanna—a region rich in silver and iron ore mines. In 1479, after Tiloka had successfully repulsed a Vietnamese attack, the Chinese court granted him the title of pre-eminent ruler west of the Mekong River and asked for tribute in iron and gold. Significantly, Tiloka refused.[45]

## Upheavals in the Interior

Fra Mauro's *World Map* of 1450 had conceived of a unit of 'Bengala-Machin' wherein Bengal, Upper Burma and Laos were seen as one.[46] Ralph Fitch, travelling through north Bengal and Bhutan a century later, noted north Bengal's connectivities with Cambodia/ Laos through the various branches of the Southwest Silk Route: the first going to Burma and India, the second to Vietnam, and the third connecting Yunnan with Laos, Thailand, and Cambodia. All three routes were used by merchants, emissaries, and pilgrims. Routes were disturbed in the seventh century. The *Biographies of Eminent Monks* notes that before 644, some seven hundred monks used the Buddhist Route, and only six hundred or so used it between 645 and 988. After 1036 there is no mention of a western monk at the Chinese court.[47] The fortunes of the Tang-Sassanid silk trade through Yunnan Nepal and Bengal were linked to these routes until about 650. Gold coins in Samatata and Pundravardhana indicate trade with the uplands, a capillary route connecting the sea routes of the Bay of Bengal with the Nepal-Tibet route. Around mid-century this route collapsed, judging from decreasing coin hoards in Bengal.[48] The silk trade used the Nepal route, the silk probably imported from China by sea into Samatata, going upland to Harshavardhana's Pataliputra, Nepal, Tibet and Bukhara and thence transmitted to Sassanian Iran.[49] The Lichhavi kingdom of

Nepal fragmented by the ninth century, how routes were further impacted is not known.

The political turmoil in Chinese Central Asia and consequent diminishing metal supplies into Bengal had been offset by the Pyu who emerged around 638. Their central places became a significant source of silver for Bengal until the Pyu decline in 832. But Bagan, emerging in 849, diverted much of the silver away from the northern Bay of Bengal polities, as had Nan Zhao which had emerged in 729, and Bagan reputedly carried out an expedition against Nan Zhao to re-open the routes to China. Stargardt suggested that by blocking the Irrawaddy basin's overland links to China, tenth-century disorders in the Nanzhao region induced Bagan to tap the increasingly prosperous coast for commercial revenue.[50] According to Hall and Whitmore, the Chola raids reinforced the coastal orientation in the eleventh century, creating a power vacuum in the upper Malay peninsula which Bagan, Angkor, Sri Lanka, and the Malay rulers sought to fill.[51] In southern India between 900 and 1300, overseas demand encouraged new merchant associations and larger textile exports to the Mideast and Southeast Asia.[52] The Chinese traded directly with the Indian peninsula, the Tang Abbasid network bypassed Bengal.

The reorientation of the eastern sea board was reflected in confusion in the uplands. Nan Zhao declined by 902, the Dali kingdom appeared in 937, but was conquered by the Mongols in 1253. Bagan fell to the Mongols in 1287; others such as Kamarupa decayed in this century from Mongol onslaughts. New polities rose in Kamarupa's place between the eleventh and thirteenth centuries: the Cachari polity lasting the longest (1086-1830), Srihatta and the Ahom state. The Khen polity rose *c.* 1185 in the Tista-Karatoya belt. The Tripura state consolidated itself at this time, while polities such as Udessa and Tarap, the former reminiscent of south Indian campaigns into Bengal through Orissa, emerged between the eleventh and thirteenth centuries. [53]

There are T'ang notices on the overland route from China to Bengal via northern Burma in 691, in 807 or 810, in 863, and in 1060.[54] The tenth century *Xin Tang Shu* (New History of the Tang

Dynasty) referred to a route linking Annam with India (Tianzhu), starting in Tonkin, and continuing via Yunnan and Prome (Sriksetra) to Magadha, a mix of land, river and sea routes.[55] This well-travelled route passed from the region of the Upper Yangtse-Mekong-Salween Rivers through Tibet. Passes through Bhutan and Nepal led respectively to Kamarupa and India.[56] A Fatimid map of *c.* the late eleventh century showed a route from China running through northern India. Kanauj was mentioned.[57]

Three routes went from Assam to Bengal, one of them by water, the Brahmaputra being an excellent example of connectivity into Tibet. Of the two land routes, one was from Tezpur (Darang district of Assam) to Lakhnauti through the districts of Kamarupa and Goalpara, north of Brahmaputra; the route from Sibsagar and that of Nowgong-Gauhati, south of the Brahmaputra, crossing over it, joined this path, respectively at Tezpur and Barpeta in Kamrup. The other route went from Sibsagar, across the Jayantia hills to Suvarnagrama-Dhaka via Srihatta and Mymensingh. As the latter had a connection with the river ports of Bengal, it was favoured by those interested in sea-trade. Lakhnauti had a line of connection with Tibet via Kamarupa, through 35 passes, Mahamhai darah being the nearest to Tibet. Lakhnauti joined a route from Kashmir to Yunnan via Koh-i-kara-chal (Kumaon mountains), the Patkai Hills and the upper districts of Myanmar. Some portions of the three routes, Lakhnauti-Tezpur, Lakhnauti-Tibet and Lakhnauti-Yunnan, probably intersected.[58]

It is tempting to link the political turmoil to the numismatic history of the northern Bay of Bengal. The lines of two currency zones—gold in Samatata and silver in Harikela—blurred in the seventh century with decreasing gold circulation. The silver coins of Harikela, linked with the early Chandra coins of Arakan, filled the gap, but stopped circulating from the tenth century. There was no Pala or Sena coinage. Coins were back in Bengal only after the thirteenth century.

## The System Stabilizes

The chaos resolved itself with the advent of the Mongol age which united these disparate polities through a silver axis, the 'Eurasian silver century' of the Mongols being a vital trigger for the northern Bay of Bengal economies. The pacification of the Shan states, the renewal of contacts with China and increased silver production from the Bawdingyi silver mines impacted Bengal. There are four instances of the southeast supplying the western delta with bullion in the early sultanate period: Rukn al-Din Kaikaus' conquest of southeastern Bengal in 1291; Mubarak Shah's expansion toward the coast; Sikandar Shah's conquest in Kamarupa in 1358; and Jalal al-Din Muhammad's re-conquest of eastern Bengal in 1420. From 1339 (AH 740) numismatic evidence from the Sylhet find confirms the continuous issuance of silver rupees. Those bearing the inscription of Mubarak Shah, were issued in consecutive years from 1339 to 1349 (AH 740–50). We may argue that political and military developments in Yunnan and Bengal seem to have caused a flow of silver from China to India, via Burma, from 1339. Conversely, the decay of Shan rule in Burma, and the collapse of the Mongol empire in China, 'appears to have shut off the stream of silver in the early 1360s'.[59] The southeastern delta remained significant in the monetary history of Bengal. Fathabad, bordering Arakan and home of the seventeenth-century Arakan court poet Alaol, was an entrepot between Chittagong, the maritime entry-point for silver, and Lakhnauti, the inland capital, its mint emerging as a significant point of coin production. A high customs duty of 37.5 per cent was paid in imported specie or bullion and generated a strong flow of silver into Bengal's coffers.[60] Obviously these Bay economies felt the need to re-adopt a coin-based economy.

## Multiple Bays

This chapter has so far traced political and monetary developments, focussing on the puzzle of the absence of coined money operating in the northern Bay of Bengal world and trying to link the two. Looking further east, R. le May commented for the Khmer civilization:

> It is strange that an Empire which lasted for at least six centuries; which stretched from Annam in the East . . . (to) Burma in the West . . . and which could produce such a wonder of civilised culture as the great temple at Angkor, still never found it necessary or expedient to employ

any standard system of gold and silver coinage, as distinct from weights, throughout its territories.[61]

Like the Khmer polity, the Pala-Sena economy in Bengal remains an enigma for several reasons. While ordinary transactions were carried on with cowries, as Deyell has argued elsewhere, Bengal's mode of payment in long-distance trade remains unclear.[62] Did this lacuna suggest the diminishing role of Buddhist merchant communities, as Prasad argues for Samatata-Harikela? Griffiths' study of two copperplates from Pundravardhana mention only Brahmins as donees.[63] Yet, Suchandra Ghosh's study of land grants in Harikela reveals mercantile initiative from the seventh to tenth centuries. The contradictory data suggests a modification of the four subdivisions I mentioned at the outset. We will see in this volume smaller sub-regions playing differing roles by virtue of expanding networks varying both spatially and chronologically.

Ghosh's conclusion about merchant involvement in Harikela's circulations, visible in the burgeoning of incipient urban centres, is reinforced by a recent essay by Bautze-Picron. Bautze-Picron found substantial mercantile involvement in the sculptural domain of ninth-tenth centuries Mainamati and Vikrampur in south and southeast Bengal (Samatata, now in Bangladesh) and also the names of three merchant donees, possibly Buddhist—Jambhalamitra (also referenced by Ghosh, see her discussion of the same)—Buddhamitra and Lokadatta. Significantly, Bautze-Picron located a sculpture atelier in Mainamati having significant interaction with both Magadha, via Lakhi Sarai and Jamui in south Bihar, and very likely with Bagan as well. Bronze images from the Mainamati atelier were also exported to Java and western Tibet. Bautze-Picron concludes that the dissemination of artistic styles and conventions followed these little-studied routes from southern Bengal and that since Bengal was at the crossroads between Tibet and Nepal in the north, China and maritime and peninsular Southeast Asia in the east, and the Ganga valley, it became the gateway through which Buddhist images created in Magadha left the subcontinent.[64]

How these items were paid for is not clear, nor do we know what precisely was imported in their place. Goods exited and entered through ports unknown to us; while there were no recorded sailings from Tamralipita after the seventh century, we know from the testimony of Yjing (who disembarked there like Fa Xian before him) that the Chinese monk Wu Hing, his contemporary disembarked on his travels from Sri Lanka and Nagapattinam at an unspecified port in *harikela*, a place regarded by Yjing as the easternmost limit of east India, [in fact] seen by him as a part of *Jambudvipa*, or Java, where Fa Xian too had made landfall. There were thus two routes into Bengal: one, through the more popular gateway, Tamralipta, a port as well as a land entry to overland routes that seems to have had a direct run via *Ka-cha*, an unspecified port in the Nicobar island chain—probably *Katchal*—but also sometimes equated with Barus on the northwest Sumatra coast or Kedah on the Malay peninsula coast to Palembang in Yjing's time. The second route embarked through an unspecified gateway in *harikela*—probably the Samandar/Chittagong port that was emergent at this time—which networked with Java, and in doing so must have passed through the Andaman Islands chain.

Bengal's horse trade with the upland economies of Bhutan, Tibet and Yunnan is another case of an economy functioning without coined money. Both Pala (750-1175) and Sena (1096-1225) Bengal imported horses; Marco Polo and Minhaj noted various horse-marts and staging posts along the metal corridor leading to Bengal. Within Bengal, whose physical location played a significant role in this trade, Lakhnauti and Nadia were possibly horse-markets, Chakravarti writing: 'as Bengal was the only *asamudrahimacala* (from the sea to the Himalayas) region in land-locked north India watered by the Ganga system, it could simultaneously function as a receiving point of imported horses from the northwest and northeast and an outlet for maritime trade in war horses in the eastern sector of the Indian Ocean.' [65]

How was the payment for horses made? While Pala-Sena records yield no clues in this regard, Chakravarti and Hussain suggest that it was either made in cowries or through commodity trade, thereby linking the economy of Bengal with upland economies.[66]

This linking of the maritime with the terrestrial world brings to mind David Armitage's threefold typology of Atlantic history: *circum*-Atlantic history or the history of the ocean as an arena of exchange, interchange, circulation, and transmission; *trans*-Atlantic history or the history of meaningful comparisons between otherwise distinct histories; and *cis*-Atlantic history or the history of any particular place (nation, state, region, specific institution, etc.) in relation to the wider Atlantic world.[67] Armitage saw his three-fold classification as, the transnational history of the Atlantic world; the international history of the Atlantic world; and national or regional history within an Atlantic context.

Can these categories be applied to the medieval Bay of Bengal world? While the chapters in this volume show trade braided into diverse circulations, we should also remember that the tenth-eleventh centuries were a period of transition as new powers emerged to assume control over the major centres of contemporary civilization: the Fatimids in Egypt (969); the Cholas in southern India (985); the Khmers at Angkor (944), the Dali kingdom in Yunnan (937), the Burmese at Bagan (1044), and the Ly in northern Vietnam (1009) on the Southeast Asian mainland and the Song dynasty in China (960). Among other results, these consolidations seem to have stimulated Indian Ocean commerce and precipitated a burst of energy in the community of international traders who travelled the navigation channels connecting eastern and western Asia, leading Chaudhuri and Kulke to discern on 'eleventh century trade revolution'.[68]

Linked with the impulses of a maritime economy were religious stimuli seen from the tenth century in three new centres of international Buddhism. India's Bihar-Bengal region, with Tibet and Central Asian connections, was a centre of evolution of an esoteric or Tantric Buddhism, under the patronage of the Pala rulers. The *Sarvabuddhasamāyogaḍākinījālaśaṃvara*, copied during the late eleventh century and instrumental in introducing significant Śaiva elements into Buddhism, may have been a product of a scriptorium located in the Pala Empire, or a Nepalese scriptorium closely imitating the style of Pala scribes and manuscript production. This kind of Tantric or Vajrayana Buddhism was also visible in Bagan and Yunnan. That there were commercial implications to this Buddhist pilgrimage networking is demonstrated in the Chola raids against the wealthy commercial centres of the Bengal coastline prior to their naval expeditions against the Srivijaya commercial realm in 1024/5. Sri Lanka became the centre of a revitalized Theravada Buddhism with contacts to Bagan and Lan Na, and flourished after a period of Chola interregnum that ended in the late eleventh century. Meanwhile, China emerged as the new centre of Buddhism's Mahayana sects. Significantly, each of these new Buddhist schools was centred in a strategically important region of international trade.[69] We should note that this was the time when the Mainamati atelier discussed by Bautze-Picron flourished.

## NOTES

1. Ranabir Chakravarti, 'The Pull Towards the Coast: Politics and Polity in India (*c.* 600-1300 CE)', Presidential Address, Section I: Ancient India, Indian History Congress, 72nd Session, Punjab University, Patiala, 2011, pp. 1-48, especially pp. 11-13.
2. Victor Lieberman, *Strange Parallels: Southeast Asia in Global Context, c. 800–1830*, vol. 2: *Mainland Mirrors: Europe, Japan, China, South Asia, and the Islands*, New York: Cambridge University Press, 2009, p. 713.
3. I am indebted to Dr. Samuel Berthet of Shiv Nadar University, Noida, for much of the formulation in this section.
4. Keith Dowman, 'A Buddhist Guide to the Power Places of the Kathmandu Valley', *Kailash*, pp. 183-291, http://himalaya.socanth.cam.ac.uk/collections/journals/kailash/pdf/kailash_08_0304_03.pdf accessed on 17 December 2013, pp. 193-4, 211-12, 218-19.
5. Sylvain Levi, 'The History of Nepal', I, *Kailash*, pp. 5-60, http://himalaya.socanth.cam.ac.uk/collections/journals/kailash/pdf/kailash_03_01_01.pdf. accessed on 17 December 2013, p. 17.
6. Alexander C. Soper and Helen B. Chapin, 'A Long Roll of Buddhist Images', I, *Artibus Asiae*, vol. 32, no. 1, 1970, pp. 5-41, especially pp. 38-9. My thanks to Dr. Bin Yang of the University of Macau, who brought the images to my notice.
7. Bhrikuti may have been Amshuvarman's daughter or the Lichhavi king Narendradeva's sister. Songtsen Gampo's invasion of Nepal *c.* 642 placed Narendradeva on the throne. Dowman, 'A Buddhist Guide', pp. 242-4.

8. Chapin Soper, 'Long Roll', pp. 16, 37-8.
9. N. Karashima and Y. Subbarayalu, 'Goldsmiths and Padinen-vishayam: A Bronze Buddha Image of Nagapattinam', in Noboru Karashima, ed., *Ancient and Medieval Commercial Activities in the Indian Ocean: The Testimony of Inscriptions and Ceramic Sherds*, Tokyo: Taisho University, 2002, pp. 57–61. See fn. 10, p. 59.
10. Amitabha Bhattacharyya, 'Trade Routes of Ancient Bengal', in *History and Archaeology of Eastern India*, ed. Asok Datta, New Delhi: Books and Books, 1998, 9, pp. 157–72.
11. Thakurlal Manandhar, 'Nepal and South India', *INAS Journal*, Institute of Nepal and Asian Studies, pp. 119-22. Not dated. Available at http://www.thlib.org/static/reprints/contributions/CNAS_02_01_10.pdf Accessed 10 December 2016.
12. Ibid, pp. 120-1.
13. Burton Stein, 'Circulation and the Historical Geography of Tamil Country', *The Journal of Asian Studies*, vol. 37, no. 1. (November 1977), pp. 7-26.
14. Volker Grabowski, 'Population and State in Lan Na Prior to the Mid-Sixteenth Century', *Journal of the Siam Society*, vol. 93, 2005, pp. 1-68, especially p. 4.
15. Gordon H. Luce, 'The Early Syam in Burma's History', *Journal of the Siam Society*, vol. 46.2, 1958, pp. 123-213, especially pp. 135, 139; A. B. Griswold, 'The Buddha Images of Northern Siam', *Journal of the Siam Society*, vol. 41.2, 1954, pp. 95-152.
16. R. le May, 'The Coinage of Siam', Bangkok: *Journal of the Siam Society*, vol. 25, 1932, pp. 1-78, especially p. 16.
17. Keat Gin Ooi, *Southeast Asia: A Historical Encyclopedia from Angkor Wat to Timor*, Santa Barbara, Calif.: ABC-CLIO, 2004, pp. 327-9; E.W. Hutchinson, 'Sacred Images in Chiengmai', *Journal of the Siam Society*, 28, 1935, pp. 115-43.
18. Goh Geok Yian, 'The question of 'China' in Burmese Chronicles', *Journal of Southeast Asian Studies*, 41(1), pp 125-52, February 2010, p. 150; Geoff Wade, 'An Annotated Translation of the *Yuan Shi* Account of Mian (Burma)', in Perry Link, ed., *The Scholar's Mind: Essays in Honor of Frederick W. Mote*, Hong Kong: Chinese University of Hong Kong, 2009, pp. 17-49.
19. Hermann Kulke, ed., *The State in India 1000–1700*, revised and enlarged second edition, Delhi: Oxford India Paperbacks, 1997, 2003, pp. 40-1; Tilman Frasch, 'In an Octopussy's Garden: Of

Chakravartins, Little Kings and a New Model of the Early State in South and Southeast Asia', in Georg Berkemer and Margret Frenz (eds.), *Sharing Sovereignty: The Little Kingdom in South Asia.* Berlin: Klaus Schwartz Verlag, 2003, pp. 93-114; Burhard Schnepel and Georg Berkemer, 'History of the Model', in Berkemer and Frenz (eds.), *Sharing Sovereignty*, pp. 11-20.

20. Victor B. Lieberman, *Burmese Administrative Cycles: Anarchy and Conquest, c. 1580-1760*, Princeton: Princeton University Press, 1984; idem, 'The Political Significance of Religious Wealth in Burmese History: Some Further Thoughts', *The Journal of Asian Studies*, vol. 39, no. 4. (August 1980), pp. 753-69; Michael Aung-Thwin, 'Spirals in Early Southeast Asian and Burmese History', *Journal of Interdisciplinary History*, vol. 21, no. 4. (Spring), 1991, pp. 575-602; idem, 'Origins and Development of the Field of Prehistory in Burma', *Asian Perspectives.*
21. Victor Lieberman, *Strange Parallels,* vol. 1, New York: Cambridge University Press, 2003, pp. 77-8.
22. Jesse Ross Knutson, 'History beyond the Reality Principle: Literary and Political Territories in Sena Period Bengal', *Comparative Studies of South Asia, Africa and the Middle East*, vol. 32, no. 3, 2012, pp. 613-43.
23. Chakravarti, 'The Pull Towards the Coast…', pp. 10-11.
24. Victor Lieberman, 'Maritime Influences in Southeast Asia, *c.* 900–1300: Some Further Thoughts', *Journal of Southeast Asian Studies*, vol. 41, issue 3, October 2010, pp. 529-39; John K. Whitmore, 'The Rise of the Coast: Trade, State and Culture in Early Đai Viêt', *Journal of Southeast Asian Studies*, 37(1), 2006, pp 103-22; idem, 'Literati Culture and Integration in Dai Viet, *c.* 1430-*c.*1840', *Modern Asian Studies*, 31, 3, 1997, pp. 665-87, especially pp. 669, 674; Li Tana, 'A View from the Sea': Perspectives on the Northern and Central Vietnamese Coast', *Journal of Southeast Asian Studies*, 37 (1), 2006, pp. 83-102.
25. Geoff Wade, 'An Early Age of Commerce in Southeast Asia, 900-1300', *Journal of Southeast Asian Studies*, 40, 2 (2009), pp. 221-65.
26. Lieberman, *Strange Parallels,* vol. 1.
27. Chakravarti, 'The Pull Towards the Coast', pp. 13-14; idem, 'Vibrant Thalassographies of the Indian Ocean: Beyond Nation States', *Studies in History* 31(2), 2015, pp. 235-48, especially p. 238.
28. Roderich Ptak, 'The Sino-European Map (Shanhai yudi quantu)'

in the Encyclopaedia 'Sanchai tuhui', in Angela Schottenhammer and Roderich Ptak (eds.), *The Perception of Maritime Space in Traditional Chinese Sources*, Wiesbaden: Harrasowitz Verlag, 2006, pp. 191-207.

29. Chakravarti, 'The Pull Towards the Coast', p. 35.
30. Hermann Kulke, 'The Naval Expeditions of the Cholas in the Context of Asian History', in Hermann Kulke, K. Kesavapany and Vijay Sakhuja, eds., *Nagapattinam to Suvarnadwipa: Reflections on the Chola Naval Expeditions to Southeast Asia*, Singapore: ISEAS, 2009, pp. 1-19; Karashima, ed., *Ancient and Medieval Commercial Activities*; Kenneth R. Hall, *Networks of Trade, Polity and Societal Integration in Chola-Era South India, c. 875-1279*, Delhi: Primus Books, 2013.
31. Friedrich Hirth and W.W. Rockhill (tr.), *Chau-Ju-Kua: His work on the Chinese and Arab Trade in the Twelfth and Thirteenth Centuries, Entitled Chu-Fan-Chi* (St. Petersburg, 1911).
32. May, 'The Coinage of Siam', p. 16.
33. Eusebius Renaudot, *Ancient Accounts of India and China by Two Mohammedan Travellers Who Went to Those Parts in the Ninth Century*, London, 1733, rpt., Delhi: Asian Educational Services, 1995.
34. Sulaiman, *Salsilat ut-Tawarikh*, in John Elliott and H.M. Dowson, *The History of India as Told by its Own Historians* (1867-77), Allahabad: Kitab Mahal, rpt, 1964, vol. I, p. 5; Renaudot, *Ancient Accounts of India and China*, p. 17; Minhaj Siraj Juzjani, *Tabakat-i-Nasiri*, tr. H.G. Raverty, 1881 rpt. Delhi: Oriental Books Reprint Corp., 1970, 2 vols., see vol. 1, p. 554; Ma Huan, *Ying-yai Sheng-lan, The Overall Survey of the Ocean's Shores 1433*, tr. J.V.G. Mills, with Foreword and Preface, London: Hakluyt Society, 1970, rpt. Chonburi, Thailand: White Lotus Press, 1997; H.A.R. Gibb and C.F. Beckingham, tr. and ed., *The Travels of Ibn Battūta, A.D. 1325-1354* (full text), 4 vols., London: Hakluyt Society, 1958, 1962, 1971, 1994, 2000; C. Defrémery and B.R. Sanguinetti, tr. and ed., *Voyages d'Ibn Batoutah*, A. Cortesao, tr., *The Suma Oriental of Tome Pires, An Account of the East, From the Red Sea to China, written in Malacca and India in 1512–1515 and the Book of Francisco Rodrigues, Pilot Major of the Armada that Discovered Banda and the Moluccas*, 2 vols., London: Hakluyt Society, 1944 rpt., Delhi: Asian Educational Services, 1990/2005.
35. Tribute was paid in silk equivalents. Robert M. Hartwell, *Tribute Missions to China: 960-1126*, Philadelphia: publisher unmentioned, 1983; Hans Ulrich Vogel and Sabine Hieronymus, 'Cowry Trade and

Its Role in the Economy of Yunnan, the Ninth to the Middle of the Seventeenth Century', in Roderich Ptak and Dietmar Rothermund (eds.), *Emporia, Commodities and Entrepreneurs in Asian Maritime Trade, c. 1400-1750*, Stuttgart: Franz Steiner Verlag, 1991, pp. 231-62, p. 234; Feng Zhao and Le Wang, 'Glossary of Textile Terminology (Based on the Documents from Dunhuang and Turfan)', London, *Journal of the Royal Asiatic Society*, vol. 23, no. 2, April 2013, pp. 349-87.

36. George Coedès, 'Some Problems in the Ancient History of the Hinduized States of South-East Asia', *Journal of Southeast Asian History*, 5, 2, 1964, pp. 1-14.
37. Pamela Gutman, 'The Ancient Coinage of Southeast Asia', *Journal of the Siam Society*, vol. 66, no. 1, 1978, pp. 8-21, pp. 9-10; May, *The Coinage of Siam*, pp. 9-11.
38. Sithu Gamani Thingyan, *Zinme Yazawin: Chronicle of Chiang Mai*, Yangon: UHRC, 2003, pp. 13, 54-5. Henceforth *ZY*.
39. Janice Stargardt, 'Burma's Economic and Diplomatic Relations with India and China from Early Medieval Sources,' pp. 53-8, 60; Robert S. Wicks, *Money, Markets and Trade in Early Southeast Asia: The Development of Indigenous Monetary Systems to* AD *1400,* Ithaca, Cornell Press, 1992, p. 123.
40. Wicks, *Money, Markets and Trade.*
41. John N. Miksic, 'Early Burmese Urbanization: Research and Conservation', p. 99.
42. J. Takakusu Yjing, tr., *Buddhist Practices in India*, pp. 30-1.
43. K.A. Nilakanta Sastri, 'I. Sri Vijaya', pp. 291-2.
44. For Song financial initiatives and constraints, Christian Lamouroux, 'Militaires et financiers dans la Chine des Song', W.W. Rockhill, 'Notes on the Relations and Trade of China', *T'oung Pao*, Second Series, October 1915, pp. 435-67, especially pp. 420-1.
45. *ZY*, pp. 43-4.
46. Rila Mukherjee, 'Maps, Concealed Geographies, Ambiguous Connectivities', in Lipi Ghosh and Rila Mukherjee (eds.), *Rethinking Connectivity: Region Place and Space in Asia,* Delhi: Primus Books, 2016, pp. 136-69. For routes in the region, see Luce, 'The Early Syam', pp. 128-9.
47. Vadime Elisseeff, 'Introduction: Approaches Old and New to the Silk Roads', in Vadime Elisseeff, *The Silk Roads: Highways of Culture and Commerce* UNESCO/Berghahn Books, 2000, pp. 1-26, especially p. 5; Marianne Yaldiz, 'These Boots are Made for Walking: Travellers from East to West?' in Osmund Bopearachchi and Marie-Francoise

Boussac, eds., *Afghanistan: Ancien Carrefour entre l'Est et l'Ouest*, Turnhout, Belgium: Brepols, 2005, pp. 403-11, especially p. 405. Tansen Sen, *Buddhism, Diplomacy, and Trade: The Realignment of Sino-Indian Relations, 600-1400*, Asian Interactions and Comparisons, University of Hawai'i Press, 2003, mentions armed conflicts along the Taklamakan and the Yunnan-Myanmar border as one of the reasons for the decline of the land routes and the rise of a maritime trade between China and India from the ninth century, pp. 211, 213.

48. Nicholas G. Rhodes, 'Trade in Southeast Bengal in the First Millennium CE: The Numismatic Evidence', in Rila Mukherjee (ed.), *Pelagic Passageways: The Northern Bay of Bengal before Colonialism*, Delhi: Primus Books, 2011, pp. 263-75.
49. Edouard Chavannes, 'Voyage de Song Yun dans l'Udyana et le Gandhara', *Bulletin de l'Ecole d'Extrême-Orient*, 1903, vol. 3, no. 1, pp. 379–441, especially pp. 386-7; Bhattacharyya, 'Trade Routes of Ancient Bengal', p. 160; Rhodes, 'Trade in Southeast Bengal', p. 266.
50. Stargardt, 'Burma's Economic and Diplomatic Relations', pp. 51-3.
51. Kenneth Hall and John Whitmore, 'Southeast Asian Trade and the Isthmian Struggle, 1000-1200 A.D.', in K. R. Hall and John Whitmore, eds., *Explorations in Early Southeast Asian* History, Michigan: Ann Arbor, 1976, pp. 303–40.
52. Lieberman, *Strange Parallels*, vol. 1: pp. 93-4; Jan Wisseman Christie, 'The Medieval Tamil-language Inscriptions in Southeast Asia and China,' *Journal of South East Asian Studies* 29, 1998: 239-68; idem, 'Asian Trade between the tenth and thirteenth Centuries and Its Impact on the States of Java and Bali,' in Himanshu Prabha Ray, ed., *Archaeology of Seafaring* (Delhi, 1999), pp. 221-70; idem, 'Javanese Markets and the Asian Sea Trade Boom of the Tenth to Thirteenth Centuries A.D.', *Journal of the Social and Economic History of the Orient*, 41, 3, 1998, pp. 344–81.
53. Kali Prasanna Sen, ed., *Sri Rajamala*, 4 vols., Agartala: Tribal Research Centre, rpt., 2003 (in Bangla); Wade, 'An Annotated Translation of the *Yuan Shi*; Goh, 'The question of 'China'.
54. Sun Laichen, 'Chinese Historical Sources on Burma', *Journal of Burma Studies*, vol. 2, Special Issue, 1997, pp. 1-53, especially pp. 13, 15-16.
55. Bin, Yang, 'Horses, Silver, and Cowries: Yunnan in Global Perspective', *Journal of World History*, vol. 15, no. 3, September 2004, pp. 281-322, especially pp. 287-8; Hartwell, *Tribute Missions*; Geoff

Wade, tr. *Southeast Asia in the Ming Shi-lu: An Open Access Resource*, Singapore: Asia Research Institute & Singapore E-Press, National University of Singapore, http://epress.nus.edu.sg/msl/

56. John Deyell, 'The China Connection: Problems of Silver Supply in Medieval Bengal,' in Sanjay Subrahmanyam, ed., *Money and the Market in India 1100-1700*, Delhi: Oxford University Press, 1994, pp. 112-36, especially p. 128.
57. Yossef Rapoport and Emilie Savage-Smith, 'Medieval Islamic View of the Cosmos: The Newly Discovered Book of Curiosities', *The Cartographic Journal*, vol. 41, no. 3, pp. 253-9, December 2004, p. 259; Jeremy Johns and Emilie Savage-Smith, 'The Book of Curiosities: A Newly Discovered Series of Islamic Maps', *Imago Mundi*, 55: 1, 2003, pp. 7-24, especially p. 11.
58. Nisar Ahmad, 'Assam-Bengal Trade in the Medieval Period: A Numismatic Perspective', *Journal of the Economic and Social History of the Orient*, vol. 33, no. 2, 1990, pp. 169-98.
59. Akinobu Kuroda, 'The Eurasian Silver Century, 1276-1359: Commensurability and Multiplicity', *Journal of Global History*, vol. 4, 2009, pp. 245-69, especially p. 255; Richard M. Eaton, *The Rise of Islam, and the Bengal Frontier, 1204-1760,* Berkeley: University of California Press, 1993, paperback 1996, p. 96.
60. John S. Deyell, 'Cowries and Coins: The Dual Monetary System of the Bengal Sultanate', *The Indian Economic and Social History Review*, vol. 47, no. 1, 2010, pp. 63-106, especially p. 86.
61. May, '*The Coinage of Siam*', p. 11.
62. Deyell, 'Cowries and Coins'; John Deyell, 'Monetary and Financial Webs: The Regional and International Influence of Pre-Modern Bengali Coinage', in Rila Mukherjee (ed.), *Pelagic Passageways: The Northern Bay of Bengal before Colonialism*, Delhi: Primus, 2011, pp. 279-314.
63. Birendra Nath Prasad, 'Votive Inscriptions on the Sculptures of Early Medieval Samataṭa-Harikela, Bengal: Explorations in Socio-religious History', *Religions of South Asia* 4.1, 2010, pp. 27-43; Arlo Griffiths, 'New Documents for the Early History of Pundravardhana: Copperplate Inscriptions from the Late Gupta and Early Post-Gupta Periods', *Pratna Samiksha*, New Series 6, 2015, pp. 15-38.
64. Claudine Bautze-Picron, 'Moving Images between Bihar and Bengal in the Ninth and Tenth Centuries', *Pratnatattva*, Journal of the Dept. of Archaeology Jahangirnagar University, vol. 22, June 2016, pp. 85-96.

65. Ranabir Chakravarti, 'Early Medieval Bengal and the Trade in Horses: A Note', *Journal of the Economic and Social History of the Orient*, 42, 2, 1999, pp. 194-211, p. 208; Ranabir Chakravarti, 'Equestrian Demand and Dealers: The Early Indian Scenario (up to *c.* 1300)', in Bert G. Fragner, Ralph Kauz, Roderich Ptak, Angela Schottenhammer (Hg.), *Horses in Asia: History, Trade and Culture*, Vienna: Verlag der Osterreichischen Akademie der Wissenschaft, 2009, pp. 145-59; Syed Ejaz Hussain, 'Silver Flow and Horse Supply to Sultanate Bengal with Special Reference to Trans-Himalayan Trade (13th-16th Centuries)', *Journal of the Economic and Social History of the Orient* 56 (2013), pp. 264-308; Ratna Sarkar and Indrajit Ray, 'Two Nineteenth Century Trade Routes in the Eastern Himalayas: The Bhutanese Trade with Tibet and Bengal', available at http://www.bhutanstudies.org.bt/admin/pubFiles/15-3.pdf, pp. 56-83, especially p. 62, accessed on 27 May 2010.
66. Chakravarti, 'Equestrian Demand', p. 157; Hussain, 'Silver Flow and Horse Supply', p. 303.
67. David Armitage, and Michael J. Braddick, 'Three Concepts of Atlantic History', in David Armitage and Michael J. Braddick, *The British Atlantic World, 1500-1800*, Basingstoke: Palgrave Macmillan, 2002, pp. 11-27.
68. Kenneth R. Hall, 'International Trade and Foreign Diplomacy in Early Medieval South India', *Journal of the Economic and Social History of the Orient*, vol. 21, no. 1 (January 1978), pp. 75-98, p. 75; K.N. Chaudhuri, *Trade and Civilization in the Indian Ocean: An Economic History from the Rise of Islam to 1750*, Cambridge: Cambridge University Press, 1985; Hermann Kulke, 'Rivalry and Competition in the Bay of Bengal and Its Bearing on Indian Ocean Studies', in Om Prakash and Denys Lombard (eds.), *Commerce and Culture in the Bay of Bengal 1500-1800,* New Delhi: Manohar/ICHR, 1999, pp. 17–35.
69. Kenneth R. Hall, 'Local and International Trade and Traders in the Straits of Melaka Region: 600-1500', *Journal of the Economic and Social History of the Orient*, vol. 47, no. 2 (2004), pp. 213-60; Coedès, 'Some Problems', p. 8; Péter-Dániel Szántó and Arlo Griffiths, 'Sarvabuddhasamāyogaḍākinījālaśaṃvara', in Jonathan A. Silk, ed., *Brill's Encyclopedia of Buddhism*, vol. I, 2015, pp. 367-72.

## BIBLIOGRAPHY

Ahmad, Nisar, 'Assam-Bengal Trade in the Medieval Period: A Numismatic Perspective', *Journal of the Economic and Social History of the Orient*, vol. 33, 2, 1990, pp. 169-98.

Armitage, David and Michael J. Braddick, 'Three Concepts of Atlantic History', in David Armitage and Michael J. Braddick (eds), *The British Atlantic World, 1500-1800*. Basingstoke: Palgrave Macmillan, 2002, pp. 11-27.

Aung-Thwin, Michael, 'Spirals in Early Southeast Asian and Burmese History', *Journal of Interdisciplinary History*, 21, 4, 1991, pp. 575-602.

———, 'Origins and Development of the Field of Prehistory in Burma', *Asian Perspectives*, vol. 40, no. 1, 2002, pp. 6-34.

Bautze-Picron, Claudine, 'Moving Images Between Bihar and Bengal in the Ninth and Tenth Centuries', *Pratnatattva*, Journal of the Dept. of Archaeology, Jahangirnagar University, vol. 22, June 2016, pp. 85-96.

Bhattacharyya, Amitabha, 'Trade Routes of Ancient Bengal', in Asok Datta, ed., *History and Archaeology of Eastern India*, Delhi: Books and Books, 1998, pp. 157-72.

Chakravarti, Ranabir, 'The Pull Towards the Coast: Politics and Polity in India (*c.* 600-1300 CE), Presidential Address, Section I: Ancient India, Indian History Congress, 72nd Session, Punjab University, Patiala (2011), pp. 1-48.

———, 'Vibrant Thalassographies of the Indian Ocean: Beyond Nation States', *Studies in History* 31, 2, 2015, pp. 235-48.

———, 'Early Medieval Bengal and the Trade in Horses: A Note', *Journal of the Economic and Social History of the Orient*, 42, 2, 1999, pp. 194-211.

———, 'Equestrian Demand and Dealers: The Early Indian Scenario (up to *c.* 1300)', in Bert G. Fragner, Ralph Kauz, Roderich Ptak and Angela Schottenhammer (Hg.), eds., *Horses in Asia: History, Trade and Culture*, Vienna: Verlag der Osterreichischen Akademie der Wissenschaft, 2009, pp. 145-59.

Chaudhuri, K.N., *Trade and Civilization in the Indian Ocean: An Economic History from the Rise of Islam to 1750*, Cambridge: Cambridge University Press, 1985.

Chavannes, Edouard, 'Voyage de Song Yun dans l'Udyana et le Gandhara',

*Bulletin de l'Ecole Française d'Extrême-Orient*, vol. 3, no. 1, 1903, pp. 379-441.

Coedès, George, 'Some Problems in the Ancient History of the Hinduized States of South-East Asia', *Journal of Southeast Asian History*, 5, 2, 1964, pp. 1-14.

Cortesao, A., tr., *The Suma Oriental of Tome Pires, An Account of the East, From the Red Sea to China, written in Malacca and India in 1512-1515 and the Book of Francisco Rodrigues, Pilot Major of the Armada that Discovered Banda and the Moluccas*, 2 vols., London: Hakluyt Society, 1944, rpt., Delhi: Asian Educational Services, 1990/2005.

Defrémery, C. and B.R. Sanguinetti, tr. and ed., *Voyages d'Ibn Batoutah* (Arabic and French text), 4 vols., Paris: Société Asiatique, 1853–8.

Deyell, John S., 'Cowries and Coins: The Dual Monetary System of the Bengal Sultanate', *The Indian Economic and Social History Review*, vol. 47, no. 1, 2010, pp. 63-106.

______, 'Monetary and Financial Webs: The Regional and International Influence of Pre-Modern Bengali Coinage', in Rila Mukherjee, ed., *Pelagic Passageways: The Northern Bay of Bengal before Colonialism*, Delhi, 2011, pp. 279-314.

______, 'The China Connection: Problems of Silver Supply in Medieval Bengal', in Sanjay Subrahmanyam, ed., *Money and the Market in India 1100-1700*, Delhi: Oxford University Press, 1994, pp. 112-36.

Dowman, Keith, 'A Buddhist Guide to the Power Places of the Kathmandu Valley', *Kailash*, vol. 8, nos. 3-4, 1981, pp. 183-291, http://himalaya.socanth.cam.ac.uk/collections/journals/kailash/pdf/kailash_08_0304_03.pdf

Eaton, Richard M., *The Rise of Islam, and the Bengal Frontier, 1204-1760*, Berkeley: University of California Press, 1993.

Elliott, John and H.M. Dowson, 'Sulaiman, *Salsilat ut-Tawarikh*', in *The History of India as Told by its Own Historians (1867-77)*, Allahabad: Kitab Mahal, rpt, 1964, vol. I.

Elisseeff, Vadime, 'Introduction: Approaches Old and New to the Silk Roads', in Vadime Elisseeff, *The Silk Roads: Highways of Culture and Commerce* UNESCO/Berghahn Books, 2000, pp. 1-26.

Feng Zhao and Le Wang, 'Glossary of Textile Terminology (Based on the Documents from Dunhuang and Turfan)', *Journal of the Royal Asiatic Society*, Special Issue, *Textiles as Money on the Silk Road*, vol. 23, issue 2, April 2013, pp. 349-87.

Frasch, Tilman, 'In an Octopussy's Garden: Of Chakravartins, Little Kings and a New Model of the Early State in South and Southeast Asia', in Georg Berkemer and Margret Frenz (eds.), *Sharing Sovereignty: The Little Kingdom in South Asia*, Berlin: Klaus Schwartz Verlag, 2003, pp. 93-114.

Gibb, H.A.R. and C.F. Beckingham, tr. and ed., *The Travels of Ibn Battūta, A.D. 1325–54* (full text), 4 vols., London: Hakluyt Society, 1958, 2000.

Grabowski, Volker, 'Population and State in Lan Na Prior to the Mid-Sixteenth Century', *Journal of the Siam Society*, vol. 93, 2005, pp. 1-68.

Griffiths, Arlo, 'New Documents for the Early History of Pundravardhana: Copperplate Inscriptions from the Late Gupta and Early Post-Gupta Periods', *Pratna Samiksha*, New Series 6, 2015, pp. 15-38.

Griswold, A.B., 'The Buddha Images of Northern Siam', *Journal of the Siam Society*, vol. 41.2, 1954, pp. 95-152.

Gutman, Pamela, 'The Ancient Coinage of Southeast Asia', *Journal of the Siam Society*, vol. 66, no. 1, 1978, pp. 8-21.

Hall, Kenneth R., *Networks of Trade, Polity and Societal Integration in Chola-Era South India, c. 875-1279*, Delhi: Primus Books, 2013.

———, 'International Trade and Foreign Diplomacy in Early Medieval South India', *Journal of the Economic and Social History of the Orient*, vol. 21, no. 1, 1978, pp. 75-98.

———, 'Local and International Trade and Traders in the Straits of Melaka Region: 600-1500', *Journal of the Economic and Social History of the Orient*, vol. 47, no. 2, 2004, pp. 213-60.

Hall, Kenneth and John Whitmore, 'Southeast Asian Trade and the Isthmian Struggle, 1000-1200 A.D.', in K.R. Hall and John Whitmore (eds.), *Explorations in Early Southeast Asian History*, Michigan: Ann Arbor, 1976, pp. 303-40.

Hansen, Valerie and Xinjiang Rong, 'How the Residents of Turfan used Textiles as Money, 273-796 CE', *Journal of the Royal Asiatic Society*, Special Issue, *Textiles as Money on the Silk Road*, vol. 23, issue 2, April 2013, pp. 281-305.

Hartwell, Robert M., *Tribute Missions to China: 960-1126*, Philadelphia, publisher not mentioned, 1983.

Hirth, Friedrich and W.W. Rockhill (tr.), *Chau-Ju-Kua: His Work on the Chinese and Arab Trade in the Twelfth and Thirteenth Centuries, Entitled Chu-Fan-Chi*, St. Petersburg: 1911.

Hussain, Syed Ejaz, 'Silver Flow and Horse Supply to Sultanate Bengal with Special Reference to Trans-Himalayan Trade (13th-16th Centuries)', *Journal of the Economic and Social History of the Orient*, 56, 2013, pp. 264-308.

Hutchinson, E.W., 'Sacred Images in Chiengmai', *Journal of the Siam Society*, 28, 1935, pp. 114-15.

Johns, Jeremy and Emilie Savage-Smith, 'The Book of Curiosities: A Newly Discovered Series of Islamic Maps', *Imago Mundi*, 55: 1, 2003, pp. 7-24.

Juzjani, Minhaj Siraj, *Tabakat-i-Nasiri*, tr. H.G. Raverty, 1881, rpt, New Delhi: Oriental Books, Reprint Corp., 1970, 2 vols.

Karashima, N. and Y. Subbarayalu, 'Goldsmiths and Padinen-vishayam: A Bronze Buddha Image of Nagapattinam', in Noboru Karashima, ed., *Ancient and Medieval Commercial Activities in the Indian Ocean: The Testimony of Inscriptions and Ceramic Sherds*, Tokyo: Taisho University, 2002, pp. 57–61.

Knutson, Jesse Ross, 'History beyond the Reality Principle: Literary and Political Territories in Sena Period Bengal', *Comparative Studies of South Asia, Africa and the Middle East*, vol. 32, no. 3, 2012, pp. 613-43.

Kulke, Hermann, 'The Naval Expeditions of the Cholas in the Context of Asian History', in Hermann Kulke, K. Kesavapany and Vijay Sakhuja, eds., *Nagapattinam to Suvarnadwipa: Reflections on the Chola Naval Expeditions to Southeast Asia*, Singapore: ISEAS, 2009, pp. 1-19.

______, 'Rivalry and Competition in the Bay of Bengal and Its Bearing on Indian Ocean Studies', in Om Prakash and Denys Lombard (eds.), *Commerce and Culture in the Bay of Bengal 1500–1800*, New Delhi: Manohar/ICHR, 1999, pp. 17-35.

______ ed., *The State in India 1000–1700*, revd. and enlgd 2nd edn., Delhi: Oxford University Press, 2003.

Kuroda, Akinobu, 'The Eurasian Silver Century, 1276-1359: Commensurability and Multiplicity', *Journal of Global History*, vol. 4, 2009, pp. 245-69.

Lamouroux, Christian, 'Militaires et financiers dans la Chine des Song', *Bulletin d'Ecole Francaise d'Extreme Orient*, vol. 87, no. 1, 2000, pp. 283-300.

Levi, Sylvain, 'The History of Nepal', I, *Kailash*, pp. 5-60, http://himalaya.socanth.cam.ac.uk/collections/journals/kailash/pdf/Kailash_03_01_01.pdf. accessed on 17 December 2013.

Lieberman, Victor, *Strange Parallels: Southeast Asia in Global Context, c. 800-1830,* 2 vols., New York: Cambridge University Press, 2003, 2009, vol. 1: *Integration of the Mainland;* vol. 2: *Mainland Mirrors: Europe, Japan, China, South Asia, and the Islands.*

Lieberman, Victor B., *Burmese Administrative Cycles: Anarchy and Conquest, c. 1580-1760,* Princeton: Princeton University Press, 1984.

———, 'The Political Significance of Religious Wealth in Burmese History: Some Further Thoughts', *The Journal of Asian Studies,* vol. 39, no. 4. August 1980, pp. 753-69.

Lieberman, Victor, 'Maritime Influences in Southeast Asia, *c.* 900-1300: Some Further Thoughts', *Journal of Southeast Asian Studies,* vol. 41, issue 3, October 2010, pp. 529-39.

Li, Tana, 'A View from the Sea: Perspectives on the Northern and Central Vietnamese Coast', *Journal of Southeast Asian Studies,* 37, 1, 2006, pp. 83-102.

Luce, Gordon H., 'The Early Syam in Burma's History', *Journal of the Siam Society,* vol. 46.2, 1958, pp. 123-213.

Ma Huan, *Ying-yai Sheng-lan, The Overall Survey of the Ocean's Shores 1433,* tr. J.V.G. Mills, with Foreword and Preface, London: Hakluyt Society, 1970; rpt. Bangkok: White Lotus Press, 1997.

Manandhar, Thakurlal, 'Nepal and South India', *INAS Journal,* Institute of Nepal and Asian Studies, pp. 119-22. n.d. Available at http://www.thlib.org/static/reprints/contributions/CNAS_02_01_10.pdf

May, R. le, 'The Coinage of Siam', *Journal of the Siam Society,* 25, 1932, pp. 1-78.

Miksic, John N., 'Early Burmese Urbanization: Research and Conservation', *Asian Perspectives,* vol. 40, no. 1, 2002, pp. 88-107.

Mukherjee, Rila, 'Maps, Concealed Geographies, Ambiguous Connectivities,' in Lipi Ghosh and Rila Mukherjee, eds., *Rethinking Connectivity: Region, Place and Space in Asia,* Delhi: Primus Books, 2016, pp. 136-69.

Ooi, Keat Gin, *Southeast Asia: A Historical Encyclopedia from Angkor Wat to Timor,* Santa Barbara, Calif.: ABC-CLIO, 2004.

Prasad, Birendra Nath, 'Votive Inscriptions on the Sculptures of Early Medieval Samataṭa-Harikela, Bengal: Explorations in Socio-religious History', *Religions of South Asia* 4.1, 2010, pp. 27-43.

Ptak, Roderich, 'The Sino-European Map (Shanhai yudi quantu) in the Encyclopedia "Sancai tuhui"', in Angela Schottenhammer and Roderich Ptak, eds., *The Perception of Maritime Space in Traditional Chinese Sources,* Wiesbaden: Harrassowitz Verlag, 2006, pp. 191-207.

Qing Duan and Helen Wang, 'Were Textiles Used as Money in Khotan in the Seventh and Eighth Centuries?', *Journal of the Royal Asiatic Society*, vol. 23, Issue 2, April 2013, pp. 307-25.

Rapoport, Yossef and Emilie Savage-Smith, 'Medieval Islamic View of the Cosmos: The Newly Discovered Book of Curiosities', *The Cartographic Journal*, vol. 41, no. 3, December 2004, pp. 253-9.

Renaudot, Eusebius, *Ancient Accounts of India and China by Two Mohammedan Travellers who Went to Those Parts in the Ninth Century*, London: Sam Harding, 1733; rpt., Delhi: Asian Educational Services, 1995.

Rhodes, Nicholas G., 'Trade in Southeast Bengal in the First Millennium CE: The Numismatic Evidence', in Rila Mukherjee, ed., *Pelagic Passageways: The Northern Bay of Bengal before Colonialism*, Delhi: Primus Books, 2011, pp. 263-75.

Rockhill, W.W., 'Notes on the Relations and Trade of China with the Eastern Archipelago and the Coast of the Indian Ocean during the Fourteenth Century', pt. IV: *T'oung Pao*, Second Series, vol. 16, no. 4, October 1915, pp. 435-67.

Sarkar, Ratna and Indrajit Ray, 'Two Nineteenth Century Trade Routes in the Eastern Himalayas: The Bhutanese Trade with Tibet and Bengal', available at http://www.bhutanstudies.org.bt/admin/pubFiles/15-3.pdf, pp. 56-83, accessed on 27 May 2010.

Sastri, K.A. Nilakanta, 'I. Sri Vijaya', *Bulletin de l'Ecole française d'Extrême-Orient*, vol. 40, 2, 1940, pp. 239-313.

Schnepel, Bukhard and Georg Berkemer, 'History of the Model', in Berkemer and Frenz, eds., *Sharing Sovereignty*, pp. 11-20.

Sen, Kali Prasanna, ed., *Sri Rajamala*, 4 vols., Agartala: Tribal Research Centre, rpt., 2003 (in Bangla).

Sen, Tansen, *Buddhism, Diplomacy, and Trade: The Realignment of Sino-Indian Relations, 600-1400*, Asian Interactions and Comparisons, University of Hawai'i Press, 2003.

Soper, Alexander C. and Helen B. Chapin, 'A Long Roll of Buddhist Images', I, *Artibus Asiae*, 32, 1, 1970, pp. 5-41.

Stargardt, Janice, 'Burma's Economic and Diplomatic Relations with India and China from Early Medieval Sources', *Journal of the Economic and Social History of the Orient*, 14, 1971, pp. 38-62.

Stein, Burton, 'Circulation and the Historical Geography of Tamil Country', *The Journal of Asian Studies*, vol. 37, no. 1. (November 1977), pp. 7-26.

Sun, Laichen, 'Chinese Historical Sources on Burma', *Journal of Burma Studies*, 2, Special Issue, 1997, pp. 1-53.

Szántó, Péter-Dániel and Arlo Griffiths, 'Sarvabuddhasamāyoga-ḍākinījālaśaṃvara', in Jonathan A. Silk, ed., *Brill's Encyclopedia of Buddhism*, vol. I, 2015, pp. 367-72.

Thingyan, Sithu Gamani, *Zinme Yazawin: Chronicle of Chiang Mai*, Yangon: UHRC, 2003.

Trombert, Eric, 'The Demise of Silk on the Silk Road: Textiles as Money at Dunhuang from the late Eighth Century to the Thirteenth Century', *Journal of the Royal Asiatic Society*, Special Issue, *Textiles as Money on the Silk Road*, vol. 23, issue 2, April 2013, pp. 327-47.

Vogel, Hans Ulrich with the assistance of Sabine Hieronymus, 'Cowry Trade and Its Role in the Economy of Yunnan, the Ninth to the Middle of the Seventeenth Century', in Roderich Ptak and Dietmar Rothermund, eds., *Emporia, Commodities and Entrepreneurs in Asian Maritime Trade, c. 1400-1750*, Stuttgart: Franz Steiner Verlag, 1991, pp. 231-62.

Wade, Geoff, 'An Annotated Translation of the *Yuan Shi* Account of Mian (Burma)', chap. 2 in Perry Link, ed., *The Scholar's Mind: Essays in Honor of Frederick W. Mote*, Hong Kong: Chinese University of Hong Kong, 2009, pp. 17-49.

———, 'An Early Age of Commerce in Southeast Asia, 900-1300', *Journal of Southeast Asian Studies*, 40, 2, 2009, pp. 221-65.

———, tr., *Southeast Asia in the Ming Shi-lu: An Open Access Resource*, Singapore: Asia Research Institute & Singapore E-Press, National University of Singapore, http://epress.nus.edu.sg/msl/

Wang, Helen, 'Textiles as Money on the Silk Road?' *Journal of the Royal Asiatic Society*, Special Issue, *Textiles as Money on the Silk Road*, vol. 23, issue 2, April 2013, pp. 165-74.

Whitmore, John K., 'The Rise of the Coast: Trade, State and Culture in Early Đai Viêt', *Journal of Southeast Asian Studies*, 37, 1, 2006, pp. 103-22.

———, 'Literati Culture and Integration in Dai Viet, *c.*1430-*c.*1840' *Modern Asian Studies*, 31, 3, 1997, pp. 665-87.

Wicks, Robert S., *Money, Markets and Trade in Early Southeast Asia: The Development of Indigenous Monetary Systems to* AD *1400*, Ithaca: Cornell University Press, SEAP Publications, 1992.

Wisseman Christie, Jan, 'The Medieval Tamil-language Inscriptions in Southeast Asia and China,' *Journal of South East Asian Studies*, 29, 1998, pp. 239-68.

———, 'Asian Trade between the 10th and 13th Centuries and Its Impact on the States of Java and Bali,' in Himanshu Prabha Ray, ed., *Archaeology of Seafaring*, Delhi: Pragati Publications, 1999, pp. 221-70.

______, 'Javanese Markets and the Asian Sea Trade Boom of the tenth to Thirteenth Centuries A.D.', *Journal of the Social and Economic History of the Orient*, 41, 3, 1998, pp. 344-81.

Yaldiz, Marianne, 'These Boots are Made for Walking: Travellers from East to West?', in Osmund Bopearachchi and Marie-Francoise Boussac, eds., *Afghanistan: Ancien Carrefour entre l'Est et l'Ouest*, Turnhout, Belgium: Brepols, 2005, pp. 403-11.

Yang, Bin, 'Horses, Silver, and Cowries: Yunnan in Global Perspective', *Journal of World History*, vol. 15, no. 3, September 2004, pp. 281-322.

Yian, Goh Geok, 'The Question of "China" in Burmese Chronicles', *Journal of Southeast Asian Studies*, 41, 1, 2010, pp. 125-52.

Yjing, J. Takakusu, tr., *Buddhist Practices in India*, Clarendon: Oxford University Press, 1896.

2

# Media of Exchange under the Pālas and the Senas as Reflected in their Inscriptions

SAYANTANI PAL

The Pālas and the Senas, two of the major regional powers of eastern India are often cited as classic examples of empires that existed without the issuance of coins. The monetary scenario of early medieval north India is characterized by the general reluctance of a particular rulers to issue varieties of coins, as was the case for the Kuṣāṇas or the Guptas. It is said that coins ceased to be used as political propaganda by rulers and minting of coins was not considered as a state prerogative.[1] The proponents of Indian feudalism would take this absence of the varieties of coin types and that of precious metal, as an indicator of monetary anaemia, connected with the decline of long-distance trade, and decay of urban centres, resulting in 'economic decline'.[2] The Pālas and Senas who did not issue any dynastic coins fit into this framework.

The Pāla-Sena period in Bengal corresponds to the period between the eighth and twelfth centuries. However, the Pālas never held effective control in areas outside the northern part of the Bengal Delta. In contrast, the Senas were the first power in Bengal who brought almost the entire delta under their authority, except its southeastern part. This is evident from the location of their land donations that practically cover all the four subregions of Bengal.[3] None of these regional rulers issued dynastic coins. This has encouraged scholars to think over the issue of the media of exchange under the Pālas and Senas. The present article attempts to explore the data regarding media of exchange in the records of the Pālas and Senas. The area of study is restricted to the northern part of the Bengal delta during the Pālas. Under the Senas land grant areas included the northern, western, southern and central parts of the Bengal Delta. None of these powers have any land grant records in the southeastern part of the delta which is thus outside my area of study.

Coin names appear in the inscriptions of the Pālas and Senas. D.C. Sircar, on the basis of the Gaya inscription of Govindapāla (1175) came to the conclusion that coin names like *dramma, purāṇa, kārṣāpaṇa* all counted as equal to 1280 cowries. All these terms are found in Pāla inscriptions and they had the same value in cowrie shells.[4] B.B. Dey has discussed in detail the epigraphic reference to coins in early Bengal.[5] B.D. Chattopadhyaya has taken into account not only the inscriptions but also the literary sources and physical evidence of coins discovered in Bengal from the earliest period up to the thirteenth century. Regarding the major issues on currency in early Bengal he has stressed the continuous use of cowries as a medium of exchange in Bengal and further he has linked up its emergence as a unit of value in the context of agricultural villages. Metallic currency, according to him, was not an integral part of the 'local' economy of Bengal. As early as the Mahasthan inscription, the coins approved as official currency were *gaṇḍaka* and *kākanik*a. Both could be counted in terms of cowries.[6]

The existence of separate monetary zones in early Bengal has been pointed out by several scholars. B.N. Mukherjee clearly defined two currency zones: Vaṅga and Gauḍa-Vaṅga and Samataṭa within his period of study. These were the zones where minted currency was in use.[7] S. Basu Majumdar has again pointed to the existence of different localities issuing coins as early as the third century BC. Besides, in the northern part of the Bengal delta as well as in some other parts, the punch marked Magadhan coinage of a little lesser weight than the *kārṣāpaṇa* standard was in use.[8] In the Gupta period *dīnāras* had to be paid as the price of land in the administrative unit of Puṇḍravardhana *bhukti*. The absence of dynastic issues of the Pālas and Senas has been attributed to the steady decline in the qualitative aspect of metal by Basu Majumdar. Regarding the cause for adopting shell currency in the Indian sub continent, especially Bengal, Basu Majumdar points out that, the debasement of coins and their low reliability in trade might have prompted these regions to adopt shells as currency. They 'cannot be forged or debased.' She has pointed to the participation of Bengal in the long distance trade in the Southern Silk Route which exposed this region to a common currency zone of cowrie shells extending up to China that was using cowries as currency and ritual objects since the eleventh century BC.[9]

S. Ghosh has cited cases where the medium of exchange was something like a kind of spice or a measure of grain etc. and not metallic money. On the basis of a discussion of exchangeable products like paddy and sugarcane and the different categories of the centres of exchange like *haṭṭa*s and ports she questions the view of the early medieval period as a non-active trading period on account of the paucity of metal money. She has pointed out the abundance of coins of the Samataṭa Harikela region and references to coin names in case of other areas.[10] Several scholars have attempted to argue against the theory of monetary anemia in Bengal with the help of these Samataṭa gold and Harikela silver coins. However, as B.D. Chattopadhyaya points out that they do not represent the coinage of the whole of Bengal Delta.[11] Besides, Ghosh brings out a situation which indicates the supplanting of coins as an exchange medium by other monetary usages, a situation once described as 'under-monetization' by John S. Deyell (now modified in this volume).[12]

Let us compare the epigraphic data of the third century BC to the fifth-eighth centuries, with that of the post eighth century. There is a striking contrast that needs explanation. Whereas the inscriptions of the early period regularly refer to transactions in coins, the inscriptions of the latter period do not. Further the latter point to the practice of counting cowries against the value of coins called *purāṇa* (a silver coin of 32 *ratis*, also known as *kārṣā-paṇa*)[13] which indicates something old that was not in use when the records concerned were written.

The status of the rulers with whose inscriptions we are dealing with needs also be taken into consideration in this connection. The rulers of the pre-eighth century period were the Guptas whose core territory was the mid-Ganga valley. They succeeded in introducing the *dināra* coins for high value transactions in northern and central Bengal. Such coins were again used for payment of the price of land in the Faridpur area in the latter part of the sixth century. We have physical evidence of gold coins of Śaśāṅka, Jayanāga, Samācāradeva in Gauḍa-Vaṅga and those of Śaśāṅka and the local rulers of Samataṭa or southeastern Bengal up to the eighth century. These rulers, however, did not rule for long. Besides their coins of high value appear to be tokens: how far they were used as a medium of exchange is not clear since the land grants never mention transactions through coins. Base metal coins in multiple denominations are totally absent in early medieval Bengal both in textual as well as physical evidences.

In a recently edited copper plate charter of Pradyumnabandhu, a ruler assigned to *c.* 550-650 CE, a *mahāpratihāra* wanted to purchase a village. As the authority decided that the *uparikara* (additional tax) of the village for the coming years would be 45 *kārṣāpaṇas*, they were in need of *hiraṇyas* (cash) for the district (viṣaya). They did not have the money. So they decided to sell the village for 1000 *curṇikās*.[14] The area of this land transfer appears to have been somewhere in north Bengal. Thus the charter gives an indication of the replacement of the practice of payment by *dināra* coins in such cases by *kārṣāpaṇa* and *curṇikā*. Though inadequate, it gives an indication that with the decline of the Gupta authority their coins also lost relevance for high value transactions in north Bengal. Taxes had to be paid in *kārṣāpaṇa*s, but since the *kārṣāpaṇas* were by this time almost 700 years old, they hardly could have been in circulation. Most probably this was a money of account (value) that was paid in cowries or paddy or some other means. Later when the Pālas captured power in this subregion, they had to reorganize the collection of land revenue.

The Pālas had their core territory in south Bihar and north Bengal. They were more interested in the politics of north India than that of Bengal proper. Most of their *jayaskandhāvāra*s (military camps) can be located in Bihar along the Ganges and north Bengal.

The physical evidence of coins during the Pala rule are mostly reported from the southeastern part of present Bangladesh which was never under their effective control. B.N. Mukherjee has cited the statements made by early Muslim geographers regarding the medium of exchange in the kingdom of 'Ruhmī, Rāhmī, Dahum', etc. He thinks that all these references can be understood in the context of the Pāla empire since all such names appear to have been derived from Dharma, i.e. Dharmapāla, the Pāla king of the end of the eighth and the early ninth centuries.[15] He explains that the account of Sulaiman actually dates to the period of the Pālas and the same information was repeated by the later Muslim writers.[16] However, it appears that most of the authors other than Sulaiman actually referred to the southeastern part of the Bengal delta, the area which was familiar to them in connection with maritime trade, and they were not speaking about Varendrī or the northern part of the Delta, far away from the sea. Whether the Pālas captured power in southeastern Bengal is a much debated question as it had its own succession of regional and local rulers from the tenth century (the Candras, Varmans and the Devas were major ruling houses in that area).

In the middle of the twelfth century the Senas captured Vikramapura and developed it as their seat of power. Vijayasena captured Raḍha (southwestern Bengal) and north Bengal, the stronghold of the Pālas. As has already been mentioned, the Senas were the first power which granted land in almost all the subregions of Bengal: North Bengal (Puṇḍravardhana *bhukti*), western and southwestern Bengal (Rāḍha and Vardhamāna *bhukti*) southern Bengal (Khāḍi *maṇḍala*) and central Bengal (Vaṅga). Besides, they regularly referred to the granted plot of land in terms of its annual income counted in *kapardakapurāṇas* (standard silver coins actually counted in cowrie shells).[17]

We may now turn our attention to the analysis of exchange in the inscriptions of the Pālas and Senas. The Bodhgaya inscription of the 26th year of Dharmapāla datable to the beginning of the ninth century records the establishment of Mahādeva Caturmukha by Keśava, the son of a stone carver in the Mahabodhi temple of Bodhgaya. On this occasion he excavated a deep lake at the expense of 3000 *drammas*.[18] Since the cost appears to be high, it could have included the price of the plot of land, the labour cost, and the cost of implements. It is difficult to ascertain which *drammas* the inscription refer to. Vigrahapāla *drammas* have been reported from various findspots such as Raghugarh in Munger, Naula, etc.[19] *Dramma* denoted Indo-Sassanian currency inspired by the broad, thin coinage of the Sassanian emperors of Iran. The Huṇas spread these coins in northern and western India in the sixth century. The Gurjara Pratihāras were influenced by this coinage and it is generally believed that they introduced this currency in Uttar Pradesh and Bihar conquest by Bhoja I (836 CE). Bhoja's coins are known as Ādivarāha *dramma*. We also have another class of coins known as Vigrahapāla *drammas* as they usually contain the legend *śri vigra*. Both these types have been found in western India, U.P., and Bihar, areas controlled by the Gurjara Pratihāras. Deyell points out that Ādivarāha *drammas* have a greater concentration in the Rajasthan borderlands and a lighter representation in the Bihar region while Vigrahapāla *drammas* have a greater concentration in Bihar. On the basis of the evolution of the design Deyell is inclined to believe that Vigrahapāla *drammas* were issued prior to Ādivarāha *drammas*.[20] In any case we are yet to prove the circulation of Vigrahapāla *drammas* in Bihar during Dharmapāla's reign (775-810 CE). In this situation we may take the *drammas* mentioned in the Bodhgaya inscription as referring to Indo-Sassanian coins in general.

A stone inscription of Mahendrapāla from Bihar states that one cowrie shell (*varāṭikā*) was to be charged for each fish shop at Ajāhaṭṭa.[21] This probably refers to a small levy to be collected by the state.

Land grants of the Pālas often refer to a granted locality without specifying the unit of measurement, e.g. Suvaṇakārikā-daṇḍa which measured 4,000 standard units (*suvarṇṇakārikā-daṇḍāt catuḥsahasra-pramāṇāt*, l.26, C.P. no.1 of Gopāla II).[22] The granted part from it is said to have measured 457 standard (unspecified units) accompanied with 9 *paṇas* and 10 *gaṇḍakas*.[23] R. Furui thinks that the terms like *pramāṇa* or *parimāṇa* refer to the production or yield of a plot or village that used to be counted in *purāṇas*, a unit of silver currency which was notional.[24] In support of his argument he has cited the Bhaturiya Stone inscription of Rājyapāla. It records the grant of a village with a tax of 100 *purāṇas* withheld.[25] The Rajbhita stone inscription of Mahīpāla I fixes the annual income to be paid in cash (*hiraṇya*) as 3 *paṇas* per coconut tree and 1 *paṇa* per arecanut tree for the worship of the deity.[26] In view of this fixation of income from land plots in terms of *purāṇa*, *paṇa*, etc. the suggestion of Furui seems to be reasonable since the granted plot in the charter of Gopāla II is said to have measured 457 standard accompanied with 9 *paṇas* and 10 *gaṇḍakas* indicating that the standard is meant for the income and not for the measurement. Thus if the silver currency called *purāṇa* is a notional unit rather than a real coined currency in this period, *paṇa* and *gaṇḍaka* could have been its lower denominations.

In the Rajibpur plate no. 1 of Madanapāla we have reference to the granted land as the production of three hundred by the standard of ploughed land and household (*kṛtahalakulapramāṇena triśatikopettau*, l. 37).[27] Here again the unit is unspecified and depended on the size of the cultivated tracts and number of households. The Manahali plate of the same king refers to *viṁśatikāyāṁbhūmau* (yielding an income of 20).[28] All these unspecified units may be taken in the sense of *purāṇas*.

Thus with the Pālas a new method of the statement of the quantity of land was introduced, referring to the yield (preferably annual). It combines two methods, one calculating the area by land measuring units, though not specified, another with reference to the yield. It is clear that both of the methods of measurement by yield and by land measuring units were followed simultaneously. In cases where yield has been specified, the plots were definitely under regular cultivation and thus their annual yield was estimated and recorded in state documents. But in cases where traditional land measuring units like *kulyavāpa*, *āḍhavāpa*, etc., have been mentioned, the plots are likely to have been not under cultivation. They could have been homesteads (e.g. Rajibpur plate no. 2), or parts of village/locality not under cultivation or meant for cultivation.

The practice mentioned above may be regarded as a general

trend of the age concerned as it is noticed not only in the charters of the Pālas but also in those of the Senas and Varmans and thus was not limited to any particular dynasty. In this way, the income of the recipient from the granted land was fixed on the one hand and the exact amount of the loss of income for the state was also specified on the other.[29]

The Gaya inscription of Govindapāla (1161-5/6 CE)[30] states that a brāhmaṇa named Vidyādhara created a deposit (*dhana*) at the temple of Gadābhṛt for the brāhmaṇas. The amount was 50 *kārṣāpaṇas* yielding an annual interest of 16 *kārṣāpaṇas* (silver coin of 32 *rati* also known as *purāṇa*).[31] D.C. Sircar thinks that these coins were actually not in circulation in this period and the transaction could have been conducted in cowrie-shells. This is proved by a line of the inscription in the left margin along the border of the inscription. It states that these *kapardaka*s were given in the presence of the image of the god. This shows that the sum of 16 *kārṣāpaṇas* was paid in cowrie-shells. This was handed over to the temple authorities for arranging the feeding of brāhmaṇas. Sircar further thinks that this fact was entered in the margin of the original document a little later.[32] The question is why there should be a difference between the currency media in which the deposition had been made, and the actual things handed over to the brāhmaṇas. Should we conclude that when the original deposit had been created the inconvenience of paying 16 *kārsāpaṇas* by coins had not been taken into account? But later considering this, the line had been added at the margin? Besides, for meeting their daily requirements the brāhmaṇas would need the cowries.

Data from the Pāla inscriptions indicate that cowries became the most common media of exchange under their rule. In the early period, transaction could be made by payment of *dramma* or *kārṣāpaṇa* in Bihar, but gradually this was supplanted by cowries in the twelfth century.

Transaction in *paṇas* was practised in Puṇḍravardhana, the core territory of the Pālas. This is suggested by a statement of Lāmā Tāranātha that upāsaka Śāntivarman was given a large sum of *paṇas* as his travelling expense and maintenance in Puṇḍravardhana and he spent it in purchasing food and drink there.[33] Unfortunately the date of this piece of evidence is uncertain.

The absence of any officer in charge of currency-related matters in the kingdom in the list *rājopādopajivins* (dependents at the feet of the king) in the Pāla land grants is also indicative of the absence of any agency for minting coins. The inhabitants of the gift villages have been asked to transfer the customary taxes (*kara*), *piṇḍaka* (taxes assessed in lump sum) and other kinds of *pratyāya* (dues) to the recipient. Although such statements are conventional and have been adopted from the *smritis*, the question arises as to whether all such payments were to be made either in cowries or in kind. The use of cowries in Bengal as the medium for the payment of salary for service has been mentioned in the *Rāmacarita*. It refers to the practice of maintaining the large army (*mahāvāhinī*) of Madanapāla by cowries and daily bread (IV, 36).[34] Cowries again functioned as media of exchange in trade as Sulaiman states that in the kingdom of Ruhmī (the Pāla territory) trade is carried on by means of cowries which were the current money of the country.[35] Cowries were given as gifts by Lakṣmaṇasena. Minhaj-ud-din Abu Umar says that in the thirteenth century in Laksmaṇasena's kingdom cowrie shell was the current money in place of silver, and the least gift he used to bestow was a lakh of cowries.[36] All these data point to the use of cowries as the medium of exchange in trade, as salary, as gifts, etc. Besides there is archaeological evidence: the discovery of cowries in hoards from Paharpur and other sites.[37]

We may now turn our attention to the inscriptions of the Senas regarding media of exchange. The Senas systematized the land measuring system. They regularly refer to the system of measurement of land by *nalas* (reeds) prevalent in the respective regions, the exact amount of land granted (even in case of the grant of whole villages) as well as the yield from the donated land. Table 2.1 shows the system of the statement of the quantity of land and its yield in the 12 charters of the Senas:

Table 2.1 shows that there were different modes by which annual income was indicated: (1) by *kapardaka purāṇa*; (2) without reference to any unit, simply a figure, (3) by *purāṇa*; (4) by *cūrnī* and *purāṇa*.

We may recall that in the charter of Pradyumnabandhu, the price of a village was 1,000 *curṇikās* which could be a smaller denomination of *cūrnī*. Besides, reference to *purāṇas* was absent

TABLE 2.1: TWELVE LAND CHARTERS OF THE SENAS

| *Land Grant* | *Amount of land granted* | *Produce from the land at the time of donation* |
|---|---|---|
| 1. Barrackpur copper plate of Vijayasena (*c*. AD 1096-1159) | 4 *pāṭakas* | 200 *kapardakapurāṇas* |
| 2. Naihati copper plate of Vallālasena (*c*. AD 1159-79) | 7 *bhū-pāṭakas*, 9 *droṇas*, 1 *ādhaka*, 34 *unmānas*, 3 *kākas* | 500 *kapardakapurāṇas* |
| 3. Govindapur copper plate of Laksmaṇasena (c. AD 1179-1206) | 60 *bhū-droṇas*, 17 *unmānas* | 900 *purāṇas* annually, at the rate of 15 *purāṇas* to the *drone* |
| 4. Tarpandighi copper plate of Laksmaṇasena | 120 *ādhāvāpas*, 5 *unmānas* | 150 *kapardakapurāṇas* annually |
| 5. Sundarban copper plate of Laksmaṇasena | 3 *bhū-dronas*, 1 *khādikā*, 23 *unmānas*, 2½ *kākinīs* | 50 *purāṇas* annually |
| 6. Anulia copper plate of Laksmaṇasena | 1 *pāṭaka*, 9 *droṇas*, 1 *ādhāvāpa*, 37 *unmānas*, *1 kākinikā* | 100 *kapardakapurāṇas* per year |
| 7. Saktipur copper plate of Laksmaṇasena | 6 *pāṭakas* | 500 (*kapardaka-purāṇas*) was the total income annually |
| 8. Bhowal/Rajavadi/India Office plate of Laksmanasena | a *droṇika*, one quarter plus 22 *yaṣṭis* | 400 *kapardakapurāṇas* annually |
| 9. Madhainagar copper plate of Laksmaṇasena | 100 *bhū-khādis*, 91 *khādikās* | 168 *kapardakapurāṇas* annually |
| 10. Madhyapara / Vangiya Sahitya Parishat plate of Viśvarūpasena (*c*. AD 1206-25) | a total of 336½ *unmānas* | total annual income was 500 |
| 11. Madanpara copper plate of Viśvarūpasena | not mentioned | 500+127=627 *purāṇas*/ *cūrṇīs* |
| 12. Edilpur plate of Keśavasena/ Viśvarūpasena | -do- | 200 (unit unspecified) |

in this record of the sixth-seventh centuries when there was no need to refer to a coin as *purāṇa* or old.

Cowries were certainly a measure of value for land under the Senas. Land values were calculated in terms of cowries called *kapardaka purāṇas*. It may be noted that the total income is always in round figures. Does this mean that where the income was 200 *kapardaka purāṇa* or 500 *kapardaka purāṇa*, it included *purāṇas* as well as a small sum of *kapardakas*, less than the value of a full *purāṇa*? In the Madhainagar plate we have reference to 100 *purāṇa* 68 *kapardaka* =168 *kapardakapurāṇas* as the annual income. Sometimes the charters only refer to *purāṇas* (no. 3) but they are probably the same as *kaparddakapurāṇas* of other charters. In later charters sometimes only the figure referring to the income appears (e.g., *samvatsarena pañca-śatotpattikam* – 1.36, Saktipur plate) without reference to any coin. Sometimes contractions like *sām bhū-hi* (i.e., *sāmvatsarika bhūmi hiraṇya*) = annual revenue income from land were used to refer to the income (no. 11).

This tendency of measuring the granted land in terms of the income from it proved to be so useful and effective that later charters, such as the Madanpara and the Edilpur plates even solely describe the plots of land donated as '*sāṁ śāsana bhū hi* 627' (yielding an income of 627 – Madanpara plate, l. 52) and '*sāṁ śāsana bhū hi* 200', thereby measuring them not by any locally used units of land measurement, but by the annual income they yielded to the state prior to the grant. Thus the practice of referring to the yield of the land prior to its donation initiated by the Pālas was continued by their successors, the Senas, and ultimately replaced the use of units of land measurement to describe the donated land.

The rate of revenue has been mentioned in the Govindapur copper plate as 15 *purāṇas* per *droṇa*. But as C. Gupta has shown, this rate was not uniform everywhere.[38] The rate was lower in the Tarpandighi plate. Gupta concludes that the land of a tenant was measured and the average production from it was also taken into account at the time of revenue assessment. Her study indicates that cultivable lands were distinguished from gardens and plantations and were recorded separately in revenue rolls.[39]

In some cases the term used is only *purāṇa* and not *kapardaka purāṇa*. Besides in the Sahitya Parishat and the Madanpada charter of Viśvarūpasena mention is made of *cūrṇṇīs*. The former refers to the amount of 500 *cūrṇṇīs*, neither *purāṇa* nor *kapardaka purāṇa*. The latter, more interestingly refers to 100 *cūrṇṇī* 32 *purāṇa* and 100 *cūrṇṇī* 27 *purāṇa*, thereby indicating that *cūrṇṇī* could be a higher denomination than the *purāṇa*. At the end while summarizing the amount only the figure 627 (500+127) has been mentioned, without reference to any unit. It may indicate that in case where no unit has been mentioned, we have to understand it as *purāṇa*.

D.C. Sircar, on the authority of the Alagum inscription of the time of Anantavarman thinks that *cūrṇṇī* is another name of *purāṇa*.[40] The inscription uses the expression *pañca-purāṇ-ādhika-cūrṇṇī-śat-aikena*, i.e., one hundred *cūrṇṇī*s exceeded by (the amount of) five *purāṇas* which was deposited at the temple. Again in line 24, where the donation is noted in numerical figure, the abbreviation *pu* is mentioned (*aṅke hi pu 105* ), implying thereby that the currency mentioned there was *purāṇa*. This would mean that 100 *cūrṇṇīs* and 5 *purāṇas* can alternatively be recorded as 105 *pu*, i.e. *purāṇas*. This may suggest that *cūrṇṇī* and *purāṇa* are same. The Mehar copper plate of Damodaradeva also uses both the terms in the same sense.[41] On the authority of the same Alagum inscription S. Basu Majumdar argues that *cūrṇṇī* means 'break up' into small denomination and it indicates that there were higher valuation currency units that required to be broken up into smaller change, e.g. in case of the conversion of the currency into cowrie-shells.[42] But the combined evidences of the Madanpada copper plate referring to 100 *cūrṇṇī* 32 *purāṇa* and 100 *cūrṇṇī* 27 *purāṇa* together with that of the Alagum inscription do not lend support to her view. Rather they indicate that *cūrṇṇī* could be the higher denomination and could not be a 'break up' into small denominations.

B.N. Mukherjee earlier suggested that *cūrṇṇī* is a unit of silver dust having the weight of a silver *kārṣāpaṇa* (i.e. 57 grains) and the value equal to that of 1280 *kapardaka*s. The Jayarampur plate of Gopacandra (sixth century) declared that the annual rent of the land granted by the charter was 100 *ārya-piṇḍaka* (lump sum) of 100 *cūrṇṇīs*.[43] Another suggestion made by S. Ghosh is that *cūrṇī* could be metal pieces / lumps equivalent to the weight of *purāṇa* as the Sena inscriptions never mention *cūrṇṇī* or *purāṇa* when the revenue is collected in *kapardaka purāṇas* and vice versa. This, according to Gupta points to the independent existence of *kapardaka purāṇa* as medium of exchange apart from *cūrṇṇī* and *purāṇa*.[44] In the absence of any evidence it is really difficult to determine the nature of the *cūrṇṇī*.

Thus we may conclude that the Senas used to collect land revenue either through cowries or through *cūrṇṇīs* that consisted of *purāṇas*, counted in *kapardakas*. The *cūrṇṇīs* were not minted currency. We may recall here the charter of Pradyumnabandhu of the sixth-seventh century referring to the *uparikara* of a village as 45 *kārṣāpaṇas*, indicating the practice of the payment of land tax by coins. Yet at the time of the transaction it was done through 1000 *curṇikās*. *Curṇikā*s could have been the lower denomination of *cūrṇṇī*.

The circulation of coins in urban centres, have, however, been indicated by the Deopara *praśasti* of Vijayasena.[45] In connection to the description of the favour shown by Vijayasena to the Vedic brāhmaṇas, the poet says that they shifted to the cities and their wives had to be taught by the wives of the townsmen to differentiate between *rūpya* and bottle-gourd flowers along with other things (verse 23). The term *rūpya* has been taken in the sense of silver coins.[46] This may suggest, although very inadequately, that the townsfolk were acquainted with silver coins. The *Vallālacarita*, although a late text (sixteenth century), refers to gold coins like *niṣka* and *suvarṇa* that Vallalasena wanted to borrow from a *suvarnavaṇik* (goldsmith). This may suggest that the merchants had an adequate supply of gold in the form of coins. But again the late date of the text does not allow us to be certain regarding the circulation of gold coins in the Sena territory.

Considering the above data regarding media of exchange in Pāla-Sena inscriptions it is clear that the state adopted the system of the use of cowries for various purposes: for the payment of salary, for gifts, for land tax, etc. Thus cowries operated in different exchange spheres. The question is why metallic money could not serve such purposes. Was there really a dearth of precious metal? Elsewhere in the other parts of the Indian subcontinent we find an attempt to handle the crisis of precious metal for minting coins by the use of mixed metal coinage and by using copper as a carrier medium as John Deyell has shown.[47] The availability of gold and silver in the region under study is suggested by the accounts of Sulaiman, Ibn Khurdadba, and others.[48] The Silimpur (Bogra) inscription from the northern part of Bangladesh records that nine hundred *hemas* were donated to a brāhmaṇa by Jayapāladeva of Kāmarūpa (*c.* twelfth century).[49] *Hema*, again was probably small pieces of gold and was not a minted currency. On the authority of a Tibetan account B.N. Mukherjee is, however, inclined to believe that each piece of *hema* denoted gold weighing 80 *ratis*.[50] However, even accepting this interpretation, *hema* would still refer to unminted currency. Besides the data cited by Mukherjee is in relation to the Vikramaśīlā monastery to which the gold was sent to facilitate Atīśa's visit to Tibet. This on the other hand indicates that minted currency was practically non-existent in the areas near the routes connecting Tibet with south Bihar.

My discussion shows that the use of cowries as official money was adopted throughout the delta in the eleventh to twelfth centuries with the help of the Senas. This is a case in which the use of coins was supplanted by the use of cowries. However, it is to be remembered that in the records under study the chief function of the cowries and the metallic lumps/dusts/ingots were to serve as the medium for tax collection. This would indicate that this medium was convenient for the villagers. Robert S.Wicks points out that farmers used the medium of exchange out of obligation. If forced to pay in metal they would have to purchase it, may be at discriminatory rates. The most convenient way may thus be to pay it either in grain or in cowrie which they were already using for their day-to-day transactions.[51] The fact that metallic lumps/dust/ingots and cowries were adopted by the state as official media of exchange indicates that there could not have been a shortage of metals in the rural areas. What was lacking was the desire to mint these metals into coins on the part of the state.

R.S. Sharma raised the question how far cowries could make up for the absence of metallic coins. He is of the opinion that the use of cowries denotes a 'backward economy' in which both local and long-distance trade could not play a substantial role. Cowries are inconvenient for large scale transactions.[52] However, he locates the end of the paucity of metal money in *c.* 1000 CE when a revival in trade could be noticed.[53]

Is there really any justification in labelling the use of cowries as the marker of a 'backward economy'? Cowries, were never a local product in Bengal. Bengal used to buy cowries from the Maldives in exchange of rice, as Ibn Battuta suggests.[54] Bin Yang has discussed the migration of cowrie shells from the Maldives to various parts of Asia as precious goods in the prehistoric era, later becoming a commodity and currency.[55] In fact it is through Bengal that cowries used to be imported to Yunnan from the Maldives. Thus cowries do operate in long-distance trade, but only in those economies that use them.

B.N. Mukherjee has cited abundant data relating to trade in early Bengal from the eighth to the twelfth centuries. His discussion shows that cotton, spices of various kinds, sugar, etc., were the items of export from Vaṅgāla in the thirteenth century.[56] But how far the rulers of the interior like the Pālas and Senas had interest in promoting this trade is not clear. It required control over the coastal tracts. Unfortunately, we lack any evidence of a land donation under the Pālas in its other parts of Bengal, suggesting their authority and control there. Image inscriptions donated by merchants from Kumilla refer to the reign of Gopāla III and Mahīpāla I (925 to 1025 CE). Although images are portable things and the stone used for manufacturing them is also not local,[57] this may indicate Pāla interest in the coastal tracts of southeastern Bengal, perhaps to control the maritime trade.[58] This may also explain why the early Muslim geographers mention that Rum (Pāla empire) as a vast country stretching to the sea.[59] But the nature and extent of the Pāla hold over southeastern Bengal remains unclear.

R. Mukherjee suggested that the drawbacks of using cowries as currency are that it could circulate only in those economies that were relatively marginal and had notably low levels of production and consumption.[60] In view of the agrarian expansion, existence of local level exchange centres like *haṭṭas* suggested by the inscriptional data[61] and also the rise of a centre of power like Rāmāvatī under the Pālas, this opinion does not seem to be correct. Certain commodities like textiles and rice could be traded with the countries which required them. There are instances for the adoption of cowries due to the stoppage in the supply of the usual media of exchange. In the state of Nanzhao in Yunan the practice of using silk as currency had been displaced by cowries from the ninth century onwards.[62] This was due to the disturbances in the Chinese silk routes through Central Asia. This situation is similar to Bengal in the Pāla-Sena era where cowries could serve all the purposes as a medium of exchange. No doubt the cowries as currency served the biggest to the smallest value transactions and adopting them as the official media of exchange proved to be useful. Besides, cowries had an advantage. As pointed out by Deyell, although the relative exchange ratio of cowries to silver was in flux, varying over seasons and year to year, they did not suffer from exchange variability that was the case with gold-silver exchanges elsewhere.[63] The question that remains unanswered is the factors which resulted in such a situation. Of course there could be a shortage in the supply of silver. But cowries continued to be counted in terms of silver standards like *purāṇa, cūrṇṇī,* and *paṇa.*

The establishment and the development of a dual denomination monetary system of silver *taṅka* coins and cowries under the Bengal Sultanate in the thirteenth century in order to meet the needs to pay an army heavily dependent on armed horsemen have been discussed by John Deyell.[64] On the basis of the data presented above, we may however locate the beginning of the integration of two dissimilar mediums of exchange into a single monetary system under the Bengal Sultans, from the ninth century, under the Pālas. Cowries counted in terms of a notional unit of silver currency of a specific weight began to figure in the Pāla inscriptions from the time of Gopāla II and gradually became much more organized, to stabilize under the Senas. The Bengal Sultans who could organize the import of silver bullion[65] brought back the use of real silver coins, although cowries were so deeply rooted in the economic transactions in the Bengal Delta, that they continued to exercise their influence in the revenue collecting apparatus.[66] Therefore it is not perhaps apt to remark that Bengal proper did not have any organized currency prior to the establishment of Turkish rule.[67]

## Acknowledgement

I am immensely grateful to Prof. Ranabir Chakravarti of the Centre for Historical Studies, Jawharlal Nehru University for providing important insights for this chapter.

### NOTES

1. B.N. Mukherjee, *Media of Exchange in Early Medieval North India*, New Delhi: Harman Publishing House, 1992, p. 41.
2. R.S. Sharma, *Early Medieval Indian Society: A Study in Feudalisation*, Kolkata: Orient Longman, 2001, pp.149-50.
3. B.M. Morrison, *Political Centres and Cultural Regions in Early Bengal*, Jaipur/Delhi: Rawat Publications, 1980, pp. 47, 51, figures 9 and 10.
4. D.C. Sircar, 'Coins in the Inscriptions of the Pālas and Senas in Eastern India', *Journal of the Numismatic Society of India*, vol. 36, 1974, pp. 71-6.
5. B.B. De, 'Epigraphic Accounts of the Numismatic History of Bengal', in *Early Indian Indigenous Coins*, D.C. Sircar, Calcutta: University of Calcutta, 1970, pp. 141-6.
6. B.D. Chattopadhyaya, 'Currency in Early Bengal', *Journal of Indian History*, vol. 55, 1977, pp. 41-60, especially p. 56.
7. B.N. Mukherjee, *Coins and Currency Systems of Post-Gupta Bengal (c.* A.D. *550-700)*, New Delhi: Munshiram Manoharlal, 1993, pp. 4-15.
8. S. Basu Majumdar, 'Monetary History of Bengal: Issues and Non-Issues', in *The Complex Heritage of Early India: Essays in Memory of R.S. Sharma*, ed. D.N. Jha, New Delhi: Manohar, 2014, pp. 585-605.
9. Ibid., p. 599.
10. S. Ghosh, 'Monetary Scenario of Early Medieval Bengal: Gleanings from Epigraphs', in *Essays on Early Bengal Epigraphy*, ed. M. Banerjee, Kolkata: Sanskrit Pustak Bhandar, 2005, pp. 156-5.
11. Chattopadhyaya, 'Currency in Early Bengal', p. 56.
12. John S. Deyell, *Living without Silver: The Monetary History of Early*

*Medieval North India*, New Delhi: Oxford University Press, 1990, p. 244.

13. D.C. Sircar, *Indian Epigraphical Glossary*, Delhi: Motilal Banarsidass, 1966, p.265.
14. Arlo Griffiths, 'New Documents for the Early History of Puṇḍravardhana: Copper Plate Inscriptions from the Late Gupta and Early Post Gupta Periods', *Pratnasamiksha*, New Series, vol. 6, 2015, pp. 15-38.
15. B.N. Mukherjee, 'Commerce and Money in the Western and Central Sectors of Eastern India (*c.* A.D. 750-1200)', *Indian Museum Bulletin*, vol. 17, 1982, pp. 65-83.
16. Ibid., p. 76, n.17.
17. Sircar, *Indian Epigraphical Glossary*, 1966, p.145.
18. N. Chakravarti, 'Pāla Inscriptions in the Indian Museum', *Journal and Proceedings of the Asiatic Society of Bengal*, vol. 4, 1908, pp. 101-9.
19. A. Ghosh, 'Numismatic and Treasure Trove', *Indian Archaeology: A Review*, vol. 1959-60, ed. A. Ghosh, Delhi: Archaeological Survey of India, 1966, p.65.
20. Deyell, *Living without Silver*, p. 30.
21. G. Bhattacharya, 'The British Museum Stone Inscription of Mahendrapāla', *South Asian Studies*, vol. 23, 2007, pp. 69-74.
22. R. Furui, 'Re-Reading Two Copper Plate Inscriptions of Gopāla II, Year 4', in *Prajñādhara: Essays on Asian Art, History, Epigraphy and Culture in Honour of Gouriswar Bhattacharya*, ed. G.R. Mevissen and A. Banerji, Delhi: Kaveri Books, 2009, pp. 319-30.
23. *Paṇa* is a coin of 80 *ratis*, the same as the copper *kārṣāpaṇa* and equal to 80 cowrie shells according to the Lilāvatī, cited by D.C. Sircar, *Indian Epigraphical Glossary*, p. 228; *gaṇḍaka* is also the name of a coin, p.111.
24. R. Furui, 'Rangpur Copper Plate Inscription of Mahīpāla I, year 5', *Journal of Ancient Indian History* , vol. 27, 2011, pp. 232-5, especially p. 237.
25. Furui, 'Re-reading Two Copper Plate Inscriptions of Gopāla II', p. 322.
26. R. Furui, 'Merchant Groups in Early Medieval Bengal: With Special Reference to the Rajbhita Stone Inscription of the Time of Mahīpāla I, Year 33', *Bulletin of the School of Oriental and African Studies*, vol. 73, 2013, pp. 391-412, p. 395.
27. R. Furui recently suggested that it actually belongs to Gopāla IV

who was then on the throne and Madanapāla at that time was his regent. R. Furui, 'Rajibpur Copper Plate Inscriptions of Gopāla IV and Madanapāla', *Pratnasamiksha*, New Series, vol. 6, 2015, p. 56.

28. N.N. Vasu, 'Copper Plate Inscription of Madanapāla', *Journal of the Asiatic Society of Bengal,* vol. 69, no.1, 1900, pp. 66-73.
29. The Bangladesh National Museum Stone Inscription of Bhojavarman, Year 7 probably refers to the grant of *kapardaka* and land with *haṭṭa* to a *brāhmaṇa*. The reading and interpretation is, however, doubtful due to the non-availability of a photograph. See Shariful Islam, 'Unpublished Stone Inscription of the Seventh Regnal Year of Bhojavarman', *Journal of the Asiatic Society of Bangladesh, Humanities*, vol. 55, no. 1, 2010, pp. 113-19.
30. D.C. Sircar, 'Three Pāla Inscriptions', *Epigraphia Indica,* vol. 35, 1966, pp. 233-8.
31. Sircar, *Indian Epigraphical Glossary*, p. 149.
32. Sircar, 'Three Pāla Inscriptions', pp. 233-8.
33. *Tāranatha's History of Buddhism in India*, ed. D. Chattopadhyaya, tr. Lama Chimpa, A. Chattopadhyaya, Simla: Indian Institute of Advanced Study, 1970, p. 193.
34. *Ramacaritam of Sandhyākaranandin,* H.P. Sastri (ed.), R.G. Basak, (tr.), Calcutta: The Asiatic Society, 1969, p. 93
35. H.M. Elliot and J. Dowson, *The History of India as Told by its own Historians: The Muhammadan Period*, vol. 1, London: Trübner and Co., 1867, p. 5.
36. *Tabaqat-i-Nasiri,* Section XX, 5, cited by B.N. Mukherjee, 'Commerce and Money in the Western and Central Sectors of Eastern India (*c.* A.D. 750-1200)', *Indian Museum Bulletin,* vol. 17, 1982, p. 68.
37. Chattopadhyaya, 'Currency in Early Bengal', p.53.
38. C. Gupta, 'Land Measurement and Land-revenue System in Bengal Under the Senas', in *Explorations in Art and Archaeology of South Asia: Essays Dedicated to N.G. Majumdar,* ed. D. Mitra, Calcutta: Directorate of Archaeology and Museums, Govt. of West Bengal, 1996, pp. 573-94, especially pp. 585-6.
39. Ibid., p. 585.
40. D.C. Sircar, 'Alagum Inscription of Anantavarman; Regnal Year 62', *Epigraphia Indica,* vol. 29, rpt., 1987, pp. 44-7, especially p. 45.
41. S. Ghosh, 'Use of Coin Terms in the Epigraphs of Early Medieval Bengal and Related Issues,' *Numismatic Digest,* vols. 36-7, 2012-13, pp. 94-112.
42. Basu Majumdar, 'Monetary History of Bengal', p. 598.

43. Mukherjee, *Coins and Currency Systems of Post-Gupta Bengal*, p. 5.
44. Ghosh, 'Use of Coin Terms in the Epigraphs', p. 102.
45. N.G. Majumdar, *Inscriptions of Bengal*, Kolkata: Sanskrit Pustak Bhandar, New Edition, 2003, pp. 42-56.
46. Ibid., p. 54.
47. Deyell, *Living without Silver*, p. 190.
48. Cited by Mukherjee, 'Commerce and Money', p. 66.
49. R.G. Basak, 'Silimpur Stone Slab Inscription of the Time of Jayapāladeva', *Epigraphia Indica*, vol. 13, rpt., 1982, pp. 283-95.
50. Mukherjee, 'Commerce and Money', p. 71.
51. Robert S. Wicks, *Money, Markets and Trade in Early Southeast Asia: The Development of Indigenous Monetary Systems to AD 1400*, Ithaca NY: Cornell Southeast Asia Programme Publications, 1992, p. 14.
52. R.S. Sharma, *Early Medieval Indian Society: A Study in Feudalisation*, Kolkata: Orient Longman, 2001, pp. 127-8.
53. Ibid. 151.
54. Ibn Battuta, *Travels in Asia and Africa 1325-1354*, cited by Bin Yang, 'The Bay of Bengal Connection to Yunan', in Rila Mukherjee, ed., *Pelagic Passageways: The Northern Bay of Bengal Before Colonisation*, Delhi: Primus Books, 2011, pp. 317-43.
55. Bin Yang, 'The Rise and Fall of Cowrie Shells: The Asian Story', *Journal of World History*, vol. 22, no. 1, March 2011, pp. 1-25.
56. Mukherjee, 'Commerce and Money', p. 66.
57. Three image inscriptions, all donated by merchants from south-eastern Bengal bear the name of Pāla rulers Gopāla II and Mahīpāla I (mid tenth to mid eleventh century). The stone is, however, not a product of Samataṭa. F. Asher has argued that the source of the dark grey or black rock from which most of the stone sculptures of Bihar and Bengal are carved out was Dalma hills, just north of present-day Jamshedpur. See F. Asher, 'Stone and the Production of Images', *East & West*, vol. 48, nos. 3-4, 1998, pp. 313-28. He further thinks that the extension of Pāla rule to southeast Bengal led to the introduction of this rock there. Thus it used to be transported 600 km from the quarry site. See F. Asher, 'The Effect of Pala Rule: A Transition in Art', *Journal of Indian Society of Oriental Art*, vols. XII, XIII, 1981-3, pp. 1-7. However, that must have been very expensive and the whole idea of transportation of rocks from such far-off places appears to be far-fetched. So the idea of penetration of Pāla power in Samataṭa, on the basis of these evidences is not strong. The merchant family could have been originally functioned somewhere in south Bihar

wherefrom they could have bought the said images to their village residence at Bilakindaka during one of their visits to their country residence.

58. R. Chakravarti also postulates this interest of the Pālas in coastal trade. See R. Chakravarti, 'The Pull Towards the Coast: Politics and Polity in India (*c.* 600-1300 CE)', *Presidential Address, Section I (Ancient India),* Patiala: Indian History Congress, 2011, pp. 17-18.
59. Mukherjee, 'Commerce and Money', p. 66.
60. R. Mukherjee, 'Bengal and the Northern Bay of Bengal', in Mukherjee ed., *Pelagic Passageways,* p. 145.
61. Transactions at the locality level served as the linkage between the agrarian and non-agrarian sector, R. Furui pointed to the frequent references to local markets or *haṭṭa* in the inscriptions of Bengal from the ninth century. Trade in coconut, areca nut, etc., used to be carried on in these local markets. At the same time inter-local trade used to be carried on through rivers and they were also exchanged in such *haṭṭas*. The flow of cowrie shells to the rural areas could have been facilitated by rural merchants and kept connections with the outer world. See R. Furui, 'Merchant groups', pp. 403-4.
62. H.U. Vogel, 'Cowry Trade and its Role in the Economy of Yunan', *Journal of the Economic and Social History of the Orient,* vol. 36, no. 4, 1993, pp. 309-53, cited by Rila Mukherjee, 'Bengal and the Northern Bay of Bengal', p. 27.
63. J.S. Deyell, 'Precious Metals, Debasements, and Cowrie-shells in the Medieval Indian Monetary Systems, *c.*1200-1575', in J.H. Munro, ed., *Money in the Pre-Industrial World: Bullion, Debasements and Coin Substitutes,* Pickering and Chatto, 2012, pp. 163-216.
64. J.S. Deyell, 'Cowries and Coins: The Dual Monetary Systems of the Bengal Sultanate', *The Indian Economic and Social History Review,* vol. 47, no. 1, 2010, pp. 63-106.
65. Deyell is of the opinion that Bengal sourced its silver from the Shan states (north eastern Burma) and neighbouring Yunnan. Ibid., p. 88. He further suggests that this silver bullion movement depended on a series of entrepots, one of which could be directly overland from Tibet and Burma. Ibid., p. 90.
66. Ibid., p. 68.
67. S.E. Hussain, 'Silver Flow and Horse Supply to Sultanate Bengal with Special Reference to Trans-Himalayan Trade (13th-16th Centuries),' *Journal of the Economic and Social History of the Orient,* vol. 56, 2013, pp. 264-308.

## BIBLIOGRAPHY

Asher, F., 'The Effect of Pāla Rule: A Transition in Art', *Journal of Indian Society of Oriental Art*, vols. 12-13, 1981-3, pp. 1-7.

______, 'Stone and the Production of Images', *East & West*, vol. 48, nos. 3-4, 1998, pp. 313-28.

Basak, R.G., 'Silimpur Stone Slab Inscription of the Time of Jayapāladeva', *Epigraphia Indica*, vol. 13, rpt. 1982, pp. 283-95.

Basu Majumdar, S., 'Monetary History of Bengal: Issues and Non-Issues', in *The Complex Heritage of Early India: Essays in Memory of R.S. Sharma*, ed. D.N. Jha, New Delhi: Manohar, 2014, pp. 585-605.

Bhattacharya, G., 'The British Museum Stone Inscription of Mahendrapāla,' *South Asian Studies*, vol. 23, 2007, pp. 69-74.

Chakravarti, R., 'The Pull Towards the Coast: Politics and Polity in India (*c.* 600-1300 CE),' *Presidential Address Section I (Ancient India)*, Patiala:Indian History Congress, 2011.

Chakravarti, N., 'Pāla Inscriptions in the Indian Museum,' *Journal and Proceedings of the Asiatic Society of Bengal*, vol. 4, 1908, pp. 101-9.

Chattopadhyaya, B.D., 'Currency in Early Bengal,' *Journal of Indian History*, vol. 55, 1977, pp. 41-60.

Chattopadhyaya, D., ed., Lama Chimpa, A. Chattopadhyaya, tr., *Tāranatha's History of Buddhism in India*, Simla: Indian Institute of Advanced Study, 1970.

De, B.B., 'Epigraphic Accounts of the Numismatic History of Bengal,' in *Early Indian Indigenous Coins*, ed. D.C. Sircar, Calcutta: University of Calcutta, 1970, pp. 141-6.

Deyell, J.S., *Living without Silver: The Monetary History of Early Medieval North India*, New Delhi: Oxford University Press, 1990.

______, 'Cowries and Coins: The Dual Monetary Systems of the Bengal Sultanate', *The Indian Economic and Social History Review*, vol. 47, no. 1, 2010, pp. 63-106.

______, 'Precious Metals, Debasements and Cowrie-shells in the Medieval Indian Monetary Systems, *c.*1200-1575,' in *Money in the Pre-Industrial World: Bullion, Debasements and Coin Substitutes*, ed. J.H. Munro, Pickering and Chatto, 2012, pp. 163-216.

Elliot, H.M. and J. Dowson, *The History of India as Told by its Own Historians: The Muhammadan Period*, vol. 1, London: Trübner and Co., 1867.

Furui, R., 'Re-Reading Two Copper Plate Inscriptions of Gopāla II, Year 4', in *Prajñādhara: Essays on Asian Art, History, Epigraphy and*

*Culture in Honour of Gouriswar Bhattacharya*, ed. G.R. Mevissen, A. Banerji, New Delhi: Kaveri Books, 2009, pp. 319-30.

———, 'Rangpur Copper Plate Inscription of Mahīpāla I, Year 5', *Journal of Ancient Indian History*, 27, 2011, pp. 232-45.

———, 'Merchant Groups in Early Medieval Bengal: With Special Reference to the Rajbhita Stone Inscription of the Time of Mahīpāla I, Year 33', *Bulletin of the School of Oriental and African Studies*, vol. 73, 2013, pp. 391-412.

———, 'Rajibpur Copper Plate Inscriptions of Gopāla IV and Madanapāla', *Pratnasamiksha*, New Series, vol. 6, 2015, pp. 39-61.

Ghosh, A. 'Numismatic and Treasure Trove', in *Indian Archaeology: A Review*, 1959-60, ed. A. Ghosh, New Delhi: Archaeological Survey of India, 1966, p. 65.

Ghosh, S., 'Monetary Scenario of Early Medieval Bengal: Gleanings from Epigraphs', in *Essay on Early Bengal Epigraphy*, ed. M. Banerjee, Kolkata: Sanskrit Pustak Bhandar, 2005, pp. 156-65.

———, 'Use of Coin Terms in the Epigraphs of Early Medieval Bengal and Related Issues', *Numismatic Digest*, vols. 36-7, 2012-13, pp. 94-112.

Griffiths, A., 'New Documents for the Early History of Puṇḍravardhana: Copper Plate Inscriptions from the Late Gupta and Early Post Gupta Periods,' *Pratnasamiksha*, New Series, vol. 6, 2015, pp. 15-38.

Gupta, C., 'Land Measurement and Land-revenue System in Bengal Under the Senas', in *Explorations in Art and Archaeology of South Asia: Essays Dedicated to N.G. Majumdar*, ed. D. Mitra, Calcutta: Directorate of Archaeology and Museums, Govt. of West Bengal, 1996, pp. 573-94.

Hussain, S.E., 'Silver Flow and Horse Supply to Sultanate Bengal with Special Reference to Trans-Himalayan Trade (13th-16th Centuries)', *Journal of the Economic and Social History of the Orient*, vol. 56, 2013, pp. 264-308.

Islam, S., 'Unpublished Stone Inscription of the Seventh Regnal Year of Bhojavarman,' *Journal of the Asiatic Society of Bangladesh, Humanities*, vol. 55, no. 1, 2010, pp. 113-19.

Majumdar, N.G., *Inscriptions of Bengal*, Kolkata: Sanskrit Pustak Bhandar, New Edition, 2003.

Morrison, B.M., *Political Centres and Cultural Regions in Early Bengal*, Jaipur/Delhi: Rawat Publications, 1980.

Mukherjee, B.N., 'Commerce and Money in the Western and Central

Sectors of Eastern India (*c.*AD 750-1200)', *Indian Museum Bulletin*, vol. 17, 1982, pp. 65-83.

______, *Media of Exchange in Early Medieval North India*, New Delhi: Harman Publishing House, 1992.

______, *Coins and Currency Systems of Post-Gupta Bengal (c.* AD *550-700)*, New Delhi: Munshiram Manoharlal, 1993.

Mukherjee, R., 'Bengal and the Northern Bay of Bengal', in *Pelagic Passageways: The Northern Bay of Bengal Before Colonisation*, ed. Rila Mukherjee, New Delhi: Primus Books, 2011.

Sastri, H.P., ed., R.G. Basak, tr., *Rāmacaritam of Sandhyākaranandin*, Calcutta: The Asiatic Society, 1969.

Sharma, R.S., *Early Medieval Indian Society: A Study in Feudalisation*, Kolkata: Orient Longman, 2001.

Sircar, D.C., 'Three Pāla Inscriptions', *Epigraphia Indica*, 35, 1966, pp. 233-8.

______, *Indian Epigraphical Glossary*, Delhi: Motilal Banarsidass, 1966.

______, 'Coins in the Inscriptions of the Pālas and Senas in Eastern India.', *Journal of the Numismatic Society of India*, vol. 36, 1974, pp. 71-6.

______, *Pāl O Sen Yuger Vaṁśānucharit* (in Bengali), Kolkata: Sahityalok, 1982.

______, 'Alagum Inscription of Anantavarman, Regnal Year 62', *Epigraphia Indica*, vol. 29, rpt. 1987, pp. 44-7.

Vasu, N.N., 'Copper Plate Inscription of Madanapāla', *Journal of the Asiatic Society of Bengal*, vol. 69, no. 1, 1900, pp. 66-73.

Vogel, H.U., 'Cowry Trade and its Role in the Economy of Yunan', *Journal of the Economic and Social History of the Orient*, 36, 4, 1993, pp. 309-53.

Wicks, R.S., *Money, Markets and Trade in early Southeast Asia: The Development of Indigenous Monetary Systems to* AD *1400*, Ihaca NY: Cornell Southeast Asia Programme Publications, 1992.

Yang, B., 'The Bay of Bengal Connection to Yunan', in *Pelagic Passageways: The Northern Bay of Bengal Before Colonisation*, ed. Rila Mukherjee, New Delhi: Primus Books, 2011, pp. 317-43.

______, 'The Rise and Fall of Cowrie Shells: The Asian Story', *Journal of World History*, vol. 22, no.1, March 2011, pp. 1-25.

3

# Understanding the Economic Networks and Linkages of an Expanded Harikela

SUCHANDRA GHOSH

The Bay of Bengal is a significant maritime zone connecting South and Southeast Asia. It looms large in Arabic and Persian travel accounts from the mid-ninth century, designated as *Bahr-i-Harkand* in the *Silsilat al-Tawārikh* by Sulayman Tajir in 851, the earliest known source to so name it.[1] Harkand derives from Harikela, a subdivision of Bengal identified with the present Chittagong area. Again, the Bay of Bengal was clearly defined as *Bahr Harkal* or the sea of Harikela by the anonymous author of the *Hudud al-A'lam* (*c.* 982).[2] This refers to 'H.rk.nd' (taken to be the same as Harikela) as a place on the sea coast together with 'N. myas', Urshin, 'S.m.n.d.r.' and Andras. The reference to 'H.rk.nd' along with Samandar as places on the seacoast is significant, being either a misinterpretation by the author that the port of Samandar lay within the Harikela country, or by the fact that Harikela was the name of a kingdom as well as the name of a place identifiable with present-day Chittagong. Associated with Harkand or Harkal we come across a port town called Samandar located in the same area.[3]

The Moroccan traveller al Idrisi, in 'The delight of those who seek to wander through the regions of the world' (*Nuzhatu-l Mushtak*), of the mid-twelfth century, writes,

> Samandar is a large town, commercial and rich, and where there are good profits to be made . . . it stands upon a river which comes from the country of Kashmir. Rice and various grains, especially excellent wheat

are to be obtained here … Aloe wood is brought here from the country of Karmut (Kāmarūpa) 15 days distance by a river of which the waters are sweet….One day's sail from this city, there is a large island well peopled and frequented by merchants of all countries. . . .[4]

Al Idrisi based a large portion of his work on the *Kitabu-l Masalik Wa-l Mamalik* (Book of Roads and Kingdoms) written by Ibn Khurdādba in the late ninth century, who also wrote about Samandar.[5] The descriptions point to the fact that Samandar was a premier port of southeastern Bengal at that time. Thus it can be surmised that by the mid-ninth century both the sea and its port attracted the attention of Arabic and Persian writers and became part and parcel of the Arab world. That a sea was named after a particular unit—Harikela—speaks for the region's importance and also its popularity among the seafarers of the time.

Chinese monks and pilgrims referred to Harikela earlier. I-jing[6] met Wu-hing near Nālanda in the first year of Ch'ui-king period (685), the latter sailing from Simhala towards the northeast and coming to 'Harikela, which was the eastern limit of Eastern India [Tung T'ien (-chu)] and of *Jambudvīpa*[7].' This suggests that Harikela must have had a littoral within its limits. Harikela is mentioned in indigenous sources at about the same time: the *Ārya Mañjuśrī Mulakalpa* (eighth century)[8] cites Vaṅga, Harikela and Samataṭa as distinct entities. Closely linked with Harikela was Samataṭa, identified with present Comilla and Noakhali districts of Bangladesh. I-jing refers to Samataṭa, indicating that Harikela was that region which lay to the east or southeast of the Comilla and Noakhali districts. Thus Harikela denoted by the second half of the seventh century only the coastal area of Chittagong, located within the ambit of the trans-Meghna region. I shall focus on the trade networks of Harikela and emphasize its linkages, so that Samataṭa, Kāmarūpa, and Arakan will come into the discussion for their networked relationship with Harikela.

## Political Overview

Our knowledge of the political situation of Harikela suggests it was ruled by the Buddhist kings Devātideva, Kāntideva, and

Attākaradeva, although no connection can be established between them.[9] A land grant of Devātideva dated 715 refers to *Harikelayam* (the people of Harikela). To date this is the first epigraphic reference to Harikela.[10]

The Chittagong area over which Devatideva ruled is described as *Khasa-maka*. Probably Devātideva belonged to the non-Aryan Khasa tribe mentioned as mercenaries in the Pāla land grants. The Khasas have been described in the early literary texts as a primary people from a hilly region—perhaps the Chittagong Hill Tracts—their kshatriya character and military prowess are highlighted.[11] The kshatriya character of the Khasas is apparent in the metal vase inscription wherein Devātideva is seen as Khasa. It is specifically mentioned in the inscription that land transactions were made to Haritakadharmasabhā vihāra by the residents of the Chandrabhaṭṭārika grāma situated in the *Khasa maka* (Khasa kingdom).

Under Kāntideva (*c.* 800-25) Harikela came to form a *maṇḍala* with its capital (*vāsaka*) at Vardhamānapura—identified with present Bara-Uthan village of the Patiya Upazila in Chittagong.[12] Although a *maṇḍala,* the name of Kāntideva's kingdom is unknown. Harikela continued as a *maṇḍala* under *Rājādhirāja Samaramṛgāṇka* Attākaradeva (early tenth century), with the capital still at Vardhamānapura. According to G. Bhattacharya, he was from Arakan, ruling over the region, but there is no evidence to substantiate this claim; he was probably a subordinate of Trailokya Chandra (*c.* 905-925), the father of Śrīchandra.[13] Recently a coin, in conformity with the Ākara coins, has been found with the name Attākara.[14] If they are the same person, then he belonged to the Ākara family of Chittagong, a family known by the coins issued by them.

According to the Rāmpāl and Bogra plates[15] of Śrīchandra, Trailokya Chandra (*c.* 900-25) became king at Chandradvipa (Bakharganj), and was the 'mainstay' of the royal family of Harikela (*harikelarājakakudacchatrasmitānāmśriyām*). This statement is taken to mean that this family rose to supreme power from a subordinate status in Harikela.[16] We have no idea of their overlords. Later, Vaṅga, Samataṭa and Śrihaṭṭa formed the Chandra kingdom, thereby becoming a regional power.[17] Our sources for this study are land grant documents and coins.

From the shadowy politics of this region, I now move on to the economy of this expansive unit, discussing the linkages between the agrarian and non-agrarian sectors of the economy. The early medieval period in South Asia experienced a remarkable agrarian expansion. Our sources indicate that Harikela, seemingly peripherally located far from the Ganga valley, developed trade, a monetized economy, and an impressive port like Samandar that was in turn linked with the riverine feeder ports Devaparvata in Samataṭa and *Vaṇgasāgarasambhaṇḍariyaka* in Vaṅga (the present Dhaka area). This suggests a dynamic economic landscape in contrast to the languishing economic portrayal of the period in Marxist historiography.[18]

## A Braided Economic Network: Agrarian and Non-Agrarian Sectors

The agrarian history of early medieval India is understood primarily through the study of land grants, ubiquitous in each region. The expansion of the agrarian economy gave a fillip to the non-agrarian sector, deriving its raw material largely from the former. Though the Harikela land grant documents are limited in number, they are of significance, grants being recorded on metal vases as well as copper plates. The names of rural residents and their involvement with land plots inform us of the nature of social relations prevailing in the region, since a diverse range of social groups possessing land holdings resided in rural settlements.

These grants, when studied against the backdrop of the Samataṭa grants, reveal a clear picture of the agrarian sector and the use of metallic currency for the purchase of land. An initial study of the Samataṭa land grants suggests its rulers were keen on expanding their agrarian base by way of creating new settlements or by granting large areas of *khila* (cultivable lands) which were then cultivated. This was not the case in Harikela. Two different patterns are apparent in the nature of donations: one relating to large-scale settlements of Brāhmaṇas, the other relating to donations of cultivated land plots scattered around several settlements to the Buddhist *vihāras*. This pattern of donation also reveals scarcity and corresponding pressure on land, noted in the Ashrafpur copper plates of Deva Khaḍga (*c.* 675) where donated lands were taken away (*apaniya*) from their enjoyers (*bhujyamanaka*) and granted to the donee.[19]

Agrarian spread in eastern India in general was marked by a profusion of paddy cultivation, of which the boro variety of paddy finds frequent mention in the Samataṭa inscriptions. This is clear from the name ending 'voraka' attached either to persons or to an entire village, as in the Mainamati copper plates of Laḍahachandra.[20] In both grants we have the expression *Voraka* or *Voraka grāma* attached to the name of a person or village. Sircar identifies *voraka* occurring in the names of some of the villages in the two plates with the Bengali *boro*, a variety of rice sown in low, swampy grounds and along riverbanks. The area being near the Meghna flood plain, this identification is perfect: boro rice is always cultivated in flood plains which are fertile, being rich in minerals. Sircar interprets *Baleśvaravardhaki voraka* as a plot of boro-sown land owned by, and named after, the carpenter Baleśvara while *Kaṁsākārakaddapolaka-grāma* might have been a village named after the *kamsakara* Kaddapolaka. B.D. Chattopadhyaya observes that the recurrence of the suffix *voraka* in the villages named after individuals (e.g. *Vappasimhavoraka-grāma*) suggests small, dispersed settlements adapted to a particular type of terrain and form of cultivation.[21] In a recently studied copper plate of Śrīchandra found from Bogra, we find the village Vyāghravoraka in Samataṭa mandala in Śrīnagara district,[22] the name vyāghra indicating that the terrain was a swampy forest tract perhaps infested by tigers at one point—suitable for boro cultivation. The existing cultivation of the boro variety of paddy occurs mostly on the sites between streams or beside rivers. Devaparvata—the famous port of Samataṭa—was located on such a ridge.

When we move to the non-agrarian sector in Samataṭa from Gunaigarh,[23] we find occupational and professional groups mentioned in boundary demarcations of granted lands. Here individual owners of land and tanks belong to different occupational groups like that of carpenter (*vardhaki*) and mechanic (vilāla) and also we find the presence of a cloth merchant community (*dosi*) along with the Vaidyas or practitioners of medicine. Interestingly Vilāla as a professional group is also visible in a new copper-plate grant of Vainyagupta edited by Furui.[24] Thus the presence of rich agrarian tracts populated with artisans allows us to envision the potentials of local level exchanges of agricultural products and craft goods. The Mainamati Plate (1) of Laḍahachandra of regnal year 6 (late tenth century) in the Samataṭa area, while delineating boundary specifications, speaks not only of a rural society and settlements, but also of Dhritipura—a town—with its market centre (*Dhritipura hattika samet*),[25] located within a predominantly agrarian context. Dhritipura could have been an incipient urban centre. That *sārthavāhas* were present in the Samataṭa subregion is also evident from the Mandhuk image inscription of the time of Gopāla II, year 1, which has *vṛddhasārtha* Jambhalamitra as the donor.[26] The term *vṛddhasārtha* can be understood both in the sense of a senior merchant or as a leader of merchants. There are two other inscriptions from Samataṭa mentioning *vaṇikas*. One is the Baghaura image inscription of Mahīpāla I, year 3, where the donor is vaṇika Alokadatta, the son of Vasudatta belonging to Vilakīndaka in Samataṭa.[27] The other is the Narayanpur image inscription dated year 4 of the same king.[28] Here *vaṇika* Buddhamitra, son of *vaṇika* Jambhalamitra residing in Vilikandhaka of Samataṭa, is the donor. Furui has correctly argued that the two Jambhalamitras were not the same person, considering the fact that the first inscription belonged to the second half of the ninth century, while the last two can be assigned to the end of the tenth century.[29] Moreover *Vaṇika* and *sārthavāha* are two different categories of merchants, and the Jambhalamitra of the Mandhuk image was a *sārthavāha* and this Jambhalamitra was a *vaṇika,* although interchange among the categories was not unknown. We have an image of exchange, markets, and merchants in Samataṭa, and neighbouring Harikela benefitted from this economic prosperity as it acted as a hinterland of Samandar, its port.

I remarked earlier that the number of inscriptions from Harikela are few and do not match in number those from Samataṭa, yet a detailed study of these inscriptions yields an idea of a burgeoning economic situation where monetization played a significant role. I concentrate on two land grants from Harikela inscribed not on copper-plates but on metal vases. The first metal vase inscription was issued in the first half of the seventh century by the local ruler Devātideva *bhaṭṭāraka*[30]. This land grant records five different occasions of land transfer in favour of the same *Mahāyāna* Buddhist monastery—Haritaka-Dharmasabhā-Vihāra—over two years, not recorded chronologically. The first land transfer took place in the year of Mārgaśīrṣa, the third day of the bright fortnight of the month *Āṣāḍha*. Land was bought by *Mahāpradhāna Dauvārika* Saubhāgyakīrtti and *Mahāpradhāna Mantrimukhya* Nayaparākrama-gomin in the presence of a number of royal officers and village notables. Altogether thirty-three *pāṭakas*[31] of land were bought. Eleven *pāṭakas* of land of Vedago(śo?)ṅgajavī belonging to Mobhināda *khaṇḍa* were bought from Sañja, Oru, Ehiśūri, and Thihu of that village, indicating autochthonous land ownership. Another twenty-two *pāṭakas* of land of Pitisoṇda were bought from *bhaṭṭa* Mitra, Vesi, Anukula, Daddi-śurika and others of that village. Though the amount of money paid for the transaction is not mentioned, the expression *su-kreyana* indicates that the land was bought at a good price. Along with this another twenty-five *pāṭakas* of land were donated by Pṛthudāma, Jiṣnudāma, and Gaurīdāma with the tenure of 'excessive enjoyment' (*sarvātibhoga*) for the increase of merit of the king Devātideva and *Mantrimukhya* Nayaparākrama-gomin, for the repair and maintenance of the *maṭha* and the future comfort, knowledge, and protection of the *viṣaya*. The expression *sarvātibhoga* is significant as the same expression is seen much earlier in the new Vainyagupta plate from Gunaigarh, where it is mentioned as a condition of donation and its approval.[32] The term seems to denote entitlement to all incomes and privileges pertaining to donated tracts.

The second purchase occurred probably two years later, on the thirteenth of the dark fortnight of the month Puṣya in the Māgha year. Ācarya Śāntibhadra and Surakṣita . . . (the first part of the name is deleted in the inscription) prabha of the same monastery along with *karaṇi* Hastirudra and Vijayin and others purchased some sixty *droṇavāpas* of land, again with a tenure of 'excessive enjoyment' from two goldsmiths named Kulachandra and Ratnachandra. The lands were given from their own share (*sva-bhāgāt*), suggesting that they were already in use and so were located within the settled area, agrarian expansion obviously not being the motive here. The next transaction mentioned took place two years after the first incident on the seventh bright fortnight of the month of Māgha. The residents of the Saṅgha, Ācarya Śāntibhadra, Devasimha, Sucharita, and Somaprabhu, along with *karaṇi* Hastirudra and Vijayin and some others, purchased some sixty *droṇavāpas* of fallow land (*khila-kṣetra*) in Chandrabhaṭṭarika village of *Khaṣa-maka* belonging to Śarabhadatta—and other residents of the village—for one hundred and twenty *taṇḍakas.* During the fourth purchase, thirty *droṇavāpas* of land were bought by the residents of the *vihāra*, in lieu of *taṇḍakas*, and another thirty *droṇavāpas* of land along with one *vihāra* were donated to the same monastery with the tenure of 'excessive enjoyment'. The fifth case recorded in the inscription took place in the same year of the second and third transactions on the eleventh of the 'bright fortnight of the month of Āṣāḍha' in the Māgha year. A high-ranking monk of the monastery purchased one *pāṭaka* and three *droṇavāpas* of land of which twenty eight *droṇavāpas* were situated in Kālasra-kaṭaka and fifteen *droṇavāpas* belonged to *mahāvārika* Sahadeva and a few others such as Kaliśuri, Kenduśuri, Amṛtalakṣaṇi. It is striking that such a small portion of land had to be purchased from several owners. An amount of land was bought with fifty-eight *taṇḍakas.* At the end it is mentioned that a total of thirty *pāṭakas* and twenty *droṇavāpas* of land was transferred to the monastery. If we calculate the amount of *taṇḍakas* used for the purchase of the lands, it appears that over one hundred seventy eight *taṇḍakas* were spent for the purchases—a substantial amount although we do not know the value of each *taṇḍaka.* (I discuss the term *taṇḍaka* later in this essay.)

I shall now discuss the metal vase inscription issued in the first half of the tenth century CE by *rājadhirāja* Attākaradeva, the ruler of the Harikela *maṇḍala.*[33] The inscription records the construction of a cell in a small monastery (*maṭhika*) Bela-Vihāra, and the donation of land by the *mahāpratihāra* Sahadeva in favour of that monastery for the attainment of enlightenment and increase of religious merit. Present and future kings of the Harikela *maṇḍala* are mentioned, no official seal has been found on the inscription. Here land was donated on two occasions. On the first occasion some *pāṭakas* of land were taken from *kārada* Indranātha and *bhārada* Amhela. Furui explains the words *kārada* and *bhārada* respectively as 'giving tax' and 'giving labour'.[34] On the second occasion a small garden of areca nut (*guvāka*) was taken from Nāgadatta. According to Bhattacharya this donation was inscribed later on the rim of the vase. Therefore, we can detect three different categories of landholdings. Categories like *kārada* and *bhārada* indicate the offering of tribute to the political authority either by giving a share of production or labour. Donation of an areca nut garden suggests scope for a commodity donation, since areca nuts were an exchangeable product in the local-level exchange network. There is no doubt that the garden was bought from the owner Nāgadatta, though no mention of sale has been found to date. The first epigraphic reference to Chaṭṭagrāma is perhaps found in this vase grant, referring to an area as *navachaṭṭa-nava* affixed to *chaṭṭa* suggests a new settlement. That the neighbouring area of the donated land was agriculturally rich is understood by the expression *upajāyamāna kṣetra*, meaning land with good yields.

There is a distinct difference between the phraseology of the land grants from Samataṭa and the two vases from Harikela. While Samataṭa—like other parts of India—followed the Dharmaśāstric format of land grants,[35] the pattern in the vase inscriptions was different. In Harikela lands were directly purchased with coin money and then granted to the donee, while no such reference to direct purchase can be found in the Samataṭa grants. Fewer land grants and the purchases of land for donation indicate a paucity of free land. Considering the geographical scenario of Harikela where we have hill tracts on the one hand and the coast on the other, which with its saline content in the soil could not be very good for paddy cultivation, availability of cultivable land was less here compared to neighbouring Samataṭa. It also indicates, significantly perhaps, that land grants and monetization are not to be seen as contrasting categories.

## The Numismatic Scenario

The regular use of the monetary term *taṇḍaka* in the context of land transactions in the two vase inscriptions from Harikela is a clear pointer to coins called *taṇḍaka* being used for transactions. In fact it is significant that both Samataṭa and Harikela experienced monetization, though the kings of Samataṭa initially minted dynastic gold coins[36] whereas Harikela experienced a circulation of silver coins with the place name Harikela written on them and thus were clearly non-dynastic in character. The sustained minting of silver coins bearing the name Harikela is the most important evidence regarding the territory of Harikela and its expanding economic orbit. Gradually Harikela coins began to circulate in the Samataṭa area and beyond, being found at Mainamati in Samataṭa, Jobra in Chittagong, Sylhet, Belonia subdivision of Tripura, Sandoway in southern Arakan and other places.[37] Stylistically, typologically, and metrologically these pieces are related to the Chandra dynasty of Arakan. The device of a Bull and Tripartite symbol on the coins of the rulers of Arakan was imitated in the issues bearing the name Harikela and circulated from the seventh to the twelfth-thirteenth centuries, indicating that Harikela made its presence felt as a distinct territorial entity for a long time.[38] The most striking features of the Harikela silver pieces are their fine metallic purity and the maintenance of the metallic weight standard.

Recently a coin with the Harikela device bearing the name Kāntidatta has become known.[39] Kāntidatta could be the Kānti-deva of the Chittagong copper-plate which references Harikela *maṇḍala*. It is almost certain that the early Harikela coins were struck in Harikela (Chittagong) itself. When these coins were struck, a port in the area must have been in the making. This can be inferred from two indirect references. First, we know that Ijing recorded that Wu-hing sailed from *Simhala* for the northeast and 'came to *Harikela*, which was the eastern limit of Eastern India [Tung T'ien (-chu)] and of *Jambudvipa*', At that time, Tamralipta was active as port but Wu hing sailed to Harikela—natural perhaps since he was using the sea route from Sri Lanka. Second, when Xuan Zang mentioned Samatata's relations with Southeast Asian polities, movement obviously took place through a port in contiguous Harikela. Samatata did not have a sea port. It could only boast of the riverine port of Devaparvata.[40]

The silver 'Harikela' coinage in the area of Comilla and southern Tripura gradually lost weight and deteriorated in calligraphy, style, and the quality of manufacture while entering into the currency zone of Samataṭa, and influencing the silver currency of Pattikera as well. Harikela coins have been reported also from the Paglatek hoard in Assam.[41] B.N. Mukherjee's study of Harikela coins reveals that they became thinner, lighter in weight, and broader in flan after the tenth century, suggesting modifications in line with the reformed Arab dirham currency.[42] Thus while the Harikela silver coins played a stellar role in strengthening the local economy, especially of commerce in the littoral, a trade relation with the Arab world can also be postulated. Their circulation pathways increased with the rise of Samandar as port.

While there was minted currency in the subregions of Samataṭa and Harikela in southeastern Bengal, revenue was assessed and expressed in terms of cash, but paid in non-minted currency. The Mehar Copperplate of Dāmodardeva is an indicator of a complex monetary system in Samataṭa where transactions could be made or expressed in multiples of one sixteenth *purāṇas*.[43] A hoard study of Harikela coins suggests that the hoard consisted of one-eighth and one-sixteenth unit pieces.[44] The cowrie/kauri was always used as a parallel currency in the sub-regions of Bengal. Harikela was also perhaps no exception, though none of the inscriptions mention the term *kapardaka*. When Marvazi's account of Bengal (in 1120)[45] states that 'in a town called "H.DKIRA" (identified with Harikela) business is carried on by means of gold (coins) and cowrie shells but the latter are more in use . . . ' we know that these shells reached Harikela from the Maldives and then transferred to the hinterlands of the Pāla-Sena domains where they were used as a parallel currency.[46] Ibn Battuta's testimony is also evocative of the demand for cowries in Bengal. He procured cowries against gems when leaving the Maldives. But the Wazir held him back. The ensuing conversation is significant. When Ibn Battuta asked the Wazir,

'What shall I do with the Cowries I bought?', the Wazir replied 'Send one of your companies [in the translation by Gibb he writes "companies" but in the next line he refers to his "companion". Since it is a quote I maintain the spelling] to sell them for you in Bengal.'[47] It appears that major transactions such as land purchases were traded through minted currency in Harikela, a premise supported by Ejaz Hussain: 'Harikela silver coins were most likely struck for the purpose of facilitating overseas trade in warhorses along with some other articles.'[48] Horses had to be imported against payment in coins because war horses were neither bartered nor possible to purchase on a regular basis through cowries.

## Fluvial Networks and Riverine Trade Centres

Land grants helped in the burgeoning of exchange in agrarian products, mostly at locality-level exchange centres sometimes integrated with wider commercial networks into distant destinations. In the case of southeastern Bengal, though we do not have specific reference to locality level exchange centres, it is possible to show that the riverine trade centres of Vaṅga and Samataṭa could connect with the wider networks of the Samandar port in Chittagong. Distinct sub-regions of Bengal were largely formed by their hydrography. The name Samataṭa itself signifies a flat coastal area, corroborated by Xuan Zang (629-45 CE, *Travels in India*).[49] While the Bay of Bengal formed its southern boundary, its northern boundary was flanked by the river Meghna, which was joined by the river Padma. The Meghna and the Brahmaputra are again linked to each other. The interchangeability and navigability of these rivers offers excellent routes between regions and connected the interior to the sea. Fluvial networks of communication can be understood from the presence of expressions related to *nau*, be it a tax or boat parking station, *nau-bandhakas* or *nau-daṇḍakas* (parking stations for vessels plying in the river) in the epigraphic sources of Vaṅga and Samataṭa. To cite an example we have the Kailan copperplate of Śrīdharaṇarāta (*c*. 665-75 CE) where along with means to *naudaṇḍakas* (boat parking stations), we find the terms *nauprṭhvī*, *nau-sthira-vegā*, and *nau Śivabhogā* in the context of markers for boundaries.[50] The term *nauprthvī* literally signifies a world of boats (*nau*). Can we then say that *nauprthvī* means the innumerable boats that were present around Devaparvata, ancient capital of Samataṭa and riverine trade centre?

The term *kshetra* is attached to *nau-sthira-vegā* an expression difficult to explain. But since one of the boundaries of the donated plot had *villa-bhaṅga* (*bil* is a common Bengali word meaning a watery low lying moss filled land) and with it was associated the expression *niṣkrāntaka-praviṣṭaka*[51] (facilities of exit and entry of vessels), then perhaps *nausthiravega* was a space with stagnant water—a sort of flat land used as a parking station. What is interesting is that in case of boundary markers this inscription uses terms relative only to boats.

In this context of riverine communications, it will be pertinent to bring in Devaparvata—the capital of Samataṭa. R. Chakravarti suggests that apart from being an administrative centre it was also a riverine port.[52] It was located in the Mainamati ridge near Comilla; archaeological excavations and explorations in the area have revealed its extraordinary historical significance. We know of Devaparvata from five inscriptions, each giving a vivid description of its landscape.[53] The earliest epigraphic description of Devaparvata is found in the Kailan copper-plate of Śrīdharaṇarāta (about 665-75), followed by his Uḍiśvara copper-plate.[54] In the description of the landscape in the Kailan copper plate, Devaparvata is encircled by the river Kṣirodā (modern Khirnai), in which elephants bathed, and both its banks were adorned by boats, as it is described as *sarvotabhadra* meaning approachable on all sides (*atha-mattamāta. ngaśatasukhavigāhyamānovividhatīrthayā naubhir=aparimitābhir =upārachitakulayā parīkṣitād-abhimatanimnagāminyā Kṣirodayā sarvvatobhadrakād-Devaparvvatāt*). The record also refers to three boat parking stations (*naudaṇḍakas*) which indicate that it was a riverine port as well as the political centre of the Rātas.

Devaparvata can again be seen in a copper plate of Rājaputra Balabhaṭṭa, sometime in the later half of the seventh century.[55] It speaks of the issuance of the charter from his palace at Kaṭakasila of a *jayaskandhāvāra* which is surrounded by the sacred river Kṣirodā. The next reference to Devaparvata is found in the

Asiatic Society copper plate of Bhavadeva Abhinavamṛgāṅka (*c.* 765-80)[56] of the Deva dynasty of Samataṭa. Devaparvata had gained substantially in stature and glory—it was explicitly stated to have been the jayaskandhāvāra, a term coterminous with the royal capital or a major politico-administrative centre—and was still associated with the river Kṣirodā. The city and its river had become the most sacred in the region. The last known epigraphic evidence of Devaparvata is furnished by the Paschimbhag copper plate of Śrīchandra (*c.* 925-75), dated to his fifth regnal year.[57] Here too its location was on the Kṣirodā, on which plied many boats. It said in the record that Lālambīvana (present day Lalmai, close to Mainamati) was searched by hundreds of boatmen for medicinal herbs (*Lālambīvanam=atra nāvika-śatair=anviṣṭa*) reinforcing Devaparvata as riverine port.[58]

During the time of the Chandras, Devaparvata no longer figures as a jayaskandhāvāra, though it remained a riverine port. This was due to the more extensive power base of the Chandras, which necessitated a shift of capital to a more strategic location. Here mention should also be made of a typical toponym—*Vaṅgasāgarasambhāṇḍāriyaka* located in Yolāmaṇḍala—mentioned in the Madanpur copper-plate charter of Śrichandra. The implication of this toponym was brought to light by R. Chakravarti.[59] He identified *Vaṅgasāgarasambhāṇḍāriyaka* with Sabhar, an archaeological site seventeen miles northwest of Dhaka, near which the copper-plate was discovered. The site was a riverine port located on the confluence of the Vaṃśāvati (Vaṃśāi) and the Dhaleśvari, and a Buddhist centre; a large number of clay moulded tablets with Bodhisattva images, and Buddhist stone and bronze sculptures have been found. *Vaṅgasāgarasambhāṇḍāriyaka* appears to have functioned as an inland riverine exchange centre, offering warehousing facilities and fluvial communications to the Bay of Bengal (*Vaṅgasāgara*). The discovery of the Madanpur copper-plate of Śrichandra from the Sabhar area, according to Chakravarti, 'strongly suggests that a *sambhāṇḍāriyaka* (a trade centre with warehousing facilities) could very well have existed at Sabhar in the early medieval times.'[60]

An administrative centre called Navyāvakāśikā occurs in an earlier inscription from Vaṅga, meaning a new opening or a channel. Such channels were mostly navigable and would have offered additional communication with Vaṅga and the littoral areas. This linkage also comes alive in the light of a recent study of a hoard[61] discovered from the village of Sandip near Sabhar, consisting of fifteen gold coins of the Samataṭa type which circulated even after the introduction of the Gupta gold coins from the Vaṅga subregion of early Bengal. This affirms a trade relation between Vaṅga and Samataṭa. Sabhar was an important trading centre from around the sixth century until at least the tenth.[62] One can still see boats laden with merchandise plying on the Sitalakshya from Dhaka towards Barishal.

## The Arakan Connection

A discussion on Harikela or early Chittagong also brings in the Arakan coast, further reinforcing our notion of an expanded Harikela. The two formed an environmental continuum with a climate and geography fundamentally different from the Ganga and Irrawaddy plains on the northwest and southeast. Communication was provided by intersecting rivers facilitating coastal journeys and trade, overland travel being difficult as the rugged Arakan Yoma closed Arakan off from Burma proper. This is precisely the reason no coins have been found in the area of the Chittagong Hill Tracts. The coastal strip that forms the Arakan littoral is nowhere more than a hundred kilometres wide before it reaches the Arakan Yoma, leaving the littoral with its many rivers and islands very open to influences from the Bay of Bengal. West of the Chittagong hill tract is a broad plain, intersected by rivers draining into the Bay of Bengal, which rises to a final chain of low coastal hills, mostly below 200 metres and attaining a maximum elevation of 350 metres. In this wet coastal plain are located the cities of Chittagong in the north and Ramu in the south. Coastal Chittagong was definitely ancient Harikela and the present town of Ramu has a significant heritage with the oldest monastery of the region—said to have been built by Aśoka. There is no doubt that it had an early foundation; some archaeological evidence like pot sherds, bricks, etc., are housed in a museum inside the monastery. This central zone of Arakan with the riverine plains of the Mayu, Kaladan, and Lemro rivers—known by its classical name of Dhānyawati—was linked to Harikela.[63]

This geographical continuum led to frequent movements of people between the two areas and some common cultural practices enmeshed within various direct and braided networks. For instance there was cross-influence in the use of a specific script type. The Arakanese 'ha', instead of 'ha' as in late Brāhmī, was used to write the 'ha' for harikela in the Harikela coins; this usage had earlier prevented scholars from reading the place name 'harikela' on the coins. Moreover, as mentioned earlier, the coinage tradition was also borrowed from the silver coins of the Chandra rulers of Arakan. Large numbers of silver coins, part of the Harikela series of coinage and datable to the eighth century with the Bull and Tripartite device, have been found in the Salban vihāra complex.[64] The Bull and Tripartite type was the basic type of coinage favoured by the Arakan Chandras. Such coins found at Mainamati are testimony to the Arakan coinage penetrating into southeastern Bengal, indicating the Samataṭa region's economic importance and participation in Bay of Bengal trade networks. Coins of Dharmavijaya in particular have been found in Samataṭa, leading numismatists to suggest that perhaps for a brief period of time Dharmavijaya was in control of Samataṭa.[65] B.N. Mukherjee had rightly argued against the political association of Dharmavijaya with Samataṭa on the grounds that a few coins found in an area may not suggest annexation of that territory by the coin issuer.[66]

A. Griffiths has published a commentary on the Odein stone inscription (A1) from Arakan issued by Sri Dharmavijayadeva in the second year of his reign.[67] To date, apart from the coins, Dharmavijaya's name in the Ānandachandra praśastī was the only proof of his rule in Arakan. Now there is no doubt that Dharmavijaya's political centre was in Arakan. A further observation regarding the shared coinage tradition between Harikela and Arakan relates to coin terminology: the term *taṇḍaka* designating a coin in the inscribed metal vase issued by Devatideva (around 715) in Chittagong.[68] The inscription records several transactions by *taṇḍaka*, implying that it was a coin or some artefact with an exchange value. Earlier it was surmised that this term was unique to Harikela. Griffiths drew my attention to the presence of this term in the Ānandachandra praśastī where we have the expression *prati taṇḍakān*.[69]

> [upajāti of indravaṁśa/vaṁśastha]
> *dadau prarṣṭaḥ suvisuddhacetasā*
> *saddharmapūjām prati taṇḍakān vahūn**
> *narādhipo dharmakathānurāgataḥ* ||

A tentative translation by Griffiths is: 'In joy and with perfectly pure thought the king, from his attachment to Dharma-narrations, gave many *taṇḍakas*, with the approval of good people, for the purpose of worshipping the true Dharma on a daily basis.'[70]

Interestingly stanza 57 of the same inscription mentions a place called Pilakkavanaka: (At [the place] called Pilakkavanaka, formerly named Domagha (?), also there have been constructed streets, various pleasances, causeways and passages.)[71] It may be noted that there is a place called Pilak Pathar in south Tripura, a part of ancient Samataṭa. A Buddhist monastery has been excavated there and Harikela coins have been found in the nearby Belonia sub-division. Moreover we have coins with Piraka written on them like the Harikela coins, following the same tradition of locality coins with place-names,[72] suggesting again a connection with Arakan. It may be that since Pilak was a Buddhist pilgrim-site with a regular movement of monks, Ānandachandra made donations for improving roadways and causeways around Pilak for easy access from Arakan. Thus Pilak, like Mainamati, was within the Buddhist network although it was not as grand.

The connected histories of Harikela with Arakan—and also of Kāmarūpa as I show later—can be traced in the text *Mañju-śrimūlakalpa* datable to around the eighth century. Places where the cult of the Buddhist goddess Tārā was prevalent were named: 'And then Tārā is realized, with the Yakṣa-king Mahābala, in Harikela, Karmaraṅga, Kāmarūpa and [the city] called Kalaśa.' (*sidhyate ca tadā tārā yakṣarāṭ caiva mahābalaḥ/harikele karmaraṅge ca kāmarūpe kalaśāhvaye//* Mmk_53.833 //).[73] The regions of Harikela and Samataṭa abound in Buddhist monasteries where small bronze images of Tārā, along with other deities, have been found. The Mainamati copper plate dated 1220 and issued in the seventeenth regnal year of king Ranavāṅkamalla Śrī-Harikāladeva informs us that Dhadi-eba, minister of the king, donated a piece of land in favour of a vihāra dedicated to Durgottārā—a form of Tārā in the town of Paṭṭikera (Patikara or Paitkara, a paragana near Mainamati).[74] Tārā was venerated in coastal southeastern Bangladesh.

It is very difficult to identify Karmaraṅga. Sircar places it in lower Myanmar along with Kalasa as its capital.[75] Recently Griffiths[76] has identified Karmaraṅga with Arakan. In view of Karmaraṅga's close association with Harikela and with Samataṭa, the identification is natural.

## Kāmarūpa: Major Hinterland of Samataṭa and Harikela

Located on the Brahmaputra, Kāmarūpa was included in interactions between Samataṭa and Harikela—politically and economically. Two rivers and a seaport are integral to the history and geography of early Assam and southeastern Bengal. They are the Brahmaputra and Meghna rivers and Samandar port. The Brahmaputra flows southwest through Assam in India and southwards as the Jamuna through Bangladesh. In the delta, it merges with the Padma, the main distributary of the Ganga, and then with the Meghna, before emptying into the *Bahr Harkand*. Ibn Battuta undertook a long journey from Sudkawan (Samandar? or perhaps another port in the Chittagong area) to Habanq or Habiganj in Sylhet via Kāmarūpa in his travels in the first half of the fourteenth century. He does not mention Samandar but Sudkawan as the first city in Bengal—it was a large town on the coast of the great sea, obviously the Bay of Bengal. Ibn Battuta recalls setting out from Sudkawan for the mountains of Kamaru (Kāmarūpa), a month's journey from the Chittagong area. He then journeyed on to Habanq and traversed the Blue River, likely to be the Meghna. According to him this route was used by travellers to Bengal[77] and Lakhnawati.[78] Southeastern Bengal appears to have enjoyed communications and linkages with Kāmarūpa in the Brahmaputra valley. If Ibn Battuta could take this route in the fourteenth century, it is possible that it was an active route even earlier. It should be mentioned here that Ibn Battuta reached Sudkawan from the Maldives after forty-three nights at sea. Initially however, he had planned to come to Bengal from Sri Lanka via the Coromandel coast.

The famous Chandra ruler Śrichandra claimed in the Paschimbhag copper-plate[79] from Sylhet to have conquered Kāmarūpa. Verse 12 of this plate records that Śrichandra's forces, in the course of their conquest of the Kāmarūpa country, entered the woodlands near the Lohitya, i.e. the Brahmaputra, where among other things they saw numerous black aloe trees which made the woodland dark (*kāl-aguru-śyāmalaḥ).* Drowsy yaks ruminated on the plains of the Lauhitya River *(Romanthalasa baddhanidrā chāmari-samsevita prāntara Lohitasya vanasthali-parisaraḥ kāl-aguru-śyāmalaḥ*). This suggests that the raid was through the riverine network as the woodlands were near the Lohitya river. We may further speculate the location of the raid being Haṭappeśvara, the capital of the Śālasthambha dynasty, and identifiable with present Tezpur. That the banks of Brahmaputra around Tezpur abounded in black aloes is evoked in a verse of the mid-ninth century Tezpur copper-plate of Vanamāla: 'this was the river where the waves are rendered fragrant by clouds formed by the smoke of black agaru trees burnt by forest fires occurring in the parks of the city of Haruppesvara' (*tadupavanalapna-dāvānaladahya-mānakālagurudhūmsambhavāmbudharavṛnda-suganjilaugha-pravāhiṇā*).[80] Arab accounts referenced good quality aloe wood from Kāmarūpa and rated it second to the wood of Multan. They also mentioned yak tail as an important commodity of the kingdom of DHM (identified with Dharmapāla). Al Idrisi (1162) stated that aloe wood was brought to Samandar from Kamrut; it took fifteen days journey by a river identifiable with the Brahmaputra.[81] From Samandar one could reach the kingdoms of Central and mainland Southeast Asia; Abu Dulaf Misa'r Ibn Muhalhil Yanbu'i made his overland journey through Turkistan to China in 331/943, mentioning the town of Qamrun on his voyage back to India.[82] According to him this place produced aloe wood known as Qmari. Trade between the kingdom of Kāmarūpa and southwestern China through Myanmar is recorded in the Arabic tract *Al-Masalik wa'l Mamalik*.[83] In one of his notices regarding gharu wood, Zhao-ru gua[84] refers to black aloe wood, maintaining it was costlier. Transportation to the coast from the northeast made it expensive.

The presence of aloe wood as item of trade in the Chinese records is a clear indicator of the revenues earned by coastal polities. Aloe was in great demand as a ritual item, its fragrance was appreciated throughout the world from Persia to China, at Rome and later at the Abbasid court at Damascus.[85] The aloe wood trade network perhaps operated within the larger horse and silk networks.[86] The prosperity of Kāmarūpa is also linked with the presence of gold from alluvial deposits in the Brahmaputra. Rhodes suggests that Samataṭa's sources of gold for its coins may have been Kāmarūpa or Tibet.[87]

## Conclusion

The port of Samandar and later Chittagong port were used as a transit trade zone for connections between countries across the Bay of Bengal. Their location at the confluence of the Ganga and the Brahmaputra meant that merchants from eastern India used Chittagong as an entrepot. In the navigational guides of mariners like Ibn Majid of the fifteenth century, Chittagong is described as a great port in Bengal, a Imperial Chinese fleet visited it in 1405.[88] We can suggest that Chittagong's position as a central entrepôt for long distance trade in the eastern part of the Bay of Bengal had its genesis as early as the ninth century when Samandar emerged as a port of Bahr Harkand. Samandar/Sudkawan maintained linkages with both hinterland agricultural producers and foreland seafarers, reaching out to distant lands and exhibiting a vibrant economic network with a perfect balance of coined money and cowrie currency in an expanded Harikela.

K.N. Chaudhuri showed the significant degree to which Indian Ocean trading networks were integrated into a genuine regional commercial culture, which formed an économie-monde of its own.[89] Following Chaudhuri I am tempted to suggest that the region of Harikela also formed an economie-monde, including Kāmarūpa and Samataṭa on the one hand and Arakan on the other. I have used the term 'expanded Harikela' precisely for this reason. Moreover I link this to the idea of scale. Human geographers reference scale by hierarchy (level). Vertical (size) conceptualizations of scale are added on to hierarchical ones in an effort to link scale to network theory.[90] Mentifacts see scale as a cultural trait linking values, beliefs, and ideas to an agreed-upon set of conventions. But scale has a dual history. The first of these two histories, scale as a mentifact, is strongly associated with values, justice, social conditions, and politics. The second is scale as a representational analogy and practice allowing for the transcription of three-dimensional objects (whether material or immaterial) into two-dimensional representations. In the case of an expanded Harikela I use scale as mentifact in the first sense—where connecting regions shared a network of beliefs, values and ideas, forming a basis wherein exchange, trade and transactions perhaps occurred in a moral and ethical way.

## NOTES

1. M. Reinaud (ed.), *Silsilat al-Tawārikh* of Sulayman al-Tajir and Abu Zaid Hasan al-Śirafī, Frankfurt: Johann Wolfgang Goethe University, 1994, reprint of 1845 Paris edn.
2. V. Minorsky, ed. and tr., *Hudud al 'Alam*, London: Gibb Memorial Trust, 1937, p. 87.
3. For a detailed discussion on the port of Samandar see Ranabir Chakravarti, 'Seafaring in the Bengal Coast: The Early Medieval Scenario', in *Trade and Traders in Early Indian Society*, New Delhi: Manohar, 2002, pp. 160-83.
4. H.M. Elliot and J. Dowson, *The History of India as Told by its Own Historians,* vol. I, Allahabad: Kitab Mahal, p. 90.

5. Ibid., p. 16
6. J. Takakusu, tr., *A Record of the Buddhist Religion as Practiced in India and the Malay Archipelago (A.D. 671-95)* by I-tsing, Oxford: Oxford University Press, 1896, pp. xxxiii, xlvi, liii and 44.
7. B.N. Mukherjee, 'The Original Territory of Harikela', *Bangladesh Lalitkala*, vol. 1, no. 2, 1975, pp. 115-19.
8. D.C. Sircar, *Pāl-Sen Yuger Vamśānucharit* (in Bengali), Calcutta: Sahityalok, 1982, p. 48.
9. Gouriswar Bhattacharya, 'A Preliminary Report on the Inscribed Metal Vase from the National Museum of Bangladesh', in *Essays in Buddhist Hindu Jain Iconography and Epigraphy*, ed. Enamul Haque, Dhaka: International Centre for Bengal Art, 2000, pp. 471-87.
10. Bhattacharya, 'A Preliminary Report on the Inscribed Metal Vase', p. 473.
11. Suchandra Ghosh, 'Character of the Pala Army: Gleanings from Literature and Inscriptions,' *Journal of Asiatic Society of Bangladesh, Humanities*, Dhaka, 2006, pp. 41-7.
12. R.C. Majumdar, 'Chittagong Copper Plate of Kantideva,' *Epigraphia Indica*, vol. XXVI, pp. 313-18.
13. Gouriswar Bhattacharya, 'An Inscribed Metal Vase Most Probably From Chittagong, Bangladesh', *South Asian Archaeology*, 1991, pp. 323-38.
14. Shariful Islam, *New Light on the History of Ancient South-East Bengal*, Dhaka: Asiatic Society, 2014.
15. Benjamin, J. Flemming, 'New Copperplate Grant of Śrīcandra (no. 8) from Bangladesh', *Bulletin of School of Oriental and African Studies*, 73, 2010, pp. 223-44.
16. D.C. Sircar, *Pāl-Sen Yuger Vamśānucharit* (in Bengali), Calcutta: Sahityalok, 1982, p. 106.
17. The notion that in Bengal the two regional powers of the period were only the Pālas and the Senas needs to be revised.
18. R.S. Sharma, *Indian Feudalism AD 300-1200*, New Delhi: MacMillan, 1980 (2nd edn.); also D.N. Jha, ed., *The Feudal Order*, New Delhi: Manohar, 2000.
19. G.M. Laskar, 'Ashrafpur Copper-Plate Grants of Devakhadga', *Memoirs of the Asiatic Society of Bengal*, I, no. 6, Calcutta, 1906, pp. 85-91.
20. D.C. Sircar, *Epigraphic Discoveries in East Pakistan*, Calcutta: Sanskrit College, 1973, pp. 69-76.
21. B.D. Chattopadhyaya, *Aspects of Rural Settlements and Rural Society*

*in Early Medieval India*, Calcutta: Centre for Social Sciences, 1990, p. 27.

22. Benjamin Flemming, 'New Copperplate Grant of Śrīcandra', p. 223.
23. D. C. Bhattacharyya, 'A Newly Discovered Copperplate from Tippera [The Gunaighar Grant of Vainyagupta: The Year 188 Current (Gupta Era)]', *Indian Historical Quarterly*, VI (1) 1930, pp. 45-60.
24. Ryosuke Furui, 'Ajivikas, Manibhadra and Early History of Eastern Bengal: A New Copper plate Inscription of Vainyagupta and its Implications', *Journal of Royal Asiatic Society*, Series 3, 2015, pp. 1-25.
25. Sircar, *Epigraphic Discoveries*, p. 74.
26. Gouriswar Bhattacharya, 'Nalanda Vāgīśvarī and Mandhuk Gaṇeśa: Are They of the Same Period?', *Journal of Bengal Art (JBA)* 4 (1999), pp. 373-80.
27. Nalinikanta Bhattasali, 'Some Image Inscriptions from East Bengal', *Epigraphia Indica, 17*, pp. 349-62.
28. D.C. Sircar, 'Nārāyaṇpur Vināyaka Image Inscription of King Mahīpāla, Regnal Year 4', *Indian Culture* 9, 1942-3, Miscellanea, pp. 121-5.
29. Ryosuke Furui, 'Merchant Groups in Early Medieval Bengal: With Special Reference to the Rajbhita Stone Inscription of the Time of Mahīpāla I, Year 33', *BSOAS*, 76, 2013, p. 305.
30. Bhattacharya, 'A Preliminary Report . . .', pp. 471-87.
31. *Pāṭaka* is a unit of land measurement.
32. Furui, 'Ajivikas, Manibhadra and Early History of Eastern Bengal', p. 10.
33. Bhattacharya, 'An Inscribed Metal Vase Most Probably from Chittagong', *South Asian Archaeology*, 1991, pp. 323-38
34. Ryosuke Furui, 'Rural Society and Social Networks in Early Bengal', unpublished Ph.D thesis, Jawaharlal Nehru University, New Delhi, 2007, p. 176.
35. According to Sayantani Pal ('Forms and format of the land grant charters of early Bengal/Textual Structure of Bengal Land Grants,' unpublished paper), the format of the land grant charters drew their inspiration from normative texts like the Dharmaśāstras which began to be composed from the second century BC. The charters discuss the donation of land, its merit compared to other kinds of donation, the format and contents a charter should contain, etc. I thank her for sharing her essay with me.
36. Since the Harikela area is focal, I am not going into the details of Samataṭa coins. See, B.N. Mukherjee, *Coins and Currency Systems*

*of Post-Gupta Bengal (c.* AD *550-700)*, New Delhi: Munshiram Manoharlal, 1993; Nicholas Rhodes, 'The Coinage of Samataṭa: Some Thoughts', *The Quarterly Review of Historical Studies*, Kolkata, 2002, pp. XLII/1 and 1-12.

37. Rhodes, 'The Coinage of Samatata', pp. 1-12
38. B.N. Mukherjee, 'The Original Territory of Harikela', *Bangladesh Lalitkala*, vol. 1, no. 2, 1975, pp. 115-19.
39. Noman Nasir, 'Coins of King Kantideva of Harikela Kingdom', *Northeast Researches*, vol. VII, March 2016, pp. 20-6.
40. T. Watters, *On Yuan Chwang's Travels*, Delhi: Motilal Banarsidass, 1961, p. 201.
41. B.N. Mukherjee, 'The Paglatek Hoard and the Relation between Kāmarūpa and Samataṭa', in K.K. Dasgupta et al., eds., *Sraddhānjali, Studies in Ancient Indian History (D.C. Sircar Commemoration Volume)*, Delhi: Sundeep Prakashan, 1988, pp. 281-6.
42. B.N. Mukherjee, 'Commerce and Money in the Central and Western Sectors of Eastern India', *Indian Museum Bulletin*, XVI (1982), pp. 65-83; Nicholas G. Rhodes, 'Trade in South-eastern Bengal in the First Millennium CE: The Numismatic Evidence', in Rila Mukherjee ed., *Pelagic Passageways*, New Delhi: Primus Books, 2011, pp. 263-78.
43. D.C. Sircar, 'Mehar Copper Plate of Damodaradeva, Saka 1156', *Epigraphia Indica*, XXX , pp. 51ff.
44. B.N. Mukherjee, 'A Survey of Samataṭa and Harikela Coinages', *Journal of Bengal Art*, vol. 8, Dhaka, 2003, pp. 199-212.
45. V. Minorsky, tr. and commentary of *Sharaf al-Zaman Tahir Marvazi on China, The Turks and India*, London: The Royal Asiatic Society, 1942, pp. 147-8; cited by Ranabir Chakravarti in the Appendix of Niharranjan Ray et al., eds., *A Source Book of Indian Civilization*, Calcutta: Orient Longman, 2000, p. 639.
46. Bin Yang, 'The Bay of Bengal Connections to Yunnan, in Rila Mukherjee (ed.), *Pelagic Passageways: The Northern Bay of Bengal Before Colonialism*, New Delhi: Primus Books, 2011, pp. 319-29. Bin Yang suggests that Bengal was the source of *kauris* in Yunnan. From the records of the Chinese travellers he was able to trace the route from Bengal to Yunnan through mainland Southeast Asia. Thus Bin Yang correctly identifies an economic network centering on cowry which was used as a parallel currency in Bengal. For a general overview of cowries in eastern India and their role see Susmita Basu Majumdar and Sharmishtha Chatterjee, 'Cowries in Eastern India:

Understanding Their Role as Ritual Objects and Money', *Journal of Bengal Art*, vol. 19, 2014, pp. 39-56.

47. H.A.R. Gibbs (rpt., tr.), *Ibn Battuta, Travels in Asia and Africa*, Delhi: Asia Educational Services, 1997, p. 249.
48. Syed Ejaz Hussain, 'Siver Flow and Horse Supply to Sultanate Bengal with Special Reference to Trans Himalayan Trade (13th-16th Centuries)', *Journal of the Economic and Social History of the Orient*, 56, 2013, pp. 264-308.
49. Watters, *On Yuan Chwang's Travels*, p. 201.
50. D.C. Sircar,'The Kailan Copper Plate Inscription of Śridharana Rāta of Samataṭa', *Indian Historical Quarterly*, vol. XXIII, 1947, pp. 221-41.
51. Ranabir Chakravarti, 'Vaṅgasāgara-sambhāṇḍāriyaka: A Riverine Trade Centre of Early Medieval Bengal', in *Trade and Traders in Early Indian Society*, New Delhi: Manohar, 2002, p. 151.
52. Ibid., pp. 151-2.
53. A.B.M. Husain, ed., *Mainamati-Devaparvata,* Dhaka: The Asiatic Society of Bangladesh, 1997, p. 218.
54. Shariful Islam, 'Uḍiśvara Copper Plate of Śridhāraṇa Rāta' , *Journal of Asiatic Society of Bangladesh, Humanities*, vol. 57, no. 1, June 2012, pp. 61-72.
55. Kamalakanta Gupta Choudhury, 'Two Mainamati Copper Plate Inscriptions of the Khaḍga and Early Deva Times (7th and 8th Centuries AD)', *Bangladesh Archaeology,* vol. 1, no. 1, 1979, p. 43.
56. D.C. Sircar, 'Copper Plate Inscription of King Bhavadeva of Devaparvata', *Journal of the Asiatic Society,* Letters, vol. XVII, no. 2, 1951, pp. 83-94.
57. D.C. Sircar, 'Paschimbhag Plate of Śricandra, Regnal Year 5', in *Epigraphic Discoveries in East Pakistan,* Calcutta: Sanskrit College, 1973, p. 27.
58. Chakravarti, 'Seafaring in the Bengal Coast', p. 167; Suchandra Ghosh, 'Economy of Samataṭa in the Early Medieval Period: A Brief Overview', in *Prajna Dhara: Essays in Honour of Gouriswar Bhattacharyya*, ed. Gerd Mevissen and Arundhati Banerjee, New Delhi: Manohar, 2008, pp. 352-9.
59. Chakravarti, 'Vaṅgasāgara-sambhāṇḍāriyaka', pp. 144-7. Chakravarti gives a detailed analyses of both the terms *Vaṅgasāgara* and *Sambhāṇḍāriyaka* and shows that the eastern Sea or Bay of Bengal was called *Vaṅgasāgara* in the later tenth century.
60. Chakravarti, ibid., p. 149.

61. Shariful Islam, 'A Hoard of Unpublished Post-Gupta Gold Coins from Sabhar', *Journal of Bengal Art*, vol. 20, Dhaka, 2015, pp. 95-100. This hoard, presently in the possession of the Bangladesh National Museum, was discovered in 2002.
62. We should note that though we do not have much information about Sabhar as a riverine port during the heyday of Devaparvata (seventh to ninth centuries CE), it must have been to some extent active to regain primacy again during the reign of the Chandras.
63. For a detailed discussion on Arakan-Chittagong geographical continuum see S.E.A. van Galen, 'The Economic Geography of the Arakan-Bengal Continuum', doctoral thesis, Leiden University. *Arakan and Bengal: The Rise and Decline of the Mrauk U Kingdom (Burma) from the Fifteenth to the Seventeeth Century* AD, 2008, 1-32; accessed on 5 March 2016.
64. Mukherjee, 'Original Territory', pp. 115-20.
65. M. Mitchiner, *The Land of Water: Coinage and History of Bangladesh and Later Arakan Circa 300* BC *to the Present Day*, London: Hawkins Publication, 2000, pp. 75-6.
66. B.N. Mukherjee, 'A Survey of Samatata', p. 206.
67. Arlo Griffiths, 'Three More Sanskrit Inscriptions of Arakan: New Perspectives on Its Name, Dynastic History, and Buddhist Culture in the First Millennium', *The Journal of Burma Studies*, vol. 19, no. 2, 2015, pp. 281-340.
68. Bhattacharya, 'An Inscribed Metal Vase,' pp. 323-38.
69. F.H. Johnston, 'Some Sanskrit Inscriptions of Arakan', *Bulletin of the School of Oriental and African Studies*, vol. II, 1944, pp. 377-88, stanza 52.
70. Johnston was not able to understand the meaning of *tandaka*. See his note 55, p. 378.
71. Johnston, 'Some Sanskrit Inscriptions', p. 378.
72. Mitchiner, *The Land of Water*, p. 74.
73. P.L.Vaidya, ed., *Aryā Mañjuśrimūlakalpa, Mahayanasutrasamgraha*, pt. II, *Buddhist Sanskrit Texts*, no. 18, Darbhanga, The Mithila Society, 1964, p. 508.
74. D.C. Bhattacharyya, 'The Mainamati Copper-plate of Ranvankamalla Harikaladeva', *Indian Historical Quarterly*, IX, pp. 282-9.
75. D.C. Sircar, 'Indological Notes', *Journal of Ancient Indian History*, vol. IX, 1976, pp. 211-13.
76. For details of the argument see Arlo Griffiths , 'Three More Sanskrit Inscriptions of Arakan', pp. 301-8.

77. Lakhnawati was obviously the capital of Gauda but what stood for Bengal is not clear.
78. Gibbs, *Ibn Battuta*, pp. 267-71.
79. D.C. Sircar, 'Pashchimbhag Copper Plate of Śrichandra, Year 5', *Epigraphia Indica*, XXXVII, 1967-8, pp. 289-304. Also 'Paschimbhag Plate of Śricandra, Regnal Year 5', in *Epigraphic Discoveries in East Pakistan*, Calcutta, 1973, p. 27.
80. M.M. Sharma, 'Tezpur Copper Plates of Vanamala,' *Inscriptions of Ancient Assam*, Gauhati, 1978, p. 99.
81. Chakravarti, 'Seafaring in the Bengal Coast', pp. 165-7.
82. Fuat Sezgin 'Studies on the Travel Account of Ibn Fudlan and Abu Dulaf', Islamic Geography (Collected and Reprinted) by M. Reinaud, Frankfurt: Johann Wolfgang Goethe University, 1994, pp. 262-5; cited in Tansen Sen, *Buddhism, Diplomacy and Trade: The Realignment of Sino-Indian Relations, 600-1400, Asian Interaction and Comparisions*, New Delhi: Manohar, 2004, p. 212.
83. Maqbul S. Ahmad, *Arabic Classical Accounts of India and China*, Shimla: Indian Institute of Indian Study, 1989, p. 6.
84. The *Zhu Fan zhi* of Zhao Ru-gua written in 1225/6 CE is an extremely important document for history of maritime trade. Zhao Ru-gua, a customs official, looks at the maritime scenario from the perspective of Song China. The Song Government perceived the sea as an active space of activity both for its exports and imports Frederic Hirth. and W.W. Rockhill (eds., and transl.) *Chau Ju-kua: His work on the Chinese and Arab Trade in the Twelfth and Thirteenth Centuries, Entitled Chu-fan-chih,* St. Petersburg: Imperial Academy of Sciences, 1912. Also see Suchandra Ghosh, 'South-East Asia and the Eastern Sea Board of India through the Lens of Zhao Rugua', in Radhika Seshan (ed.), *Convergence: Rethinking India's Past,* New Delhi, Primus Books, 2014, pp. 41-54.
85. Rila Mukherjee (ed.), *Pelagic Passageways: The Northern Bay of Bengal Before Colonialism,* New Delhi: Primus Books, 2011, p. 27.
86. Mukherjee, ibid., p. 27.
87. Rhodes, 'Trade in South-Eastern Bengal', pp. 263-75.
88. G.R. Tibbetts, 'Arab Navigation in the Indian Ocean before the Coming of the Portuguese', being a translation of *Kitab al-Fawa'id fi usul al bahr wa'l-qawa'id of Ahmad b. Majid al-Najdi*, London: The Royal Asiatic Society of Great Britain and Ireland, 1971, p. 395.
89. K.N Chaudhuri, *Trade and Civilization in the Indian Ocean: An*

*Economic History from the Rise of Islam to 1750,* Cambridge: Cambridge University Press, 1985, p. 4.

90. Chris Lukinbeal, 'Scale and its Histories', *Association of Pacific Coast Geographers Year Book,* vol. 78, 2016, p. 5.

## BIBLIOGRAPHY


Ahmad, Maqbul S., *Arabic Classical Accounts of India and China* , Shimla: Indian Institute of Indian Study, 1989.

Bhattacharyya, D.C., 'The Mainamati Copper-plate of Ranvankamalla Harikaladeva', *Indian Historical Quarterly*, IX, 1933, pp. 282-9.

______, 'A Newly Discovered Copperplate from Tippera [The Gunaighar Grant of Vinayagupta: The Year 188 Current (Gupta Era)]', *Indian Historical Quarterly*, VI (1), 1930, pp. 45-60.

Bhattacharya, Gouriswar, 'An Inscribed Metal Vase Most Probably from Chittagong, Bangladesh', *South Asian Archaeology,* 1991, pp. 323-38.

______, 'Nalanda Vāgīśvarī and Mandhuk Gaṇeśa: Are they of the Same Period?', *Journal of Bengal Art*, 4, 1999, pp. 373-80.

______, 'A Preliminary Report on the Inscribed Metal Vase from the National Museum of Bangladesh', in Enamul Haque, ed., *Essays in Buddhist Hindu Jain Iconography and Epigraphy*, Dhaka: International Centre for Bengal Art, 2000, pp. 471-87.

Bhattasali, Nalinikanta, 'Some Image Inscriptions from East Bengal', *Epigraphia Indica*, 17, pp. 349-62.

Chakravarti, Ranabir, 'Vaṅgasāgara-sambhāṇḍāriyaka: A Riverine Trade Centre of Early Medieval Bengal', in *Trade and Traders in Early Indian Society*, New Delhi: Manohar, 2002, pp. 144-59.

______, 'Seafaring in the Bengal Coast: The Early Medieval Scenario', in *Trade and Traders in Early Indian Society*, New Delhi: Manohar, 2002, pp. 160-83.

Chattopadhyaya, B.D., *Aspects of Rural Settlements and Rural Society in Early Medieval India*, Calcutta: Centre for Social Sciences, 1990.

Chaudhuri, K.N., *Trade and Civilization in the Indian Ocean: An Economic History from the Rise of Islam to 1750,* Cambridge: Cambridge University Press, 1985.

Choudhury, Kamalakanta Gupta, 'Two Mainamati Copper Plate Inscriptions of the Khaḍga and Early Deva Times (7th and 8th Centuries A.D.)', *Bangladesh Archaeology,* vol. 1, no. 1, 1979, pp. 14-48.

Elliot, H.M. and John Dowson, *The History of India as Told by its Own Historians: The Muhammadan Period,* vol. I, Allahabad: Kitab Mahal, rpt., 1964.

Flemming, Benjamin J., 'New Copper Plate Grant of Śrīcandra (no. 8) from Bangladesh', *Bulletin of School of Oriental and African Studies,* 73, 2010, pp. 223-44.

Furui, Ryosuke, 'Merchant Groups in Early Medieval Bengal: With Special Reference to the Rajbhita Stone Inscription of the Time of Mahīpāla I, Year 33', *Bulletin of the School of Oriental and African Studies,* 76, 2013, pp. 391-412.

———, '*Rural Society and Social Networks in Early Bengal,*' unpublished Ph.D thesis, New Delhi: Jawaharlal Nehru University, 2007.

———, 'Ajivikas, Manibhadra and Early History of Eastern Bengal: A New Copper Plate Inscription of Vainyagupta and its Implications', *Journal of the Royal Asiatic Society,* Series 3, 2015, pp. 1-25.

Ghosh, Suchandra, 'Character of the Pala Army as Reflected in Inscriptions and Literature,' *Journal of the Asiatic Society of Bangladesh (Humanities),* vol. 51 (1), 2006, pp. 41-7.

———, 'Economy of Samataṭa in the Early Medieval Period: A Brief Overview', in *Prajna Dhara, Essays in Honour of Gouriswar Bhattacharyya,* Gerd Mevissen and Arundhati Banerjee (eds.), New Delhi: Manohar, 2008, pp. 352-9.

———, 'South-East Asia and the Eastern Sea Board of India through the Lens of Zhao Rugua', in Radhika Seshan (ed.), *Convergence: Rethinking India's Past,* New Delhi, Primus Books, 2014, pp. 41-54.

Gibbs, H.A.R., trans., *Ibn Battuta: Travels in Asia and Africa,* rpt., Delhi: Asia Educational Services, 1997.

Griffiths, Arlo, 'Three More Sanskrit Inscriptions of Arakan: New Perspectives on Its Name, Dynastic History, and Buddhist Culture in the First Millennium', *The Journal of Burma Studies,* vol. 19, no. 2, 2015, pp. 281-340.

Hirth, Frederic and W.W. Rockhill (eds. and trs.) *Chau Ju-kua: His Work on the Chinese and Arab Trade in the Twelfth and Thirteenth Centuries, Entitled Chu-fan-chih,* St. Petersburg: Imperial Academy of Sciences, 1912.

*Hudud al 'Alam,* ed. and tr. V. Minorsky, London: Gibb Memorial Trust, 1937.

Husain, A.B.M., ed., *Mainamati-Devaparvata,* Dhaka: The Asiatic Society of Bangladesh, 1997.

Hussain, Syed Ejaz, 'Silver Flow and Horse Supply to Sultanate Bengal with Special Reference to Trans Himalayan Trade (13th-16th Centuries)', *Journal of the Economic and Social History of the Orient*, 56, 2013, pp. 264-308.

Islam, Shariful, 'Uḍiśvara Copper plate of Śridhāraṇa Rāta' , *Journal of Asiatic Society of Bangladesh, Humanities*, vol. 57, no. 1, June 2012, pp. 61-72.

———, *New Light on the History of Ancient South-East Bengal*, Dhaka: Asiatic Society, 2014.

———, 'A Hoard of Unpublished Post-Gupta Gold Coins from Sabhar', *Journal of Bengal Art*, vol. 20, 2015, pp. 95-100.

Jha, D.N., ed., *The Feudal Order*, New Delhi: Manohar, 2000.

Johnston, F.H., 'Some Sanskrit Inscriptions of Arakan' *Bulletin of the School of Oriental and African Studies*, vol. II, 1944, pp. 377-88.

Laskar, G.M., 'Ashrafpur Copper-Plate Grants of Devakhadga,' *Memoirs of the Asiatic Society of Bengal*, I, no. 6, Calcutta, 1906, pp. 85-91.

Lukinbeal, Chris, 'Scale and its Histories', *Association of Pacific Coast Geographers Year Book*, vol. 78, 2016, pp. 1-13.

Majumdar, R.C., 'Chittagong Copper Plate of Kantideva', *Epigraphia Indica*, vol. XXVI, 1941, pp. 313-18.

Majumdar, Susmita Basu and Sharmishtha Chatterjee, 'Cowries in Eastern India: Understanding Their Role as Ritual Objects and Money', *Journal of Bengal Art*, vol. 19, 2014, pp. 39-56.

Mitchiner, M., *The Land of Water: Coinage and History of Bangladesh and Later Arakan Circa 300 BC to the Present Day*, London: Hawkins Publication, 2000.

Mukherjee, B.N., 'The Original Territory of Harikela', *Bangladesh Lalitkala*, vol. 1, no. 2, 1975, pp. 115-19.

———, 'Commerce and Money in the Central and Western Sectors of Eastern India', *Indian Museum Bulletin*, XVI, 1982, pp. 65-83.

———, 'The Paglatek Hoard and The Relation between Kāmarūpa and Samataṭa', in K.K. Dasgupta et al., eds., *Sraddhānjali, Studies in Ancient Indian History (D.C. Sircar Commemoration Volume)*, Delhi: Sundeep Prakashan, 1988, pp. 281-6.

———, 'A Survey of Samataṭa and Harikela Coinages', *Journal of Bengal Art*, 8, 2003, pp. 199-212.

———, *Coins and Currency Systems of Post-Gupta Bengal (c. AD 550-700)*, New Delhi: Munshiram Manoharlal, 1993.

Mukherjee, Rila (ed.), *Pelagic Passageways: The Northern Bay of Bengal Before Colonialism*, New Delhi: Primus Books, 2011.

Nasir, Noman, 'Coins of King Kantideva of Harikela Kingdom', *Northeast Researches*, vol. VII, March 2016, pp. 20-6.

Ray, Niharranjan et al. (eds.), *A Source Book of Indian Civilization*, Calcutta: Orient Longman, 2000.

Renaud, M. (ed.), *Silsilat al-Tawārikh* of Sulayman al-Tajir and Abu Zaid Hasan al-Śirafī, Frankfurt: Johann Wolfgang Goethe University, 1994, reprint of 1845 Paris edn.

Rhodes, Nicholas G., 'The Coinage of Samataṭa: Some Thoughts', *The Quarterly Review of Historical Studies*, vol. XLII, nos. 1 & 2, Kolkata, 2002, pp. 1-12.

———, 'Trade in South-Eastern Bengal in the First Millennium CE: The Numismatic Evidence', in Rila Mukherjee (ed.), *Pelagic Passageways*, New Delhi: Primus Books, 2011, pp. 263-78.

Sen, Tansen, *Buddhism, Diplomacy and Trade: The Realignment of Sino-Indian Relations, 600-1400*, New Delhi: Manohar, 2004.

Sezgin, Fuat, 'Studies on the Travel Account of Ibn Fudlan and Abu Dulaf', in M. Reinaud (ed.), *Islamic Geography* (collected and reprinted), Frankfurt: Johann Wolfgang Goethe University, 1994, pp. 262-5.

*Sharaf al-Zaman Tahir Marvazi on China, The Turks and India*, trn. and commentary V. Minorsky, London: The Royal Asiatic Society, 1942.

Sharma, M.M., 'Tezpur Copper Plates of Vanamala,' *Inscriptions of Ancient Assam*, Gauhati, 1978, pp. 96-105.

Sharma, R.S., *Indian Feudalism AD 300-1200*, New Delhi: MacMillan, 1980 (2nd edn.).

Sircar, D.C., 'Nārāyaṇpur Vināyaka Image Inscription of King Mahīpāla, Regnal Year 4', *Indian Culture*, 9, 1942-3, pp. 121-5.

———, 'The Kailan Copper Plate Inscription of Śridharana Rāta of Samataṭa', *Indian Historical Quarterly*, vol. XXIII, 1947, pp. 221-41.

———, 'Copper Plate Inscription of King Bhavadeva of Devaparvata', *Journal of the Asiatic Society, Letters*, vol. XVII, no. 2, 1951, pp. 83-94.

———, 'Pashchimbhag Copper-Plate of Śrichandra, Year 5', *Epigraphia Indica*, XXXVII, 1967-8, pp. 289-304.

———, 'Paschimbhag Plate of Śricandra, Regnal Year 5', in *Epigraphic Discoveries in East Pakistan,* Calcutta: Sanskrit College, 1973, pp. 19-40.

———, 'Indological Notes', *Journal of Ancient Indian History*, vol. IX, 1976, pp. 211-13.

———, 'Mehar Copper Plate of Damodaradeva, Saka 1156' , *Epigraphia Indica*, vol. XXX, 1987, pp. 51ff.

______, *Pāl-Sen Yuger Vaṁśānucharit* (in Bengali), Calcutta: Sāhityalok, 1982.

Takakusu, J., trans., *A Record of the Buddhist Religion as Practiced in India and the Malay Archipelago (*A.D. *671-695)* by I-tsing, Oxford: Oxford University Press, 1896.

Tibbetts, G.R., trans., *Kitab al-Fawa'id fi usul al bahr wa'l-qawa'id of Ahmad b. Majid al-Najdi*, London: The Royal Asiatic Society of Great Britain and Ireland, 1971.

Vaidya, P.L., ed., *Aryā Mañjuśrimūlakalpa, Mahayanasutrasamgraha*, pt. II, Buddhist Sanskrit Texts, no. 18, Darbhanga: Mithila Text Society, 1964.

van Galen, S.E.A., *Arakan and Bengal: The Rise and Decline of the Mrauk U Kingdom (Burma) from the Fifteenth to the Seventeenth Century* AD, doctoral thesis, Leiden University, 2008.

Watters, Thomas, *On Yuan Chwan's Travels*, New Delhi: Motilal Banarsidass, 1961.

Yang, Bin, 'The Bay of Bengal Connections to Yunnan', in Rila Mukherjee (ed.), *Pelagic Passageways: The Northern Bay of Bengal Before Colonialism*, New Delhi: Primus Books, 2011, pp. 319-29.

4

# Money and Communications in Sultanate Bengal and its Neighbouring Areas

## Evidence of the Coin-hoards (1205-1576 CE)

SUTAPA SINHA

This chapter encompasses a period covering more than three and a half centuries in the history of medieval Bengal (1205 to 1576), which began with the establishment of the Turkish rule under the leadership of Ikhtiyar al-din Bakhtiyar Khalji. During this period, Bengal witnessed a new and stable coinage-based system which took root from 1300 in the time of Shams al-din Firuz Shah, the governor appointed by Delhi. It gathered momentum with the initiation of independent Sultanate rule by Fakhr al-din Mubarak Shah, that continued up to the fourth decade of sixteenth century. The regular currency was a silver coin or *tanka* (average 10.6-10.8 grams in weight), generally used for revenue collection, government expenditure, and the transactions of the traders. An occasional issue of gold coins of the same weight standard was probably used for ceremonial purposes. Instead of low value copper coins or small denomination silver coins, transactions for daily necessities were carried out through cowry shells.

We have literary evidence of overseas trade between Bengal and China from the early fifteenth century and later on that between Bengal and Portugal during the late fifteenth and early sixteenth centuries. But no dependable contemporary source material is available to find any clue about the growth and development of internal trade and trade routes that flourished during this period. As a result, no investigation has ever been made to trace the inland communication routes and their probable direction in the Bengal, Bihar, and Orissa region (though in case of Assam, significant research has been done by Nisar Ahmad on the basis of numismatic evidence).[1]

As John S. Deyell pointed out,

> A fundamental concern of economic history ... is the retracing of trade routes and assessment of the direction and volume of trade patterns along these routes. Numismatic researchers have always had a contribution to make to this line of enquiry, since it has been the fate of traders throughout history to inadvertently lose some of their money in the course of their travels. The pattern of retrieval of these old coinages in modern times is one obvious indicator of the extent and amount of trade undertaken during the period of the coins' loss.[2]

Of course, it is equally evident that the geographic patterns of coin dispersal do not represent simply trade routes: money, and coins, move in the course of revenue collection, in the train of armies, and with pilgrims (to name but a few scenarios). However, it is fair to say that the movement of coins has much to teach us about the scale and influence of particular types of money, and about the principal communications routes that were utilized by officials, soldiers, pilgrims and traders alike.

It is significant to note that unlike earlier coinage, the mint name was clearly inscribed on most of the coins minted during the Islamic period, and coins of the Bengal Sultans were no exception. On them the mint names are generally inscribed along with the date or year of minting. As a consequence, an analysis of coin hoards may well provide authentic data on the mobility of a group of coins if we plot the locations of mints indicated on the coins of a single hoard against the place of discovery of that hoard. This is physical evidence of movement of currency, due to official, military and commercial activity between different regions, reflecting the many reasons for monetary transactions that used to take place in those days. It has been mentioned explicitly by Deyell in his latest article on the monetary history of the Bengal Sultans, that 'The *tanka* was used extensively in the formal economy for purposes of revenue collection but as well as the expenditures of royalty, nobility, government, military and religious establishments ... although that was not its principal purpose, the *tanka* also served internal trade.'[3] Hence if one proposes to make a systematic plotting of find spots of a hoard along with location of mint towns of the coins found from the respective hoard, it could furnish a pattern of movement of coins.

There is no contemporary written document on the mints or the minting system of the sultanate period of Bengal but the evidence of the coins themselves provides a comprehensible record of the mints in operation during various dynasties of this entire sultanate period. It may also be noted that despite the number of mints in operation, several coins were struck without any mint name and date throughout the period of more than three hundred years. Scholars like Abdul Karim tried to identify those mints by finding out their locations but some of them remained unidentified.[4] After him, several new mint names have been deciphered by scholars on the coins of Bengal Sultans and a few of them have also been identified tentatively within the territory of present day West Bengal and Bangladesh.[5] We have accepted those identifications of mint towns for our study tracing communications routes.

## Methodology

This study draws upon a large body of only partly–published coin hoard records (see Sutapa Sinha)[6] offering an initial glimpse into my research findings, and demonstrating the potential utility of this form of evidence. Data has been accumulated from fifty-six coin hoards under study[7] (listed in the Appendix, below), for the analysis of money circulation patterns and to identify any trends of the inter-regional mobility of the coins.

A number of coin hoards discovered especially from Bangladesh, still remain beyond the reach of this research due to the paucity of information and their irregular publication particularly after independence. Even in the case of Assam and Bihar, a few coin hoards might have been left out of this research if they are unpublished and lying unnoticed in some private or public collections. However, among all these reported hoards and small finds of coins of the Bengal Sultan series, some have been excluded from study either due to incomplete reporting or due to absence of required data. Therefore, this empirical study of tracing the communications routes through the coin hoards is restricted to the analysis of fifty-six large hoards and small finds.

Coins struck in a mint were subsequently issued officially from a treasury, but it is the minting place which is considered here as the place of origin. Once issued, coins followed many paths in circulation: they might be used by governments for the salaries of officials, or by army paymasters to pay soldiers, by officials to undertake public works, or by the court for the purchase of luxury goods, by traders for the conduct of their business. As a general rule of fiscal policy, a coin or a group of coins was meant to travel during their circulation period as a medium of exchange by all or any of these means. These coins might stay in place, but they could also move considerable distances from their place of manufacture to a destination in their place of deposition. They were either buried intentionally or lost accidentally and remained buried there for several hundred years before being retrieved as a hidden treasure.

An attempt has been made here to find out a relation between the places of origin with the places of deposition of the group of coins recovered from a single coin hoards. As a result of this systematic plotting of place of origin of the coins against their place of deposition on the map (of the four major geographical regions—West Bengal, Bihar, Assam and present Bangladesh), a pattern of the currency movement of different regions has been observed separately.

Quite often, in a single hoard we found coins bearing different mint names of different regions which may indicate that coins from multiple directions came to a single point where they were accumulated and ultimately buried due to certain exigency or pressure situation. It could also be a case of long time savings for generations and eventually deposited for safekeeping of the treasure. Nevertheless, such movement of currency may well indicate a linkage between the places of origin and places of eventual deposition of the coins found in a single coin hoard. It should also be mentioned here that in case of more than one mint situated in and around a particular area, the core area and the individual mint has been considered as place of origin. For example, in the capital city of Sultanate Bengal, i.e. present day Gaur in Malda district of West Bengal, more than one mint was in operation simultaneously such as Dar al-Zarb (the mint) and Khazanah (the treasury) along with the primary mint Lakhnauti, which was often re-named after the reigning Sultans, such as Mahmudabad, Nasirabad, Shamsabad, Husainabad or Jannatabad at different points of time. So, for any one of these above mints, the place of origin has been plotted as Gaur, the capital on the Ganga during the thirteenth-fourteenth and the fifteenth-sixteenth centuries.

So, coins in hoards present three types of variables: the date each coin was minted (often indeterminate), the place each coin was minted (again, often indeterminate), and the place the coin hoard was found (i.e. place of loss or burial). Two of these variables in hoard analysis can be plotted geographically, as Figures 4.1 and 4.2 show.

This information can be captured because each Sultanate coin was marked with its city of issue. I have found, however, that for a significant proportion of the coins, the mint name is not readable due to various factors of manufacture or burial. Hence this information can be determined for only a percentage of each hoard. There is no identifiable pattern for the missing mint names, so it is likely that truncated samples are reasonably representative of the whole.

Fig. 4.2 plots the coin hoard locations used in this study. This data was also aggregated into comparative charts prepared for each single hoard. Unfortunately, no pattern has emerged if we put 'where found' versus 'where from'; i.e. the place of deposition (where found = findspot of the hoard) against the place of origin (where from = mint name) in a one-to-one relation. It becomes difficult to highlight any trends, either temporal or geographic, out

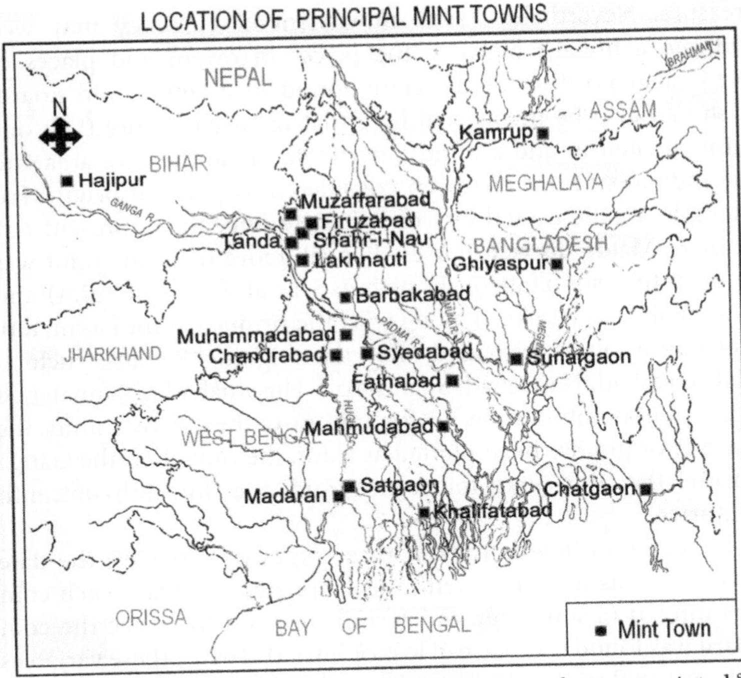


Figure 4.1: Places where Bengal Sultanate silver *tankas* were minted.[8] Modern place-names are included to assist in orientation (map drawn by the author).

of such a direct method. We had to adopt the method of analysing data in groups instead of singly, placing them time-wise and place-wise.

In order to do this, the hoard spreadsheet (summarized in the Appendix) was divided into three folders, analysing the data by century of loss of the said hoard (determined by the last dated coin found in a hoard), by place of find (the immediate political division or state of modern India and Bangladesh), and by region (the five major geographical regions of the then Bengal). For this analysis, the coin mints represented in the coin hoards have been grouped into five medieval regions: northwest (Varendra), southwest (Radha), central (Vanga), southeast (Harikela) and northeast (Srihatta/Kamru).

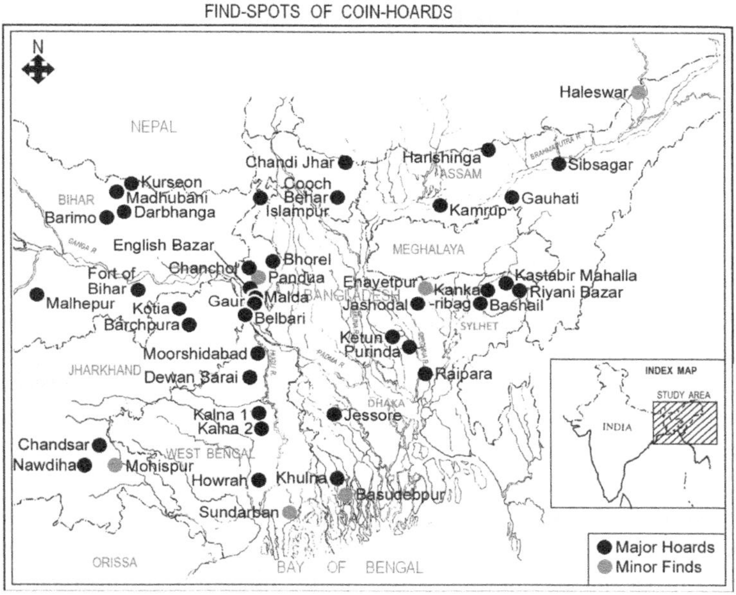


Figure 4.2: Places where Bengal Sultanate coin hoards were found (map drawn by the author).[9]

As Rila Mukherjee has shown in her contribution to this book, in some cases these regions date back into the ancient period, and were certainly well-recognized by the early medieval period. During the late medieval period these larger regional identifiers began to lose their currency, as the Sultanate population grew and as the revenue system became increasingly subdivided into smaller administrative units. Still, for purposes of general conclusions, the ancient regional classification remains useful even today.

## Presentation and Analysis of the Data

The first sorting of the coin hoard data was undertaken using a temporal filter. The fifty-six coin hoards were tagged as to the date of manufacture of the latest dateable coin in each hoard. These were grouped sequentially by 'late date' (note this refers to the coin issue date and *not* the date of recovery), within each geographic region (i.e. places where the coin hoards were found). Finally, the hoards were grouped into hundred-year intervals. The findings of this temporal or sequential sorting are given below:[10]

TABLE 4.1: HOARDS RECOVERED, BY LATE DATE

| | *Total* |
|---|---|
| 13th century | 3 |
| 14th century | 9 |
| 15th century | 22 |
| 16th century | 22 |

It is apparent that the volume of monetary transactions involving silver coinage increased steadily from the thirteenth to the sixteenth century. This has been clearly reflected in the modest number of hoards lost in the thirteenth century (three) to a peak of twenty-two in the fifteenth century. We should remark here, that this was prior to the arrival of European powers in the Indian Ocean. For the sixteenth century, the number of hoards recovered is the same, twenty-two, but since this represents only three-quarters of a century (to 1576), the number of sixteenth-century hoards was in effect one-third higher than in the previous century. Again, it is to be noted that the sample ends before the earliest arrival of New World silver in the Indian Ocean.

A second type of sorting gives a regional flavour to these chronological observations:

The gradual increase in the number of hoards lost during the four successive centuries indicates the gradual upsurge of the number of coins used in transactions, by two measures: the steady increase in production quantities per mint, as well as an increase in the number of mints in operation. In other words, it may be concluded that silver coinage had a slow start in the beginning with the establishment of the Turkish rule in Bengal in the thirteenth century and gained momentum over time. It was noticed by both Eaton and Hussain that the number of mints rose commensurately over the same period.[11] This body of data shows that the number of coins produced, and used, rose in tandem.

Second, the continued pre-eminence of the mint cities Gaur,

TABLE 4.2: COIN HOARDS GROUPED BY CENTURY AND REGION

| | *Summary (by century)* | | | | | |
|---|---|---|---|---|---|---|
| | *Minting places (grouped by region)* | | | | | |
| | *1. North-west (Varendra)* | *2. South-west (Radha)* | *3. Central (Vanga)* | *4. Southeast (Harikela / Samatata)* | *5. North-east (Srihatta)* | |
| | *No. of hoards* | *No. of hoards* | *No. of hoards* | *No. of hoards* | *No. of hoards* | *Total* |
| 13th century | 2 | 1 | 0 | 0 | 0 | 3 |
| 14th century | 8 | 2 | 5 | 0 | 0 | 15 |
| 15th century | 16 | 4 | 2 | 4 | 1 | 27 |
| 16th century | 20 | 5 | 13 | 5 | 1 | 44 |

*Source:* Prepared by the author.

*Key to regions*

1. Northwest (Varendra) mints: Lakhnauti, Firuzabad, Pandunagara, Pandua, Hussainabad, Khazana, Dar al-Zarb.
2. Southwest (Radha) mints: Nagore, Satgaon, Saptagrama, Madaran, Khalifatabad.
3. Central (Vanga) mints: Sunargaon, Muazzamabad, Suvarnagrama, Fathabad.
4. Southeast (Harikela / Samatata) mints: Chatgaon, Chattigrama, 'Arsah.
5. Northeast (Srihatta) mints: Ghiyaspur, Kamru.

Lakhnauti, Firuzabad, Pandunagara, Hussainabad, Khazana, Dar al-Zarb of Varendra cluster (i.e. northwest part of the region) is noticeable throughout the sultanate rule in Bengal. Interestingly the number of hoards from mints of four other regions, Radha (southwest), Vanga (central), Harikela/ Samatata (southeast), and Srihatta (northeast), has grown as well in a gradual increasing order. Nevertheless, the influence of the regional port mints, Satgaon in southwest Radha region and Chatgaon/Chatigrama in southeast Samatata-Harikela region was really felt only in the fifteenth and sixteenth centuries when maritime trade with China and Portugal was proceeding regularly, putting much pressure on the port towns as well as on the port mints.

The influence of the Vanga complex of mints grew with the fourteenth century expansion of the sultanate to the delta region. It is noticeable that these mints had two separate heydays: Sunargaon/Muazzamabad in the fourteenth century, and Fathabad in the sixteenth century. Sunargaon was the first independent capital of Sultan Fakhr al-din Mubarak Shah (1334-49) who was ruling independently from the eastern part of Bengal and to date innumerable silver coins of Mubarak Shah have been encountered, both from the coin hoards and from the public collections, all issued from a single mint of Hazrat Jalal Sunargaon. As a matter of fact, during this fourth decade of the fourteenth century, an upsurge took place in coin production and the Sultan consistently issued silver coins in huge number each year of his reign. This high volume occurred for the first time in the monetary history of Sultanate Bengal. It is also noticeable that coins produced from Sunargaon mint were circulated mainly in the eastern part of Bengal as these were lost and found in coin hoards unearthed in the Vanga area.

Likewise, Fathabad became the most dominant mint for the Husain Shahi rulers in the sixteenth century, especially by Ala al-din Husain Shah and his son Nasir al-din Nusrat Shah. The beginning of the sixteenth century saw growing trade relations of Bengal with the outer world as well as with other regional powers of medieval India.

This regionwise analysis of the data derived from fifty-six major and minor finds of the Sultans of Bengal is quite complex to interpret. The result is perplexing at first glance, but throws very interesting light on the nature of currency circulation which in turn is a clear indicator of inland communications. The number of mints is highest in the Varendra (northwest) region but the number of hoards recovered (either lost or buried) is highest in the 'northeast' region, i.e. Srihatta. This region comprising Sylhet, Cooch Behar, Kamta and Kamrup yielded the highest number of coin hoards of the series under review and contained predominantly coins minted from 'Varendra' and 'Vanga' regions and very few coins of the Srihatta region itself. This shows that the region with a marginal number of mints with very low production capacity used to draw large number of coins from the mints of the capital area (Varendra) or more centralized mints (Vanga)

TABLE 4.3: COIN HOARDS GROUPED BY SUBREGION

| | *Summary (by region)* | | | | | |
|---|---|---|---|---|---|---|
| | *Minting places (grouped by region)* | | | | | |
| | *1. North-west (Varendra)* | *2. South-west (Radha)* | *3. Central (Vanga)* | *4. Southeast (Harikela / Samatata)* | *5. North-east (Srihatta)* | |
| *Region found* | *No. of hoards* | *No. of hoards* | *No. of hoards* | *No. of hoards* | *No. of hoards* | *Total* |
| 1. Northwest | 12 | 3 | 5 | 2 | 1 | 23 |
| A. Tirhut | 3 | 0 | 0 | 0 | 0 | 3 |
| B. Bihar | 2 | 1 | 0 | 0 | 0 | 3 |
| 2. Southwest | 4 | 3 | 2 | 0 | 0 | 9 |
| 2A. Jharkhand | 4 | 0 | 3 | 1 | 0 | 8 |
| 3. Vanga | 4 | 2 | 3 | 1 | 0 | 10 |
| 4. Southeast | 0 | 0 | 0 | 0 | 0 | 0 |
| 5. Northeast | 16 | 3 | 11 | 6 | 3 | 39 |

*Source:* Prepared by the author.

and we must emphasize that this intense flow of currency from the highest producing region to the lowest one must have been taken place due to significant political or economic factors. I am unable to detect any strong and continuous military activities in the Sylhet region that would explain this specific flow. Nor can it be associated with the revenue regime for, as late as the eighteenth century, the revenue of Sylhet was still being collected in cowries.[12] I conclude that it is due to strong and steady commercial activity, i.e., regular internal trade between the Varendra and Vanga regions with Srihatta, more precisely with Kamta-Kamru, Sylhet and Cooch Behar that was sustained through centuries. The two mint names found for this Srihatta region are Ghiyaspur and Kamru (Chawlistan urf Arsah Kamru), the former being the official mint of Ghiyasuddin Bahadur Shah, the Governor of Bengal who was ousted by Muhammad bin Tughlaq in the third decade of fourteenth century. The mint Ghiyaspur was never restored after

Ghiyasuddin Bahadur Shah. The mint of Kamru which had an epithet 'Chawlistan' i.e. land of rice, found mention very rarely on the coins of Sikandar Shah dated only 759 AH. Until now no coins of any other sultan have been reported bearing this mint name. So the Srihatta region practically had no regular mint throughout the period but attracted the largest number of coins (reflected by 39 coin hoards found).

On the other hand, the Harikela-Samatata region in the southeast did not yield a single coin hoard to date even though Chatgaon or Chatigrama, being the most important port town and port mint, served as such for a considerable time in fifteenth-sixteenth centuries. The reason behind the complete absence of any lost/buried hoard is beyond estimation. It may well indicate that the coins of the southeast were one means of monetizing the incoming silver from the Bay of Bengal trade. But since hoards containing coins of Chatgaon/Chatigrama mint have been recovered from the distant Varendra and Radha regions, we can reasonably conclude that silver *tankas* of the southeast consistently travelled northwest towards the capital, in revenue or trade, thereby supplying the proliferate mints of that region.

The above analysis also traces coins found in different regions that either remained in, or travelled back to, their place of origin (except for the Harikela-Samatata area). It would be easier to explain if we take the example of Varendra where twenty-three hoards have been found from the core area of the capital region of which twelve comprise coins produced from the different mints of the same region, five hoards have coins from the Vanga region, three hoards have coins from the Radha region, two hoards have coins from the Harikela-Samatata region and a single hoard has coins from the Srihatta area.

Thus, an inland monetary movement due to revenue collection, military movement and trade activity was in continuous process and as a result coins originating from a mint of Radha (southwest) region found their way to somewhere in Varendra, Vanga or as far as the Harikela-Samatata region, remained buried there for a few hundred years, and were retrieved accidentally from their respective places of deposit/burial, in later times.

## Paths of Travel and Money Movement

Analysis has revealed some surprising, and consistent, patterns of coin movement in the Bengal Sultanate. The entire region under discussion is partly covered by the upper Gangetic valley, the middle Gangetic plain and the lower Gangetic delta formation and, needless to mention, the rivers and their tributaries and distributaries have always played a significant role in the inland communication system — whether for commercial purposes or for revenue gathering, administration, military activity, or pilgrimage. Sailing through these watercourses was always cheaper and quicker than land routes, especially in an age when much of the original forest cover and mangrove swamps were yet to be cleared and settled.

It is important that most of the find spots of the coin hoards and mint towns are (or were) in and around a river course, either on the bank of the principal river or near its tributaries which had direct link with the main river. As a case study, we may cite examples from Bihar and Jharkhand (one in Varendra and the other in the Radha region of our study). There were two tentative routes to be mentioned here: one from Bhagalpur district (now divided into Bhagalpur and Banka district) and the other from Santhal Pargana district, now known as Dumka in Jharkhand, both having transactions with faraway places in Bengal. The coin hoards found in different places in Bhagalpur district yielded coins minted in the Sunargaon (present Narayanganj district of Bangladesh), Chittagong and Firuzabad (Pandua in Malda district, West Bengal) mints. Bhagalpur is quite close to the Ganges and is surrounded by a network of its tributaries, and coins from far away Sunargaon mint and Chatgaon mint (one in Vanga and the other in the Harikela region) could have arrived there along with coins from the Firuzabad mint (Varendra region) by waterway. It may logically be assumed that coins from Firuzabad mint (Pandua, Malda district) moved through the river Mahananda and the Ganges to reach Bhagalpur. Sunargaon is situated on a strategically important point for trading on the Meghna river near the confluence of the Padma, Meghna and some other tributaries. Chittagong was the most important port (*porto grande*) town and was well-connected with Sunargaon through the Meghna and its estuary. Therefore, it may be stated that movement of metal currency of the Sultanate Bengal further established the fact that Bhagalpur, Pandua, Dhaka, Sunargaon and Chittagong, the chief centres of politico-economic importance of medieval Bengal were inter-connected through the Ganga-Padma-Meghna fluvial network and an internal trade route along these rivers can convincingly be drawn on the basis of this evidence.

## NOTES

1. Nisar Ahmad, 'Assam-Bengal Trade in the Medieval Period: A Numismatic Perspective', *Journal of the Economic and Social History of the Orient*, 33-2, 1990, pp. 169-98.
2. John S. Deyell, 'Numismatic Methodologies Which Answer Questions Economists Might Ask', in Amal Kumar Jha (ed.), *Coinage, Trade and Economy*, Nasik: IIRNS Press, 1991, p. 1.
3. John S. Deyell, 'Cowries and Coins: The Dual Monetary System of the Bengal Sultanate', *Indian Economic and Social History Review*, 47-1, Jan.-Mar. 2010, p. 70.
4. Abdul Karim, 'Section II: Mint-Towns', *Corpus of the Muslim Coins of Bengal (down to 1538 A.D.)*, Dhaka: Asiatic Society of Bangladesh, 1960 (rpt. 2013), pp. 157-64.
5. Stan Goron and J.P. Goenka, *Coins of the Indian Sultanates*, New Delhi: Munshiram Manoharlal, 2001.
7. My preliminary findings have been published previously as Sutapa Sinha, 'Coin Hoards of the Bengal Sultans: An Anatomy of the Hoards', *Pratna Samiksha*, vols. 6-8, Kolkata, 2001, pp. 136-241; idem, 'A Note on an Important Coin Collection of the Bengal Sultans in the Bode Museum, Berlin', in Gerd Mevissen and Arundhati Banerji, *Prajnadhara: Essays on Asian Art History, Epigraphy and Culture in Honour of Gouriswar Bhattacharya*, Delhi: Kaveri, 2009, pp. 359-66; idem, 'The Coin Collection of the Bengal Sultans in the Cabinet of the Heberden Coin Room, Ashmolean Museum, Oxford', *Pratna Samiksha*, Kolkata: Centre for Archaeological Studies and Training, Eastern India, New Series 1, 2010, pp. 163-75; idem, 'A Note on the Coins of the Bengal Sultans in the Collection of the Patna Museum, Bihar', *Journal of Bengal Art*, vol. 18, 2013, pp. 143-

58; idem., 'Coins from Gaur', *Pratna Samiksha,* New Series 3, 2012, pp. 185-90; idem, 'Coin Hoard and Small Finds of the Sultans of Bengal in the Collection of Assam State Museum, Guwahati, Assam', *Pratna Samiksha,* New Series 5, 2014, pp. 101-16.

7. The full corpus of hoard evidence is published in Sutapa Sinha, *Coin Hoards of the Bengal Sultans, 1205-1576 AD: From West Bengal, Bihar, Jharkhand, Assam and Bangladesh*, Gurgaon: Shubhi Publications, 2017.
8. *Sources*: Karim, *Corpus of the Muslim Coins,* pp. 157-64; Syed Ejaz Hussain, *The Bengal Sultanate: Politics, Economy and Coins (AD 1205-1576),* New Delhi: Manohar, 2003, map following p. 304.
9. This map is based on my own research (cited above).
10. I am deeply indebted to Dr John S. Deyell for his unstinted help, valuable advice and sincere cooperation in organizing and interpreting the statistical data, otherwise publication of this article would not have been possible.
11. Richard M. Eaton, *The Rise of Islam and the Bengal Frontier, 1204-1760,* New Delhi: Oxford University Press, 1994; Husain, *The Bengal Sultanate.*
12. Sanjay Garg, 'Non-metallic Currencies of India in Indian Ocean Trade and Economies', in Himanshu Prabha Ray and Edward A. Alpers (eds), *Cross Currents and Community Networks: The History of the Indian Ocean World*, New Delhi: Oxford University Press, 2007, pp. 252-3.

## BIBLIOGRAPHY

Ahmad, Nisar, 'Assam-Bengal Trade in the Medieval Period: A Numismatic Perspective', *Journal of the Economic and Social History of the Orient,* 33, 2, 1990, pp. 169-98.

Deyell, John S., 'Numismatic Methodologies Which Answer Questions Economists Might Ask', in Amal Kumar Jha (ed.), *Coinage, Trade and Economy*, Nasik: IIRNS Press, 1991, pp. 1-15.

———, 'Cowries and Coins: the Dual Monetary System of the Bengal Sultanate', *Indian Economic and Social History Review*, 47, 1, Jan.-Mar. 2010, pp. 63-106.

Eaton, Richard M., *The Rise of Islam and the Bengal Frontier, 1204-1760,* New Delhi: Oxford University Press, 1994.

Garg, Sanjay, 'Non-metallic Currencies of India in Indian Ocean Trade and Economies', in Himanshu Prabha Ray and Edward A. Alpers (eds), *Cross Currents and Community Networks: The History of the Indian Ocean World*, New Delhi: Oxford University Press, 2007, pp. 245-62.

Goron, Stan and J.P. Goenka, *Coins of the Indian Sultanates*, New Delhi: Munshiram Manoharlal, 2001.

Hussain, Syed Ejaz, *The Bengal Sultanate: Politics, Economy and Coins (AD 1205-1576)*, New Delhi: Manohar, 2003.

Karim, Abdul, *Corpus of the Muslim Coins of Bengal (Down to 1538 A.D.)*, Dhaka: Asiatic Society of Bangladesh, 1960 (rpt. 2013).

Sinha, Sutapa, 'Unpublished Coin Hoards of the Later Ilyas Shahi Sultans of Bengal', *Journal of Bengal Art*, vol. 3, 1999, pp. 109-30.

______, 'Coin Hoards of the Bengal Sultans: An Anatomy of the Hoards', *Pratna Samiksha* (Journal of the Directorate of Archaeology and Museums, West Bengal), vols. 6-8, Kolkata, 2001, pp. 136-241.

______, 'A Note on an Important Coin Collection of the Bengal Sultans in the Bode Museum, Berlin', in Gerd Mevissen and Arundhati Banerji (eds), *Prajnadhara: Essays on Asian Art History, Epigraphy and Culture in Honour of Gouriswar Bhattacharya*, Delhi: Kaveri, 2009, pp. 359-66.

______, 'The Coin Collection of the Bengal Sultans in the Cabinet of the Heberden Coin Room, Ashmolean Museum, Oxford', *Pratna Samiksha*, Kolkata: Centre for Archaeological Studies and Training, Eastern India, New Series 1, 2010, pp. 163-75.

______, 'A Note on the Coins of the Bengal Sultans in the Collection of the Patna Museum, Bihar', *Journal of Bengal Art*, vol. 18, 2013, pp. 143-58.

______, 'Coins from Gaur' *Pratna Samiksha*, New Series 3, 2012, pp. 185-90.

______, 'Coin Hoard and Small Finds of the Sultans of Bengal in the Collection of Assam State Museum, Guwahati, Assam', *Pratna Samiksha*, New Series 5, 2014, pp. 101-16.

______, *Coin Hoards of the Bengal Sultans, 1205-1576 AD, From West Bengal, Bihar, Jharkhand, Assam and Bangladesh*, Gurgaon: Shubhi Publications, 2017.

## Appendix: Coin Hoards Analysed in this Study

| *Hoard no.* | *Place found* | *District* | *State* | *Year found* | *No. of coins* | *Early date* | *Late date* |
|---|---|---|---|---|---|---|---|
| 1 | Howrah | Howrah | West Bengal | 1841 | 31 | 1342 | 1459 |
| 2 | Dinhata | Cooch Bihar | West Bengal | 1863 | 13,500 | 1265 | 1410 |
| 3 | Fort of Bihar | Patna | Bihar | 1873 | 37 | 1217 | 1229 |
| 4 | Madhubani | Tirhut | Bihar | 1874 | 36 | 1409 | 1422 |
| 5 | Sundarban | 24 Parganas | West Bengal | 1875 | 2 | 1519 | 1532 |
| 6 | Gauhati | Gauhati | Assam | 1880 | 38 | 1217 | 1255 |
| 7 | Dewan Sarai | Murshidabad | West Bengal | 1883 | 85 | 1357 | 1474 |
| 8 | Sibsagar | Sibsagar | Assam | 1891 | 44 | 1322 | 1519 |
| 9 | Kamrup | Kamrup | Assam | 1892 | 30 | 1394 | 1410 |
| 10 | Gaur | Malda | West Bengal | 1892 | 14 | 1493 | 1538 |
| 11 | Kotia | Bhagalpur | Bihar | 1892 | 28 | 1391 | 1440 |
| 12 | Narail | Jessore | Bangladesh | 1893 | 60 | 1363 | 1432 |
| 13 | Barchpura | Bhagalpur | Bihar | 1893 | 25 | 1349 | 1353 |
| 14 | Darbhanga | Darbhanga | Bihar | 1896 | 3 | 1513 | 1519 |
| 15 | Chandsar | Santhal Pargana | Jharkhand | 1897 | 20 | 1378 | 1416 |
| 16 | Jashodal | Mymensingh | Bangladesh | 1897 | 317 | 1362 | 1556 |
| 17 | Belbari | Malda | West Bengal | 1904 | 110 | 1519 | 1556 |
| 18 | Moorshidabad | Murshidabad | West Bengal | 1907 | 85 | 1210 | 1345 |
| 19 | Enayetpur | Mymensingh | Bangladesh | 1909 | 6 | 1301 | 1322 |
| 20 | Purinda | Dhaka | Bangladesh | 1910 | 24 | 1294 | 1322 |
| 21 | Rupaibari | Naugaon | Bangladesh | 1911 | 5 | 1305 | 1321 |
| 22 | Pandua | Malda | West Bengal | 1911 | 5 | 1416 | 1420 |
| 23 | Basudebpur | Khulna | Bangladesh | 1911 | 2 | 1416 | 1418 |
| 24 | Kastabir Mahalla | Sylhet | Bangladesh | 1913 | 97 | 1301 | 1387 |
| 25 | Bara Rajpur | Khulna | Bangladesh | 1915 | 100 | 1296 | 1414 |
| 26 | Kankaribag | Sylhet | Bangladesh | 1916 | 31 | 1474 | 1532 |
| 27 | Bashail | Sylhet | Bangladesh | 1917 | 10 | 1462 | 1481 |
| 28 | Mohispur | Santhal Pargana | Jharkhand | 1918 | 6 | 1518 | 1532 |
| 29 | Ketun | Dhaka | Bangladesh | 1918 | 346 | 1322 | 1431 |
| 30 | Rautkhai | Sylhet | Bangladesh | 1919 | 7 | 1488 | 1493 |
| 31 | Sonakhira | Sylhet | Bangladesh | 1919 | 3 | 1519 | 1543 |
| 32 | Kalighat | Sylhet | Bangladesh | 1919 | 6 | 1297 | 1305 |

| | | | | | | | |
|---|---|---|---|---|---|---|---|
| 33 | Raipara | Dhaka | Bangladesh | 1928 | 182 | 1493 | 1546 |
| 34 | Nawdiha | Santhal Pargana | Jharkhand | 1933 | 16 | 1493 | 1524 |
| 35 | | Santhal Pargana | Jharkhand | 1934 | 8 | | |
| 36 | Baijnathpur | Santhal Pargana | Jharkhand | 1935 | 7 | 1493 | 1532 |
| 37 | Kalna I | Burdwan | West Bengal | 1937 | 20 | 1301 | 1358 |
| 38 | Kalna II | Burdwan | West Bengal | 1939 | 72 | 1301 | 1359 |
| 39 | Malhepur | Shahabad | Bihar | 1943 | 18 | 1436 | 1538 |
| 40 | Nazirkhani | Malda | West Bengal | 1957 | 69 | 1493 | 1538 |
| 41 | Barimo | Darbhanga | Bihar | 1958 | 6 | 1414 | 1519 |
| 42 | Kurseon | Darbhanga | Bihar | 1966 | 15 | 1357 | 1414 |
| 43 | Islampur | Uttar Dinajpur | West Bengal | 1981 | 135 | 1342 | 1431 |
| 44 | Chandir Jhar | Jalpaiguri | West Bengal | 1987 | 767 | 1342 | 1582 |
| 45 | Biyani Bazar | Sylhet | Bangladesh | 1988 | 800 | 1342 | 1457 |
| 46 | Harishinga | Darrang | Assam | 1990 | 40 | 1519 | 1581 |
| 47 | Haleswar | Sonitpur | Assam | 1993 | 168 | 1296 | 1474 |
| 48 | English Bazar | Malda | West Bengal | 1996 | 50 | 1459 | 1482 |
| 49 | Chanchol | Malda | West Bengal | 1996 | 40 | 1449 | 1480 |
| 50 | Bhorel | Dakshin Dinajpur | West Bengal | 1997 | 83 | 1320 | 1516 |
| 51 | Kushmandi | Dakshin Dinajpur | West Bengal | ? | 67 | 1342 | 1531 |
| 52 | Mathanguri | Baksa | Assam | ? | 127 | 1320 | 1537 |
| 53 | Donka Mokam | Karbi Amlong | Assam | ? | 6 | 1389 | 1520 |
| 54 | Juria | Nawgaon | Assam | ? | 3 | 1296 | 1410 |
| 55 | Rajaduar | Guwahati | Assam | 1988 | 6 | 1342 | 1545 |
| 56 | Nawabganj | Rajshahi | Bangladesh | 1964 | 199 | 1329 | 1410 |

*Source*: Perpared by the author.

5

# Cashless Economy or Value for Money

## Early Medieval South India

Radhika Seshan

What was the extent of the money economy in medieval India? Was there a money economy at all? Scholars have often argued that India did not have a money economy until very late and that money entered the local markets only well into the medieval period. These theories have of course been challenged, and very effectively. As has been pointed out (by Irfan Habib,[1] Om Prakash,[2] and Sushil Chaudhuri[3] in particular), not only did India have a flourishing money economy, there were also in operation systems of cashless transfers, through the *hundis*, the bills of exchange. Until as late as the eighteenth century, we find in the Maratha records mention of money being transferred from various parts of India to Maharashtra through the *varats*, which the English also used in the seventeenth and early eighteenth centuries. That such systems were not peculiar to India is also clear from the research carried out into, for example, the *wampum* used in North America.[4]

A question that perhaps needs to be addressed is the nature of the 'cashless economy' in India in comparison with such systems elsewhere in the world. Focus has generally been on the European bill of exchange, described in 1972 by Irfan Habib as 'the European merchants' means of cashless payment between the Middle Ages and the twentieth century for transactions involving both Europe, as well as areas overseas.'[5] Habib has also highlighted the role of the Indian *hundis* in the exchange networks of, in particular, Mughal north India.

Given the importance of trade to most economies, and the role of long distance trade in the Asian world from antiquity, one should perhaps look at the idea of a 'cashless economy' both in other times and in other spaces. Globally, how would such a network work? Logically, the answer would be, through networks of family or business contacts, or through what has been called 'networks of trust'. Another question would then have to be how these networks of trust came into existence, and how, and when, the notion of non-monetary transfers gained greater currency. To this would be linked the issue of currency itself, and the validation of a particular system through such networks. We know, for example, that one of the areas where the Persian *lari* was found was Chaul on the west coast of India; but what is less known is that the *lari* was minted in Chaul as well, and thus can be seen as indicative both of the strength of the ties between the two regions, and, perhaps, the need for cash here. For the seventeenth century, Irfan Habib has pointed to fluctuations in the commission and transfer rates at Surat in response to the political instability at Yemen.[6]

It must also be pointed out that such studies have concentrated on north India, particularly Mughal north India. We know from Persian, English and Dutch sources that, in the seventeenth century, bills of exchange were commonly used to and from Surat, Burhanpur, and Agra, to name just three places. Thomas Roe was very impressed with the system and said that 'the interest [due on money borrowed from local *sarrafs*] is not the hundredth part of the charge the Company bear in attending five months with a fleet for the fitting and safety of a ship'.[7] He particularly impressed upon the English factors at Surat the convenience of transferring both principal and interest through a *hundi*. A little later, the Council at Surat instructed the factors at Burhanpur to get the payment due on a 'tapestry' sold to one 'Rao Rattan', and then to 'solicit his order for the passing and making of a Barratt [*Varat*], (the Course and manner whereof wilbe [*sic*] shown you by the Brokers)' and send it to Surat.[8] However, we do not get such information about the south of India even for this period, let alone for an earlier time.

The role of the state as guarantor, in a sense, of such transactions also needs to be underlined. In Mughal north India, the areas in which the *hundis* were in use were all within the Mughal Empire, or with areas with which there were long established contacts, but mostly across the western Indian Ocean. Can similar networks be traced for the eastern Indian Ocean? That south India had a money economy from the early medieval period is clear, if from nothing else, then from the prevalence of currency, particularly of gold coins. It was often argued that such coinage had a purely commemorative value, and could not be used in small, local purchases; but as K.R. Hall has pointed out, there has been 'insufficient consideration of specie-extractive taxation systems that might have stimulated the utilization of coinage or altered its character'.[9] The role of the temple in such utilization or alteration also needs to be further examined.

But was there another mode of payment of the kind identified in north India, which involved transfers without money being carried from one place to another? Or were there other mechanisms at play? What was the *idea* of money and / or transactions that existed in early medieval south India?[10] These are questions to which answers still have to be found, and are not the main concern here.

In another context, it has been said that the world consists of two kinds of items – that of a market, which has a price, and that of an audience, which has a value.[11] Can we then argue that there existed in early medieval south India a system in which value and price were both understood, and neither needed to be clearly stated? In other words, this was a different kind of a 'cashless economy'. Networks of circulation linked communities, products, and production centres, in a system in which money underpinned the networks, even if not used in regular transactions. 'Equivalency' is perhaps the appropriate term, for the exchanges clearly had a monetary value even if not transacted in cash as a material substance.

This chapter focuses on two questions raised by the editors – to wit, how did a cashless economy work alongside cash-using zones, and what were the networks that were generated through such zones. However, a question that needs to be asked is whether, in south India during the period between the Cholas and Vijayanagar, there were such parallel zones at all. Networks of circulation are easy to identify but such zones are not. The questions raised are addressed through a study of a series of inscriptions, covering the different time periods. What I propose to do is list some of the inscriptions below before going into analysis.

The first of the inscriptions is from Aihole, and has been dated to the eighth century CE. It states that a grant was given to the

> Five Hundred *Caturvedis* of the excellent capital Aryapura [Aihole]: A *dharana* at the ceremonies of *Annaprasana* (the first feeding of the child with boiled rice), *Pusavana* (attaining puberty) and *Caula* (tonsure); a *gadyana* at the ceremonies of *Upanayana* (investiture with sacred thread) and *Samavartana* (return home of the student after completion of study); two *gadyanas* at the *Caturmasya* (sacrifices); four *gadyanas* at the *Agnistoma* sacrifice.[12]

The Cholas, as is well known, were in many ways the most important of the rulers of the south in the period between the ninth and the thirteenth centuries. A variety of inscriptions testify to the land revenue and other arrangements that were set up by them, and, of course, to the number of irrigation projects that they set up (among the most important being the Grand Anicut, the canal that is still in use). Here, only two of the many inscriptions will be taken up. The first dates to the early eleventh century, and is concerned with the arrangements made for the maintenance of the great temple at Thanjavur. In analysing this, I have mainly followed James Heitzman's study of what he has called 'ritual polity'.[13] The other inscription dates to the early thirteenth century, and is from Piranmalai, to the southeast of Thanjavur.

The Thanjavur inscriptions give details of the arrangements for the maintenance of the temple, its rituals, and its functionaries. One requirement in all temples is for oil and ghee for the lamps; this was done by gifting cows and sheep to the temple, and appointing the required people to look after them. According to Heitzman, courtier and military groups 'arranged for annual income for the temple through deposits made with Brahmana assemblies. . . . The Brahmana assemblies were responsible for investing the money and, with accruing profits, provided the temple with an annual return.'[14] The Piranmalai inscription is rather different, in that it refers not to the king's involvement with a specific temple, but records the activities of the guild of the 500,[15] especially mentioning the areas of their operations. These are defined as being in 'the eighteen *Pattinam*, the thirty-two *valarpuram*' and the 'sixty-four *kadigaitavalam*'.[16] The first word seems to refer to market towns of all kinds, the second means 'coastal town', and the third probably means interior towns where periodic fairs or markets were held.

Moving away from the Cholas, the next inscription, of 1117, is of the dynasty of the Kakatiyas. It says that a lady named Mailamma 'built the Kadalalaya-basadi on the top of the hill and gifted two *mattar* of wet land below the bund of the tank built in her name by her husband Betana-pergade and four *mattar* of black-soil land and six *mattar* of uncultivable land (*karambam*) for the daily workshop, incense, lights and other services in the *basadi* and for food, clothing, etc., of the temple priest.'[17]

Another inscription, dated 1186, says 'Kakati Rudradevaraju, provided a perpetual lamp with metal stand (*loha-dandu*) in the temple of Bhimesvara at Daksaramamu and gifted 50 *inupa-edlu*. The gift was entrusted to the *boyas* (shepherds) of the temple cow-pen (*kilaramu*) with the stipulation that one *Tribhuvanankusa-mana* of ghee should be supplied every day for the maintenance of the lamp. It is also stated that four *boyas* stood surety.'[18]

The next five inscriptions are all of the fourteenth century and belong to the period of the Vijayanagar empire. One of 1353 AD 'records the sale for 200 *panam*, of 2 *karai* of land in the village Nayappakkam …, as *tirunamattukani* for maintaining certain festivals in the temple'.[19] The next is dated to ten years later, and says that 'all the temple trustees and functionaries of the Tiruvannamalai temple including the Head of the *matha*, *devakanmi*, accountant, the *kaikkolar* of two temple streets, the *virabhadrar*, and the *tiruvagambadiyar* sold some temple land … as *kaniyatci*.'[20] The next, dated in the same year, is from Karnataka. This states that 'Duggannan, the chief chamberlain of the palace … gave all taxes including that on looms (*makka-tirai*), oil mill (*cekkirai*), and others to the temple of Valavantaperumal at Velliyur.'[21] Another inscription of 1367 AD states that the temple trustees fixed the rates for specific taxes on some land purchased by a functionary of the temple from the people of the village near the temple, but said that the purchaser had to reclaim the land for cultivation and then pay the temple a fixed quantity of paddy and money as tax.[22] The last inscription dated to 1374 'registers the levy on the Kaikkolas of Tirukkalukkunram [modern day Kanchipuram district] of a consolidated rent including the taxes already payable by them, of 70 *panam* per annum, on the clothes taken out to Pattinam for sale and on the commodities brought home by them from there.'[23]

These are only some of the inscriptions that list networks of exchanges in the region that, during the period between the eighth century CE and the fifteenth century CE, were included in the kingdoms of the Cholas, the Chalukyas, the Kakatiyas, and the Vijayanagar rulers.

The first inscription, of the Chalukya kingdom, which covered much of present-day Karnataka state, is clearly about money payments for specific rituals – the *gadyana* was a gold coin that was current in the Deccan during the Chalukya period. What is interesting is that the inscription lists the payments, but it is none too clear whether these were the fees charged by the temple for these services, or were the fees to be paid to the Five Hundred for performing these ceremonies. How did a guild of merchants become the recipients of fees for what seem to be basically Brahmanical rituals? Could this have been linked to the goods brought in by the guilds, or to the fact that they were obviously closely involved with circulation of goods and money?

The Chola inscriptions are clearly about networks of circulation, of both goods and people, mediated by the state directly in the first instance, and by a guild of merchants in the second. The role of the state and of the temple in the economic, political, and legitimacy structures come out very clearly – far more so than the earlier Chalukya inscription, where ritual and payment mesh, but the state is not such an obvious player.

The next lot of inscriptions belong to the Kakatiyas, who ruled from Warangal in modern-day Andhra Pradesh. They ruled the area to the coast, and Motupalli, a port in their kingdom, was one of the most important of the ports of the Bay of Bengal trade network. An important inscription from Motupalli, recording in detail the concessions given to merchants at the port, has not been included here, mainly because the focus has been more on the hinterland connectivities than on the circulation networks to the coast and across the seas, but it is necessary to point out that such connections are also to be found in the inscriptions. In contrast to the earlier inscription, this inscription cited here is about the grant of land, not money; but it is significant that specific measures of land are mentioned, as are types of soil (*mattar*, wet land, and black soil). As is clear, the income from these lands was to be used for ceremonies carried out in the temple, and for the supply of goods to be used in these ceremonies. The third inscription, of the same dynasty, is not about money or land; but it does involve the gift of an item (a lamp stand, probably brass), and mentions the shepherds, who were to provide ghee, and stand surety for the community. One can go back to the Chola arrangements for the maintenance of ghee, and the shepherds as surety makes much more sense.

The Vijayanagar inscriptions indicate some more differences. For one thing, all of them involve money of some kind – sale of land, grant of taxes, fixing of sums to be paid as tax, and consolidated rent on goods taken to the port of Pattinam by the weavers, the *kaikkolars*. Money was obviously much more the medium, and apparently part of the regular economic exchanges, even when these involved the temples and the services to and by the temples. The role of the local communities through the temple, and so the working of the temple as an economic institution are very obvious, but again, what needs to be underlined is that this kind of service-economy-cash-value method of interaction does not seem to have been out of the ordinary. Rather, it seems to have evolved to the extent where they no longer need to be defined in any way other than the very matter-of-fact tone that comes through in the Vijayanagar inscriptions.

Y. Subbarayalu has described in detail the contents of a grant to the Anjuvannam guild in Kerala, which mentions '72 rights and privileges' that were to be given to them. These included remission of a part of the customs duty that they had been paying to the government, the amounts that they were permitted to collect on 'incoming and outgoing merchandise transported by carts' and a slightly smaller sum on goods coming or going by ships and boats.[24] He has also pointed to the inscriptions extant in Indonesia that refer to the same guild, and so argues for the prevalence of this guild in trading operations across the Indian Ocean world between the ninth and the thirteenth centuries in particular. Can one argue that these were the networks of trust in this world? What the medium of transaction was, whether cash or cashless, is unfortunately impossible to find, and what references we do have are all expressed in cash terms. But that they straddled the oceanic and the land based trading worlds is clear.

It must also be remembered that, while the focus here has been on the inscriptions that do not directly link to the circulation systems prevalent in the Bay of Bengal world, these were the areas that supplied the goods required in that world. It is difficult to talk of 'parallel' zones; rather, one should talk of overlapping ones, in which cash existed, was taken for granted, and used when required, but cash value was much more of a reality. The links between money as material, money as exchange, and money as marker of status need to be much more deeply studied.

What is clear from these inscriptions is that they were not 'cashless', in the sense of 'without coinage'. Coins were clearly present from the eighth century itself. While we do not have any records from this region indicating clearly the transfer of money through bills of exchange, neither do we get any indication of a system based on barter, which has often been seen as the only other form of exchange that exists – i.e. there is money and a money economy, where money is at some point handed over; or else there would have to be systems in which there was no money exchange at all. What we are arguing is that both these seem to be rather extremely stated. Can we really identify such extremes, even through the very few inscriptions cited above?

As stated at the beginning, another aspect that needs to be highlighted is the role of the state. In all of these inscriptions, the presence of the state is very obvious. Heitzman has argued that there were to be seen 'transactional networks', which, on the one hand, 'entailed a set of transactions bringing services, agricultural produce and money into the temple' and also another which involved the temple as a redistributive centre.[25] One of the major arguments against Burton Stein's segmentary state and peasant state model has been that of taxation – how can there be a peasant state in which the peasant taxes himself? That taxes were collected, in cash or kind or both, or were assigned, is clear–the inscriptions are replete with references to the grant of *maganmai* (tolls and customs collected on the roads) and *pattanapagudi* (share of the town), either granted by the merchant guilds to a town, or collected by them in a town.

What seems to be working here is a system in which value was understood, and prices were fixed. The cost of something–a ritual, a piece of land or some manufactured item – was known, and therefore the value of a gift of this kind was understood. This was a society in which value had significance and price, even if it was not expressed in cash terms alone. Multiple networks existed, in all of which money operated in a number of ways, some direct, some implied.

## NOTES

1. Irfan Habib, 'Systems of Bills of Exchange (*Hundis*) in the Mughal Empire', *Proceedings of the Indian History Congress*, Muzaffarpur, 1972, pp. 290-303.
2. Om Prakash, 'The Cashless Payment Mechanism in Mughal India: The Working of the Hundi Network', in Sushil Chaudhuri and Markus A. Denzel (eds), *Cashless Payments and Transactions from the Antiquity to 1914*, Stuttgart: Franz Steiner Verlag, 2008, pp. 131-8.
3. Sushil Chaudhuri, 'No Ready Money? No Problem! The Role of *Hundis* (Bills of Exchange) in Early Modern India, *c.* 1600-1800', in Chaudhuri and. Denzel (eds), *Cashless Payments*, pp. 139-52.
4. Claudia Schnurmann, 'Wampum as a Cultural Broker in North-eastern America, 1620-1660', in Chaudhuri and Denzel (eds), *Cashless Payments*, pp. 107-30.
5. Markus A. Denzel, 'Introduction', in Chaudhuri and Denzel (eds), *Cashless Payments*, p. 7.
6. Habib, 'Systems of Bills of Exchange'.
7. William Foster (ed.), *The Embassy of Sir Thomas Roe to India*, London:

Oxford University Press, 1926; rpt., Delhi: Asian Educational Services, 1990, p. 233.

8. *Surat Factory Records*, 'Outward Books' for 10 November 1630, London: British Library, Oriental and India Office Library Collections.
9. K.R. Hall, 'Coinage, Trade and Economy in Early South India and its Bay of Bengal Neighbours', in K.R. Hall, *Networks of Trade, Polity, and Societal Integration in Chola Era South India, c. 875-1279*, New Delhi: Primus Books, 2014, pp. 69-98.
10. Following the idea put forward by Monika Sharma, 'Idea of Money for Merchants of Gujarat in Sixteenth-Seventeenth Centuries', *IOSR Journal of Humanities and Social Science*, vol. 19, issue 5, May 2014, pp. 15-20.
11. I thank Sushruti Santhanam for this reference, which was used to talk about craft from the perspective of first the market, and then the artisans.
12. Shrinivas V. Padigar (ed.), *Inscriptions of the Chalukyas of Badami*, Bangalore: ICHR, Southern Regional Centre, 2010, Inscription no. 156, p. 255.
13. All references are from *South Indian Inscriptions*, vol. 2, Delhi, Archaeological Survey of India, 1891. The ones used here are inscriptions 9, 31, 38 and 79. A detailed study of the 'ritual polity' based on this temple has been done by James Heitzman, 'Ritual Polity and Economy: The Transactional Network of an Imperial Temple in Medieval South India', *Journal of the Social and Economic History of the Orient*, vol. 34, nos. 1-2, 1991, pp. 23-54. The Chola inscriptions have not here been given in detail, as so much research has already been published on these inscriptions, unlike the others chosen for this chapter.
14. Heitzman, 'Ritual Polity', p. 30.
15. A merchant guild, established probably in Aihole, in the eighth century CE. See M.M. Abraham, *Two Medieval Merchant Guilds of South India*, New Delhi: Manohar, 1988.
16. *Annual Report on South Indian Epigraphy*, 1903, p. 154.
17. S.S. Ramachandra Murthy (ed.), *Inscriptions of the Kakatiyas of Warangal*, Bangalore: ICHR, Southern Regional Centre, 2011, Inscription No. 8, 'Hanumakonda Inscription of Prola II, 1117', p. 18.
18. Murthy, *Inscriptions of the Kakatiyas*, Inscription no. 23, 'Draksaramam Inscription of Rudra I, 1186', p. 53.
19. Y. Subbarayalu and S. Rajavelu (eds.), *Inscriptions of the Vijayanagar*

*Rulers*, vol. V, pt. 1 (Tamil Inscriptions), Bangalore: ICHR, Southern Regional Centre, 2014, Inscription No. 6, 'Tiruvorriyur Inscription of Savana I, 1353', pp. 3-4.

20. Ibid., Inscription no. 11, 'Tiruvannamalai Inscription of Kampana II, 1363', pp. 7-8.
21. Ibid., Inscription no. 12, 'Bellur Inscription of Kampana II, 1363', pp. 8-9.
22. Ibid., *Inscriptions of the Vijayanagar Rulers*, no. 31, pp. 24-5.
23. Ibid., no. 76, p. 60.
24. Y. Subbarayalu, 'Anjuvannam, A Maritime Trade Guild of Medieval Times', in H. Kulke, K. Kesavapany and V. Sakhuja (eds), *Nagapattinam to Suvarnadwipa: Reflections on the Chola Naval Expeditions to Southeast Asia*, New Delhi: Manohar, 2010, pp. 158-67, especially p. 159.
25. Heitzman, 'Ritual Polity', p. 34.

## BIBLIOGRAPHY


Abraham, M.M., *Two Medieval Merchant Guilds of South India*, New Delhi: Manohar, 1988.

*Annual Report on South Indian Epigraphy*, Delhi: Archaeological Survey of India, 1903.

Chaudhuri, Sushil, 'No Ready Money? No Problem! The Role of *Hundis* (Bills of Exchange) in Early Modern India, *c.* 1600-1800', in Chaudhuri and Denzel (eds), *Cashless Payments*, pp. 139-52.

Denzel, Markus A., 'Introduction', in Sushil Chaudhuri and Markus A. Denzel (eds), *Cashless Payments and Transactions from the Antiquity to 1914*, Stuttgart: Franz Steiner Verlag, 2008.

Foster, William (ed.), *The Embassy of Sir Thomas Roe to India*, London: Oxford University Press, 1926; rpt. Delhi: Asian Educational Services, 1990.

Habib, Irfan, 'Systems of Bills of Exchange (*Hundis*) in the Mughal Empire', *Proceedings of the Indian History Congress*, Muzaffarpur, 1972, pp. 290-303.

Hall, K.R., 'Coinage, Trade and Economy in Early South India and its Bay of Bengal Neighbours', in K.R. Hall, *Networks of Trade, Polity, and Societal Integration in Chola Era South India, c. 875-1279*, New Delhi: Primus Books, 2014, pp. 69-98.

Heitzman, James, 'Ritual Polity and Economy: The Transactional Network of an Imperial Temple in Medieval South India', *Journal of the Social and Economic History of the Orient*, vol. 34, nos. 1-2, 1991, pp. 23-54.

Murthy, S.S. Ramachandra (ed.), *Inscriptions of the Kakatiyas of Warangal*, Bangalore: ICHR, Southern Regional Centre, 2011.

Padigar, Shrinivas V. (ed.), *Inscriptions of the Chalukyas of Badami*, Bangalore: ICHR, Southern Regional Centre, 2010.

Om Prakash, 'The Cashless Payment Mechanism in Mughal India: The Working of the *Hundi* Network', in Chaudhuri and Denzel (eds), *Cashless Payments*, pp. 131-8.

Schnurmann, Claudia, 'Wampum as a Cultural Broker in Northeastern America, 1620-1660', in Chaudhuri and Denzel (eds), *Cashless Payments*, pp. 107-30.

Sharma, Monika, 'Idea of Money for Merchants of Gujarat in Sixteenth-Seventeenth Centuries', *IOSR Journal of Humanities and Social Science*, vol. 19, issue 5, May 2014, pp. 15-20.

*South Indian Inscriptions*, vol. 2, Delhi: Archaeological Survey of India, 1891.

Subbarayalu, Y. and S. Rajavelu (eds), *Inscriptions of the Vijayanagar Rulers*, vol. V, pt. 1 (Tamil Inscriptions), Bangalore: ICHR, Southern Regional Centre, 2014.

Subbarayalu, Y., 'Anjuvannam, 'A Maritime Trade Guild of Medieval Times', in H. Kulke, K. Kesavapany and V. Sakhuja (eds.), *Naga-pattinam to Suvarnadwipa: Reflections on the Chola Naval Expeditions to Southeast Asia*, New Delhi: Manohar, 2010, pp. 158-67.

*Surat Factory Records*, 'Outward Books' for 10 November 1630, London: British Library, Oriental and India Office Library Collections.

6

# Tibet and Bengal

## Trade Routes and Long Distance Exchange with Reference to Silver

M.N. RAJESH

Bengal absorbed silver from all directions in the eighteenth century, remarks Andre Gunder Frank in *Reorient*.[1] One of the routes by which such silver and other precious metals reached Bengal was Nepal and Assam. Embarking on a trail to trace the origin of silver, the lead takes us to places as far as China and Mongolia and of course Tibet, through which the silver from both these regions in addition to gold dust found its way to Bengal. Of these many trade routes, some were large and well established while others were smaller and transient.

Previously Tibet was identified as a religious area, but the focus has now shifted largely, due to the work of economic historians, from religion to trade. This more balanced picture has opened our eyes to a new network of routes. Tibetan gold and silver, wool, rare spices and horses reached Bengal as part of a long distance network. These exchanges connected Tibet with other parts of India and Asia and commodities like precious stones, religious artifacts like conches, etc., were traded. I will try to explore references to these commodities in fragmentary sources and how, in the process of reconstruction of the economic history of Tibet, the role of Bengal as a gateway is indispensable. It would also show that new themes in the history of Tibet can be essayed while focusing on the trade with Bengal and the wider world.

Tibet is often identified as the land of snow nestled in the

Himalayas; that has been the standard characterization over the last three centuries. The counter narratives that seek to escape this Orientalist view, are also in a sense overwhelmed by the same stereotypes.[2] However, while this snowy portrayal may be partly true, it also obscures many other aspects of the Tibetan geography that includes cold deserts, rivers and their fertile banks, lakes, dense forests and also wooded eco-zones.[3] In this diverse physiographic landscape, there exists potential for different forms of production based on the different physical features, though agriculture and pastoralist animal husbandry seem to be dominant.[4] There also exists a large number of different forms of gathering: of minerals and precious stones and also of rare herbs and plants and animal products. The surplus products of pastoralism including wool, horses, and yaks comprise the major items of export.[5]

While the modern characterisation of Tibet as a high altitude cold desert is true, it also obscures the fact of Tibet as a home to major trade routes. The Silk Route highlighted Tibet's central location and established its close connection with China and other different parts of the world, bringing many new actors into the picture. This geographical corrective is needed to put things in perspective so as to establish the diversity of the Tibetan landscape and also the different forms of production and exchange.[6] Like the purported geographical unity of Tibet, so also an illusory historical unity of Tibet spanning a large spatial and temporal canvas is facilitated by the assumption of the predominance of religion. In this larger narrative that has become standard in the last 300 years, what has been emphasized is that Tibet was an isolated Buddhist country and was less known to the outside world because of the isolationist policies of the Buddhist Lamas who were inward looking.

There are three problems with this narrative. First, it draws from the normative texts of Tibetan Buddhists which are unidimensional religious texts whose primary concern is religion, theology, metaphysics, and related aspects like iconography. In addition many of the religious texts focus on the question of reincarnation traditions as Tibetan Buddhism is dominated by a large number of reincarnate lamas with their lineages and this aspect has only emphasized the diversity of the different methods of Buddhist teachings. In the larger Western narrative, Tibetan texts are predominantly religious, as also all of Tibetan art, and therefore the society is totally imbued with religion. A cursory reading of that statement would seem to be valid but again points to the problem of masking the diversity. There is a Tibetan proverb which says that every valley has its own dialect and every lama has his own way of teaching. In a simple but powerful way it captures the tremendous diversity of the Tibetan landscape, language, and practices but leaves out the geographic context and the production patterns. We see that large monasteries are situated in places with favourable eco-zones in dense agricultural settlements; medium-sized monasteries are situated in places with considerable agricultural settlements, while the smaller monasteries are situated in remote agricultural settlements, and the nomadic regions do not have any permanent monasteries.[7] We thus see that there is a correlation between religious structures and geography that has not been examined fully and therefore does not do full justice to the diversity of the landscape and production patterns. This is one of the problems of relying on religious texts that are predominantly normative.

The second problem is that the study of Tibet was heavily influenced by Orientalism that emerged in strength around the seventeenth century and this orientation is hard to dislodge. Earlier, there was scant knowledge in Europe about Tibet and it was seen as a cold desert with 'wild' people who were mentioned in passing and not in detail. By 1700, however, we find a number of European travellers travelling to China and India and from there to Tibet. In this endeavour, one of the main concerns of the travellers was to write about these regions for a European audience, addressing some of the important concerns then prevalent in Europe. One was the fabled country of lost Christians, and another the need to evangelize the pagans. Still others were to look for exotic items and send these to Europe as merchandise, i.e. a commercial interest was visible. By the late eighteenth century, a standard narrative of this region emerged which was that Tibet was an exotic region ruled by a god king, with his capital Lhasa at its centre. This isolated city could only be reached by traversing innumerable wastelands. The people living in these arid regions, (the nomads) were not given a voice and therefore this narrative became Lhasa-centric, revealing all the trappings of Orientalism.[8]

The third problem concerns a new set of Tibetan language sources on the geography of Tibet from the eighteenth century, dealing mostly with the neighbouring countries and relations with them. This contrasted with other geographical works in the Tibetan language prior to this period, that dealt largely with pilgrimage. One of the problems with this newer material is that most writings are local in scope, dealing with a particular place or region. These textual materials are mostly works on trade and also provide descriptions of geographical features that contain two practical purposes--pilgrimage routes and trade routes. A further challenge is the appropriation of these texts by the Chinese; history has become the property of nation states. The deracinated nature of these texts has led to another factor, the straightforward reading of the pilgrimage routes. One of the clearest illustrations of this lack of context is when we refer to the horse trade and find it mentioned that the regions to the west of China and more precisely the mountainous regions, are the sources of the horses.[9] The regions mentioned here clearly point to the Yunnan–Tibet borderlands and since some of the borderland regions in Yunnan did not form any durable state societies with a tradition of writing, they were referred to as vassal states of China or simply as regions that did not have a king or were barbarous in nature. Modern narratives of these regions also perpetuate this idea, despite the fact some of the texts were only written in Tibetan for the simple reason that the Tibetan language in its standard variety formed the great tradition for many of these societies (though it could not be understood by the laymen who spoke different languages, but whose culture had been thinly Tibetanized). This is one example of historiographical problems that have led to the current state of misunderstanding of the region without giving voice to it and in the process alienating texts from their context. It has led to the making of a wrong picture. In this case, the established ideas of sacred geography draw on the religious texts; no similar sources are available to explain the physical or economic spaces like the Silk Route.

What is missing here, apart from the delocalized nature of these texts, is that most of the pilgrims were also traders who combined trade with religion. We thus have a complicated picture and the simplistic division of modern-day texts into purely religious or economic is inadequate to understand this period. A recent publication titled *Muslim, Trader, Nomad, Spy* highlights the multiple roles of travellers in the same caravan[10]. The understanding that had grown from this type of reading was that Tibet was a Buddhist nation having more in common with its Buddhist neighbours Mongolia, Ladakh and the contiguous parts of China, and therefore all the traders could only be from these regions and Tibet. Such a reading, giving concession to and acknowledging the role of trade, limits it to the Buddhist regions with which Tibet had contact. The picture was corrected with a new portrayal of Lhasa not just as a holy city but also as a city where everyone had something to buy and sell without license. It included pilgrims and traders and anyone except the monks (for whom trade was prohibited). Thus the Oriental idea of Lhasa and Tibet as a religious entity is overturned by these new representations. Following from this is the question whether these activities were carried on secretly or openly, and it is found that most of them were actually carried out under the patronage of the Yellow Hat or Gelugpa establishment.

Recent works by economic historians have brought about a new understanding of pre-modern Tibet. That it had manifold contacts with many parts of the world, though surprising, is in fact a reality. To drive home this point, a list of commodities and their exchange networks are now elaborated in detail, highlighting both long-distance and cross-border trade.[11] Writings by scholars such as Luce Boulnois have illustrated the contacts over a large temporal span starting from the early centuries. One of their contributions is that the idea of Tibet as an isolated region though fanciful cannot practically work for the simple reason that Tibet was not always self-sufficient and needed many items for everyday survival. Secondly some surplus had to be generated to barter, exchange, or pay for these items. Beginning in the eighth century we see that Tibetans were slowly becoming habituated to tea as a part of the staple diet and this dependence became a very important part of the Tibetan culture[12]. While China is undeniably the source of tea, Tibet was one among the many importers of Chinese tea since the ancient period. Most of the tea was imported in the form of bricks that traversed thousands of miles on the backs of mules and yaks and ponies. In return horses were a significant item of exchange used to pay for the tea. This is evident from the fact that there was a separate department known as the 'tea horse department' in China during the different imperial periods like the Song, Yuan, Ming and Qing. Clearly the very high volume of this exchange was the reason such a department was set up in the first place. As a result, active horse breeding was one of the important occupations of the tribal people in Tibet and its borderlands and also in regions of Yunnan.

Morris Rossabi and other historians of inner Asia maintained that while plunder and raids were frequent activities of the nomadic societies and an important way of getting a surplus, another channel for the same was trade, as China was perpetually short of horses. These trade missions were actually characterized in the Chinese historical annals as tribute missions.[13] This was also one of the methods through which ritual suzerainty over the nomads could be claimed by allowing them to engage with state societies. The horse was an important item of trade with Bengal as well even in the early mediaeval period. Indeed, Bengal was one of the few places where we have horses from both the northwest and the northeast coming in simultaneously. Two important texts need to be mentioned here, *The History of Buddhism in India and Tibet*[14] authored by Taranatha whose earliest versions dated back to at least the thirteenth century and the second is the *Tabaqat i Nasiri* of Minhaj us Siraj.[15] From these sources we get the idea that at least 1,500 horses came every day to the plains of Bengal from the hills, originally from the borderlands of Yunnan and Tibet. While horses form an important commodity of trade, they were limited to Bengal and did not form an item of transshipment beyond Bengal overseas.[16] The items that came from abroad through Bengal to

Tibet are primarily luxury items which were small in volume but high in value. They will be analysed below.

It was commonly assumed that the conch shells used in the monasteries of Tibet came from South India, particularly the Palk Straits, but recent works have proved that these enormous conch shells were in fact *not* the low value south Indian variety. They were very high value, having just the right number of whorls, and only conches without any impurities, indentations, or breakages were preferred. It was difficult to source these from south India; their origin is speculated to be Southeast Asia, since the early Buddhist monasteries of that region already had a tradition of using conch shells in their religious routine.

A similar item that has escaped the attention of scholars is the small-scale trade in yak tails, an important item in both the Hindu and Buddhist religious worlds. A small but continuous volume of such trade percolated from Tibet to all parts of India, Sri Lanka, and Southeast Asia. The northwestern frontier of India, and interestingly the central Himalayas with the pilgrim route to Kailash, are the important areas of this trade.[17] Bengal also figures in the story and fragmentary records assert that some of these yak tails went from Bengal to Southeast Asia. They did not form part of the main consignment as they are of medium value and did not need much safeguarding as they could withstand the vagaries of nature.

How did the yak tails reach Bengal?[18] In Tibet there was a trade between the farmers and the nomads known as 'trade for survival' which was widely prevalent and this included various types of barter such as grain for salt, salt for tea, and tea for butter. Indeed, salt is one of the most important trade commodities in the Himalayas. It was as part of one such network of trade that we see the participation of numerous groups. The nomads traded yak tails, yak butter, and yaks and other livestock, and also salt (which was available and plentiful in many of the lakes) with the farmers for foodgrain. These networks of trade between the nomadic community and the farmers were ancient and formed a symbiotic relation between the two major producer communities in Tibet.[19] These were necessary because Tibet was perpetually short of food grains and fruit and many other vegetables that led to stunting and other health problems including vitamin deficiencies in its population.

An important item of import from Tibet was gold in the form of gold dust sourced from western Tibet, where the mines were owned by the local chieftains and later by the central government at Lhasa (from the seventeenth century onwards).[20] According to religious dictates there was no large-scale exploitation of these mines because of the fear that it would harm the earth. But gold mining was not fully banned and formed an important item of export. It was also feared that gold dust and musk would be adulterated, so to stop this adulteration the packets in the form of leather pouches were sealed in Lhasa, only to be opened later.[21] This prevented a bad name for the gold trade and gave the product greater legitimacy and established market trust. All this was necessary because of the enormity of the trade; by the seventeenth century there were around a hundred trading offices open in Lhasa, a significant number.

Many of these Tibetan trade items reached Patna and from there went to Bengal via the river. There were also many other important items of trade. Among these were medicinal plants and other *Materia medica* including rhubarb, worm seed and medicinal mallows that passed through Patna and Kabul. That these reached Europe in the form of dried secretions of roots and rhizome and were prescribed as astringents, is recorded by the French traveller Tavernier. But Bengal was also one of the most important centres of consumption of these items. In addition to the medicinal plants other animal products like bear bile, leopard bones and fresh stag horns were also important items of trade and these were used for medicinal and other aphrodisiac purposes in Europe.

Returning to silver, we see that a significant source of silver in Tibet was from Mongolia and here too one of the chief items of trade to Mongolia from Tibet were the religious texts in addition to deer horns and animal skins and butter. Mongolian silver came to Tibet by the northeastern route, which went from Tibet via Koko Nor to China, Siberia, and the Turkic regions. This was one of the four main routes from Tibet to the outside world.[22] One might also stress that Mongolia, like Tibet, was landlocked and very far from the coast and this complicated matters. Bengal was what John Deyell calls a natural outlet to the seas for the Himalayan regions and a main route was through Cooch Behar[23].

Silver and horses from Tibet entered Bengal mainly through Cooch Behar whose trade vastly expanded in the sixteenth century.[24] An important aspect of the flow of Tibetan silver is that it was erratic and dependent on a variety of factors. Two of these were the role of Nepal (which controlled both the mints and part of the trade routes) and Tibet's need for silver to pay China for tea. From the eighteenth century, our knowledge of the situation improves as we see a large number of Englishmen travelling to Nepal. Mention may be made of three of them: William Kirkpatrick, Charles Crawford and Francis Hamilton.[25] There is also a detailed description of routes through Nepal to Shigatse in Tibet on the east and other routes on the west.[26] Another important trade route was through Mustang in western Nepal where its impact on the religious sites is shown clearly. The dense settlements in northern and southern Mustang highlight the importance of trade along this route. On this axis there are more settlements than in the parallel valleys which have no trade routes or only poorly developed routes to Tibet. Even later maps like those of Col. Sidney Gerald Burrard, prepared around 1915, clearly show the channels of trade between India and Tibet. Notably important are those that pass through the Kali Gandaki valley, occupying a key place in the Himalaya.

One of the problems we see in the maps is that the markings reveal the importance of the routes by the dots that show the paths taken by the explorers and these have been rendered as trade routes on the maps. However a survey of the trail of the routes would reveal much more and here we see that religious sites are found and one example is in the south of Mustang where there is a marking indicating 'Saligram here found'. Another such stretch is from Kagbeni to Dolpo. Some routes were not used only for trade but also by pilgrims and the case of Muktinath is a good example as we have both Hindu pilgrims from the subcontinent and also Buddhist pilgrims from both Tibet and Nepal. A route from Muktinath to Manang was used for both trade and pilgrimage purposes and here one of the important items traded was salt.[27] Hindu temples, *mani* walls and *mani* stone heaps mark these routes. The high cost of labour involved in the maintenance of these pilgrim paths shows that they were important.

A fuller review of the references to the Indo-Tibetan trade through Nepal and the commodities traded, would throw more light and also emphasize its importance. The Tibetan merchants brought woollen cloths, ponies, shawls, goats, yaks, sheep, musk, gold, silver, borax and paper to Kathmandu. In exchange cotton cloth, cutlery, glassware, spices, pearls, coral and betel were exported. Most of these goods originated in Bengal; but the costly goods from Bengal did not always go via the passes of Nepal, being also conveyed through Morung and Sikkim. The name Morung was given to the Nepalese Tarai and Mustang. All this trade went on to bring horses and silver to Cooch Behar until the ascendancy of the Gurkhas of Nepal in 1769. It is from this point that the importance of the trade routes via Nepal was disrupted, the closure of the routes and the political problems between the Nepalese and the Tibetans were the factors. As Tibet had been using silver coins of Nepal since the Malla period, the ascendancy of the Gurkhas led to the minting and circulation of new coins which became debased, leading to a controversy about their value. In these circumstances, the Tibetans asked the Nepalese to issue newer coins to compensate them for losses. The Nepalese did not heed their pleas, leading to war, in the process of which the Qing Chinese were drawn into Tibet when the lamas asked for help.[28]

The silver flow to Lhasa and the countertrade emerged stronger after 1642 when the Fifth Dalai Lama was enthroned. The establishment of Lhasa as an administrative capital gave a strong impetus to its development as a centre where aristocratic and mercantile groups congregated. Thus there emerged an image of Tibet as a country that was friendly to trade and as Luce Bulnois shows, there were more than a hundred trading companies in the seventeenth century in Lhasa.[29] Cooch Behar was a natural outlet for Tibet and also functioned as a transfer point where the trade items from maritime Southeast Asia with which Bengal had linkages, were transferred to Tibet. This was also due to another important fact that Bengal till the seventeenth century (as Rila

Mukherjee points out) was more integrated with the Southeast Asian economies than with the Gangetic plains, until the currency reforms of Sher Shah.[30] The three routes from Yunnan to Bengal traced by John Deyell cover a lot of area in the mountainous regions of the borderlands of Assam and Burma and this brings into question the idea of these regions as non-state space, or zones that did not allow trade. Deyell's arguments on the flow of silver give us a clearer picture of the role of Tibet and Yunnan in Bengal as the regions from where silver was sourced. This is captured in a broader frame by Bin Yang where he quotes Deyell, 'A separate apparently well-travelled and renowned route led from the region of the Upper Yangtse-Mekong-Shalween Rivers through Tibet. Passes led through Bhutan and Nepal into Kamarupa and Hindustan respectively.'[31] Another important aspect of the flow of silver from Tibet is that while it has long been speculated that India was a source of silver and also that there was an increase in the movement of silver after the discovery of the New World, the Tibet connection prompts us to explore other possibilities. Elliot Sperling has rightly discounted the flow of Indian silver to Tibet and has pointed to China as the source. He further points out that most of this silver also came to China from the New World via the Philippines on the Spaniards' famed Acapulco-Manilla galleons.[32]

From this discussion we see that there is a paucity of literature on the role of silver in Tibet, despite its robust trade during the seventeenth century and later. These correctives about the engagement of Tibet in the larger trade networks of the world then lead us to the realization the that the Himalayan region was not isolated economically as represented in popular depictions. Further, the fact that the discovery of the New World and the introduction of new commodities even affected these far off regions, shows that the connections demonstrate the viability of trade between Bengal and Tibet and its borderlands, in which silver was an important component.

## NOTES

1. Andre Gunder Frank, *Re-Orient: Global Economy in the Asian Age*, Berkeley: University of California Press, 1998, p. 92.

2. Tsering Shakya, *Dragon in the Land of Snows: The History of Modern Tibet since 1947*, New York: Random House, 1999, 2012.
3. Jin-Ting Wang, 'The Steppes and Deserts of the Xizang Plateau (Tibet)', *Vegetatio*, vol. 75, no. 3, 1988, pp. 135-9.
4. Daniel J. Miller, 'Grasslands of the Tibetan Plateau', *Rangelands*, vol. 12, no. 3, 1990, pp. 159-63.
5. Wim Van Spengen, 'The Geo-History of Long-Distance Trade in Tibet 1850-1950', *The Tibet Journal*, vol. 20, no. 2, 1995, p. 28.
6. Ibid.
7. M.N. Rajesh, *Gompas in Traditional Tibetan Society*, Delhi: Decent Books, 2002, p. 28.
8. Dibyesh Anand, *Tibet: A Victim of Geopolitics*, London: Routledge, 2007.
9. Bin Yang, 'Horses, Silver, and Cowries: Yunnan in Global Perspective', *Journal of World History*, vol. 15, no. 3, 2004, p. 288.
10. Sulmaan Wasif Khan, *Muslim, Trader, Nomad, Spy: China's Cold War and the People of the Tibetan Borderlands*, Chapel Hill: University of North Carolina Press, 2015.
11. Wim Van Spengen, *Tibetan Border Worlds: A Geo-historical Analysis of Trade and Traders*, New York: Kegan, Paul International, 2000.
12. Luce Boulnois, 'Gold, Wool and Musk: Trade in Lhasa in the Seventeenth Century', Gray Tuttle and Kurtis R. Schaeffer, eds., *The Tibetan History Reader*, New York: Columbia University Press, 2013, pp. 457-61.
13. Morris Rossabi, *From Yuan to Modern China and Mongolia: The Writings of Morris Rossabi*, Leiden: Brill, 2014, p. 181.
14. D.P. Chattopadhyaya, ed., *Taranatha's History of Buddhism in India*, Delhi: Motilal Banarsidass, 1990, 1997.
15. Minhāj Sirāj Jūzjānī, *Tabakat-i-Nasiri*, Lahore: Sang-e-Meel Publications, 2006.
16. Bin Yang, 'Horses, Silver, and Cowries: Yunnan in Global Perspective', p. 286.
17. Sonam Joldan, 'Relationship between Ladakh and Buddhist Tibet: Pilgrimage and Trade', *The Tibet Journal*, vol. 31, no. 3, 2006, pp. 49-51.
18. *Report on the External Trade of Bengal with Nepal, Sikkim, and Bhutan, for the Year 1884-85*, Calcutta: Bengal Secretariat Press, 1885, p. 20.
19. Bulnois 'Gold, Wool and Musk', p. 459.
20. Ibid., p. 509.

21. Ibid., pp. 465-7.
22. http://www.tibetancoins.com/III%20Tibetan%20Trade.html
23. John Deyell, 'Monetary and Financial Webs: The Regional and International Influence of Pre-modern Bengali Coinage', in Rila Mukherjee, ed., *Pelagic Passageways: The Northern Bay of Bengal Before Colonialism*, New Delhi: Primus Books, 2011, p. 106.
24. http://www.tibetancoins.com/III%20Tibetan%20Trade.html
25. Matthew H. Edney, *Mapping an Empire: The Geographical Construction of British India, 1765-1843*, Chicago: University of Chicago Press, 2009, p. 82.
26. Leo E. Rose, *Nepal Strategy for Survival*, Berkeley: University of California Press, 1971, p. 13.
27. Robert W. Bradnock, *South Asian Handbook*, Bath: Trade & Travel Publications, 1993, pp. 1212-15.
28. Bulnois, 'Gold, Wool and Musk', pp. 457-65.
29. Ibid., p. 457.
30. Mukherjee, *Pelagic Passageways*, p. 106.
31. Bin Yang, 'Horses, Silver, and Cowries', p. 290.
32. Elliot Sperling, 'Some Preliminary Remarks on the Influx of New Worlds Silver into Tibet during China's "Silver Century" (1550-1650)', *The Tibet Journal* 34/35, no. 3/2 (2009), pp. 299-311.

## BIBLIOGRAPHY

Anand, Dibyesh, *Tibet: A Victim of Geopolitics*, London: Routledge, 2007.

*Archiv Für Zentralasiatische Geschichtsforschung*. VGH Wissenschaftsverlag, 1983

Boulnois, Luce, 'Gold, Wool and Musk: Trade in Lhasa in the Seventeenth Century', in Gray Tuttle and Kurtis R. Schaeffer (eds), *The Tibetan History Reader*, New York: Columbia University Press, 2013, pp. 457–76.

Bradnock, Robert W., *South Asian Handbook*, Bath: Trade & Travel Publications, 1993.

Chattopadhyaya, D.P., ed., *Taranatha's History of Buddhism in India*, New Delhi: Motilal Banarsidass, 1990, rpt. 1997.

Deyell, John, 'Monetary and Financial Webs: The Regional and International Influence of Pre-modern Bengali Coinage', in Rila Mukherjee, ed., *Pelagic Passageways: The Northern Bay of Bengal Before Colonialism*, New Delhi: Primus Books, 2011.

Edney, Matthew H., *Mapping an Empire: The Geographical Construction of British India, 1765-1843*, Chicago: University of Chicago Press, 2009.

Frank, Andre Gunder, *Re-Orient: Global Economy in the Asian Age*, Berkeley: University of California Press, 1998.

Internet, http://www.tibetancoins.com/III%20Tibetan%20Trade.html

Joldan, Sonam, 'Relationship between Ladakh and Buddhist Tibet: Pilgrimage and Trade', *The Tibet Journal*, 31, 3, 2006, pp. 43-76.

Jūzjānī, Minhāj Sirāj, *Tabakat-i-Nasiri*, Lahore: Sang-e-Meel Publications, 2006.

Khan, Sulmaan Wasif, *Muslim, Trader, Nomad, Spy: China's Cold War and the People of the Tibetan Borderlands*, Chapel Hill: University of North Carolina Press, 2015.

Miller, Daniel J., 'Grasslands of the Tibetan Plateau.' *Rangelands*, vol. 12, no. 3, 1990, pp. 159-63.

Rajesh, M.N., *Gompas in Traditional Tibetan Society*, Delhi: Decent Books, 2002.

*Report on the External Trade of Bengal with Nepal, Sikkim, and Bhutan, for the Year 1884-85*, Calcutta: Bengal Secretariat Press, 1885, p. 20.

Rose, Leo E., *Nepal Strategy for Survival*, Berkeley: University of California Press, 1971.

Rossabi, Morris, *From Yuan to Modern China and Mongolia: The Writings of Morris Rossabi*, Leiden: Brill, 2014.

Shakya, Tsering, *Dragon in the Land of Snows: The History of Modern Tibet since 1947*, New York: Random House, 1999; rpt. 2012.

Sperling, Elliot, 'Some Preliminary Remarks on the Influx of New World Silver into Tibet during China's "Silver Century" (1550-1650)', *The Tibet Journal* 34/35, nos. 3/2 (2009), pp. 3-35.

Tucci, Giuseppe and Wim Swaan, *Tibet: Land of Snows*, New York: Stein and Day, 1967.

Tuttle, Gray and Kurtis R. Schaeffer, *The Tibetan History Reader*, New York: Columbia University Press, 2013.

Van Spengen, Wim, 'The Geo-History of Long-Distance Trade in Tibet 1850-1950', *The Tibet Journal*, vol. 20, no. 2, 1995, pp. 18-63.

———, *Tibetan Border Worlds: A Geo-historical Analysis of Trade and Traders*, New York: Kegan, Paul International, 2000.

Wang, Jin-Ting, 'The Steppes and Deserts of the Xizang Plateau (Tibet)', *Vegetatio*, vol. 75, no. 3, 1988, pp. 135-42.

Yang, Bin, 'Horses, Silver, and Cowries: Yunnan in Global Perspective', *Journal of World History*, vol. 15, no. 3, 2004, pp. 281-322.

7

# *The Laws of King Mengrai*, Cowrie Shells, and Intra-Asian Interactions

BIN YANG

Cowrie shells were widely used in Eurasian societies, particularly India, China, Southeast Asia, and sub-Saharan Africa. The relatively rich cowrie finds, for example in the Yin Relics of the middle Yellow River region of north China , and in ancient Yunnan tombs in southwest China, combined with numerous textual records, illustrates the significance of cowries in early Chinese civilization and its connections with others. While much attention has been paid to the cowrie phenomenon, a few questions remain, such as the source, the distribution routes, and the functions of this marine product. The dynamics of the use of cowrie shells in various Asian societies awaits a fuller understanding.

Originating in the seas, especially those surrounding the low Maldive islands, cowrie shells migrated to various parts of Eurasia as precious goods in the prehistoric era, and over time were transformed into a commodity-money and popular currency in various societies. In China, cowries (both true cowries and their imitations in jade, stone, bone, earthenware, gold, tin, and bronze) have been found in archaeological sites. When cowries are studied, what scholars address is whether or not they served as money, and if so, when.[1] The source of these shells and the routes which made possible their diffusion are usually not taken into consideration.[2] As a result, the implications of the cowrie network with respect to the links between the Chinese world and other worlds remain unexamined.

India is well-known for its use of cowries. Enormous hoards of cowrie shells have been found through its history. The monetary system in which cowrie shells functioned as 'small money', while silver functioned as 'big money', has been vividly illustrated in many accounts of early Indian society. The cowrie trade is also connected to the slave trade, linking the Indian Ocean to Africa and the Atlantic slave markets. Surprisingly, however, the role of cowrie shells along the Silk Road seems not to have been much explored, though cowries were widely used as money in northern India, including modern Pakistan and Afghanistan, in addition to Orissa and Bengal. Little statistical work has been done on the archeological finds in these areas, a comprehensive research project is yet to be considered. Nor has the pre-1500 period been appropriately studied. As things stand, the historical expansion of the cowrie currency in India remains unclear.

In addition to northern India and Central Asia, cowries also reached Southeast Asia through both overland and maritime routes, though they functioned as money only in some places and societies. Cowrie shells were used as a medium of exchange in Assam, Arakan, Lower Burma, Thailand, Laos, and beyond.

Cowries went westward to Arabia and Africa. The latter is another well-studied area. It is clear that by the fourteenth century, the cowrie currency had reached the upper and middle Niger, first the Mali Empire, and then Songhay. The Europeans, pioneered by the Portuguese in the fifteenth and sixteenth centuries, followed by the Dutch and English in the seventeenth and eighteenth centuries, and finally joined by the French and Germans in the eighteenth and nineteenth centuries, brought cowries from the Indian Ocean to West Africa in such quantities that they eventually ruined all local monetary systems and economies, although they contributed to the prosperity of both the Atlantic slave trade and the palm oil trade. Pioneering works by Jan Hogendorn and Marion Johnson have illustrated how this Indian-Ocean-based item, shipped to West Africa at least since the fourteenth century, contributed to the spread of the European colonial machine and served to engulf various local economies, especially during the period of the Atlantic slave trade.[3]

Here medieval Yunnan deserves some special attention because of its geo-cultural affinities with the Chinese, Southeast Asian, and Indian civilizations. Yunnan is an area located in upper mainland Southeast Asia, sandwiched by Tibet and China, with a cowrie monetary system from the ninth to the seventeenth century.

## Cowries in Yunnan: Sources and Routes[4]

Although Yunnan has been a province of China since the Mongol conquest, the case of cowries in Yunnan was different from that of China proper in terms of their long-term existence and diverse usage. From 1955 to 1972, archaeologists unearthed a large number of cowries in tombs in Yunnan—amounting to more than 260,000 pieces and weighing over 700 kilograms.[5] All these tombs are dated before the Qin unification of 221 BC and demonstrate that cowries were present in Yunnan before the late third century BCE, and taken as 'a special highly prized form of money, a status marker, and a certain form of prestige goods, accumulated as stores of value and used in inter-societal exchanges between elites, exclusively'.[6] Hence, these cowries serve as strong evidence for a southern Silk Road connecting Yunnan with the Indian Ocean zone. Probably it is worthwhile to mention the cowries unearthed in Sanxingdui (Sichuan), southwest China, are dated over three thousand years ago, the same age as the cowries found in the Yin tombs of the Central Plains of north China. It is said that finds in the Sanxingdui match those in Yunnan, which, together with the geography of usage, strongly suggests that they came into China through Yunnan. While the paucity of textual sources allows us no further conclusion, it is confusing that very few cowries have been found in Yunnan date from after the Western Han. It seems that the cowrie trade was suddenly disrupted by the Han military control over Yunnan in the first century.

It was during the period when China lost authority over Yunnan that cowries again entered Yunnan in large numbers and a cowrie system took shape. But the issue of the exact date remains unknown, since the first Chinese text recording cowrie money in Yunnan is *Xin Tang Shu* (New History of the Tang dynasty).

Fan Chuo's *Yunnan Zhi*, written around 864 and presumed to be a primary source, did mention cowries, but as ornaments rather than money. Pelliot concludes it is difficult to know details before the tenth century,[7] while circumstantial evidence points to the eighth century.[8]

The Yuan and Ming have left abundant sources on cowrie money in Yunnan. Diverse usages are revealed in those texts. Cowries were used in land purchases as well as in small transactions. Cowries were also used to pay taxes, to make donations to Buddhist churches, and to pay government salaries. In addition, cowries were stored as treasure. Contrary to the common idea, cowries in Yunnan served not only in small transactions, but also in more extensive activities, such as in house sales. In short, cowrie money fulfilled the functions of modern abstract money.

From which area the cowrie shells utilized in Yunnan originated, is a key issue. Peng Xinwei thought the usage of cowrie shells in Yunnan was influenced by India;[9] Jiang Yingliang, based on his study of Chinese texts, excluded the possibility of Burma and Vietnam, and stated that Siam was the main source of cowrie shells;[10] Li Jiarui stated that cowrie shells in Yunnan came from the Indian Ocean and South China Sea;[11] and Yang Shouchun, through scientific examinations, posited that these cowries originated from the western part of the Pacific Ocean, including India, the Philippines and Taiwan, referring to the trading routes among Yunnan, Southeast Asian countries, and India as the distribution paths.[12] Vogel, through a careful analysis of Chinese sources, believes that trade routes connecting with Burma and Siam brought cowries into Yunnan.[13] Nonetheless, Chinese and Southeast Asian sources are unable to confirm the distribution route of cowries inland from mainland coasts. And it is for this reason that *The Laws of King Mengrai*, a Siamese source, is so crucial.

## Cowrie Shells in Chiang Mai: The Law Codes of King Mengrai

The kingdom of Chiang Mai was located in today's northern Thailand. King Mengrai (*r.* 1259-1317), was the ruler of Nan, conqueror of the Mon-dominated kingdom of Hariphunchai (modern Lamphun), and founder of the Lan Na Thai kingdom and its capital Chiang Mai. He promulgated a code of law, focused on restitution and to a lesser extent on repressive sanction.[14] In this law code, cowrie shells were frequently mentioned. To cite,

'4. Sexual offences

If he grasps the breasts of a woman who is willing, he will be fined 22,000 cowrie shells, equivalent to 21 pieces of silver. If he grasps her breasts inside her blouse he will be fined 11,000 cowrie shells.

5. The value of persons and offenses against persons

Consider the wound whether there is large or small. If there is blood, 522; if there is bruising, 332. If there is only pain, 1,000 cowrie shells.

6. Abuse

If one was abused and abuses in return, if there was no cause, the [first] abuser is fined 33,000 cowrie shells; 11,000 for the upper lip, 11,000 for the lower, and 11,000 for the tongue.

7. Theft

The stealing of forest animals: (compensation)

A chicken 1,100 cowries, a duck 150, a goose 300 cowries. If the value of the animals [stolen] is less than 10,000 cowries, the fine is seven times the value. If the value is over 10,000, the fine is four time the value.

For stealing a fishing net without a handle, the fine is either 10,000 [cowries?] or four times the value. For a fish trap with a handle, 10,000 or nine times the value. For a fish container and a casting net, the value being 330, the fine is nine times.

For stealing a plough and a harrow, without the metal parts, the value being 3,000, the fine is three times that.

A horse worth 330, the fine is four times, that is, 1,300 cowries [sic]. A cow or a buffalo of good condition, the same price. A cat worth 110 cowries, the fine is nine times that. An ordinary dog two pieces of silver. The fine for dogs is according to their value up to 110 pieces of silver.

8. Damage to ritual objects

For breaking the container for offering liquor to the spirits, the fine, 33,000 cowries. Even if the vessel is not broken, if any villager dies the offender must pay the cost of funeral, or he must pay wergild. He must pay for the corpse to be taken away from the village.

For cutting the inthakhin pillar, 330 cowries,

9. Theft

Stealing bird-nets or animal traps of all kinds the cost must be paid, and in addition a fine of 33,000 cowries.

Stealing the yoke of an ox, the cost must be paid, and a fine of 13,000 cowries. For stealing firewood, or a spade or a hoe with the its handle, the fine is 13,000 cowries, or nine times [the value].

10. Damage

Cutting down the fence of a house, or of the city [?], 33,000 cowries.

13. Offenses involving trespass

If a pool or the other stretch of water had been reserved, anyone stealing fish from there will be fined 11,000 and fined fourfold [?]. If bees or other honey-producing insects which have been reserved are stolen, for each hive the fine is pieces of silver. If ground-bearing creepers of all kinds are cut down, for each creeper the fine is 1,000 [amounts presumably refers to cowries].

14. Thefts of clothes

For stealing clothes, loth, white cloth of value, the cost of the cloth must be paid and [the culprit] fined 11,000 cowries.

16. Theft

If water is stolen from someone else's field and put on one's own, offerings of chickens and pigs must be made on behalf of the owner of the field. If the culprit doesn't pay, the fine is 33,000.

17. Damages

If buffaloes or cattle eat the newly-sprouting rice in swidden or field, the fine is 11,000 cowries for each rice plant. If they agree that not fine be paid, let a ceremony be done to call the khwan of the rice.

....

If an ox or a buffalo eats the young rice plants after they have been transplanted, let the owner [of the animal] get new plants and replace those destroyed. If he cannot find shoots of planting, let him be fined 51 cowries for each stalk. If the buffalo had a keeper, let him be fined 110 cowries for each stalk. This refers to newly-planted rice. If the rice was eaten when grown, the fine is 100 cowries for each stalk. If the animal had a keeper, the fine is 200 cowries per stalk. If the grain is ripe and there was no one looking after the buffalo, the fine is 300 cowries. If there was a keeper, the fine is nine times that for each.

22. Marriage

If a man courts a girl and her parents do not agree, he cannot be betrothed. If the parents agree and the daughter also agrees, he may be betrothed. If the parents agree but the daughter does not and runs away to someone else's house, let the parents return the value of the betrothal gifts, 11,000 cowries.

27. Theft

For a stealing a cock, the cost is 400 cowries; for stealing a hen 1,000 cowries and the fine is nine times the value.

For stealing knives, the fine is 3,300 cowries for each. For stealing a mortar and pestle the fine is 200 cowries, for stealing only the mortar, 660 cowries.

33. Theft

If there is a calf in womb, 11, 000 cowries; the fine is nine fold [buffalo].

....

The value of an ordinary dog is 3,000 cowries; the fine is nine times.

35. Theft

For stealing an elephant or a horse, 33,000 cowries [presumably the fine on return, rather than compensation].

49. Wife-beating

If a villager beats his wife, and the wife runs to the headman's house, if the villager pursues her there and continues beating her, let him be fined 22,000 cowries.

If the headman beats his wife, and she runs to a villager's house, if the headman follows her there and continues beating her, let the headman be fined 33,000 cowries.

51. Precedence and liability

Whether journeying or sitting, lying down, standing, walking, the cavalry officer must give way to the officer of elephants, the infantry officers must give way to the cavalry officer, the ordinary person must give way to the officers.

> Let the ordinary bearer give way to the bearer who is servant to a lord. Let the ordinary infantryman give way to the merchant, the slave of a lord, and men carrying grass [?]
>
> If he does not give way and there is a collision, and the infantryman beats the man carrying goods, let him be fined 11,000 cowries, because the bearer had a load and the other was just walking. The latter is at fault for hitting the former. He should be fined. If he holds him by the arm and hits him one, two, three times, if blood does not flow but he is bruised, the skin not broken, if he is unwell for only a single day, let the fine be 11,000 cowries.[15]

Obviously cowries functioned as currency in the kingdom of Chiang Mai. The law codes clearly state that cowries were used for fine or compensation, equivalent to silver values. Various things including production or hunting or fishing tools, domestic and forest animals, wild products, ritual objects, people's property such as water, money, clothes or slaves, had their value measured by cowries. The ratio between cowrie and silver is 1,100 cowries equal to one piece of silver.

## The Siam-Chiang Mai-Yunnan Route

The Laws of King Mengrai makes a great parallel and connection with Chinese testimony of cowrie money in Yunnan during the Ming dynasty. While his reign was earlier than the Ming period, King Mengrai once attacked the Mongols between 1301 and 1312, about half a century after the Mongols took over the Dali Kingdom in 1254. As such, this Siamese record fills in the Chinese vacuum of the Yuan period, and precedes Chinese textual details of the Ming period.

Indeed, various texts mentioned connections between Siam and Yunnan, testifying to trade routes and cultural intimacies between these societies. In general, almost all Chinese textual sources concerning cowrie shells in India and Southeast Asia matched non-Chinese sources. And from the thirteenth to the sixteenth centuries Zhao Rukuo, Wang Dayuan, Ma Huan, Gong Zhen, Fei Xin, and Huang Xingceng recorded the usage of cowrie money in Southeast Asia with more and more detail, which confirmed the Yunnan connection with Southeast Asia and the Indian Ocean. Wang Dayuan of the fourteenth century wrote for Mecca (*Tiantang*), 'Yunnan has a road to connect, and within one year (people) can reach it. For Western Ocean, (there also exists) a road.'[16] Ma Huan, an interpreter of the Treasure Fleet in the early fifteenth century, left us with more details. He noted the inland connections between Siam and Yunnan:

> When you travel something over two hundred *li* to the northwest from the capital, there is a market-town called Upper Water (*Shangshui*), whence you can go through into Yunnan by a back-entrance. In this place, there are five or six hundred families of foreigners; all kinds of foreign goods are for sale; red *ma-ssu-k'en-ti* stones are sold in great numbers here; this stone is inferior to the red *ya-ku*, [and] its brightness resembles that of a pomegranate seed. When the treasurer-ships of the Central Country come to Hsien Lo [Siam], [our] men also take small boats and go to trade [at Upper Water].[17]

Ma Huan's impression was reiterated by Huang Xingceng in the sixteenth century. [18] Not surprisingly, *Shangshui* adopted gold, silver, copper cash and cowrie shells as money.[19] Tomè Pires, the first Portuguese Ambassador to China, arrived in India in 1511 and, seeing cowries in Bengal and some ports in Southeast Asia, noted Siamese-Chinese connections as well. In Siam 'There are three ports in the kingdom of Siam on the Pegu side, and on the Pahang and *Champa* side there are many. They all belong to the said kingdom and are subject to the king of Siam. The land of Siam is large and very plenteous, with many people and cities, with many lords and many foreign merchants, and most of these foreigners are Chinese, because Siam does a great deal of trade with China.'[20] It seems that routes connecting Yunnan and Siam were crucial for the transportation of these shells, and Pelliot points out that the cowrie shells in Yunnan were probably sourced from Siam.[21]

Located between Yunnan and Siam, the Chiang Mai Kingdom served as a bridge. Indeed it had built intimate relationships with various Tai political entities in modern Xishuangbanna and southern Yunnan. Trade, ethnic connections, political interactions, and marriage alliances have been noticed in textual and archaeological studies, and also in local folklore. King Mengrai, for instance, was a son of Lao Meng of Hiram Ngern Yong and a princess of Chiang Rung (now known as Jinghong in Yunnan). And as mentioned, he once attacked the Mongols between 1301 and 1312, suggesting a well-used route in existence between Chiang Mai and Yunnan.

The source and routes by which cowries spread into Yunnan can be further indicated through a linguistic dimension.[22] The term '*cury*', or '*kauri*', used in Bengal (observed by Tomè Pires) suggests that Bengal was the source of cowries in Yunnan. The cowrie, or cowrie shell, was in Chinese *bei*, *haibei* (sea shell), or *beichi* (shell teeth),[23] but never 'kaoli', a new term that was not invented until the Yuan-Ming period, to refer to cowries. Ma Huan and Gong Zhen of the early fifteenth century record the word *kaoli* for the first time. *Kaoli*, from its pronunciation clearly refers to the transliteration of *cury* or *kauri*, suggesting the origin of cowries in Yunnan to be Bengali. It seems that both the Chinese term *kaoli* and the English term cowrie should be regarded as Indian dialectal terms akin to *kaudi* in Hindi, *kavari* in Marathi and *kabtaj* in Maldivian.[24]

Another Chinese term *ba* was invented during the Yuan-Ming period and deserves our attention. Wang Dayuan used the term *bazi* (shells).[25] Ma Huan and Gong Zhen also used the term *haiba* (sea shells). The character *ba* is the combination of two Chinese radicals, 'shell' and 'ba'. The radical 'shell' refers to its origin and feature, while the radical 'ba' is used for its pronunciation. The radical ba possibly is the transliteral abbreviation of the Sanskrit term *kaparda*, or the Hindustani derivation *kapari*.[26] The pronunciation of 'ba' resembles the Cham *bior*, the Khmer *bier*, the Siamese *bia*, and the Laotian *bia hoi* in Thai.[27] Pelliot has also brought the Malay *biya* to our attention, suggesting that the Thai probably borrowed the word from the Malays.[28] Whatever the case, linguistic connections lead us to speculate not only on the trading routes of cowries but also on the intimate relationship between Bengal, coastal mainland Southeast Asia and Yunnan (upper mainland Southeast Asia).

The foregoing discussion may lead to some tentative conclusions concerning the source and route of cowrie shells in Yunnan. These shells originated in the Maldives, were shipped to Bengal, travelled along coastal Burma to Siam, and were taken from Siam through Chiang Mai, Cheli (Jinghong or Chiang Rung) to Dali in western Yunnan. This route, a vital part of the Southern Silk Road (and the Maritime Silk Road) to which the following section will briefly refer, constituted a major source for the cowrie monetary system in medieval Yunnan from the eighth to the seventeenth centuries.

## The Southern Silk Road

Trade routes connecting ancient southwestern China and the Bay of Bengal have not been unknown to scholars; nevertheless, spatial and temporal vagaries have made it difficult to track these routes. Numerous imperial Chinese sources lead us to the existence of the so-called Shu-Yandu (Sichuan-India) Road that linked China through ancient Sichuan, Yunnan, Myanmar, Assam and India, and currently more and more scholars identify this trading network with the overland Silk Road and the maritime Silk Road by renaming it the Southern Silk Road.[29]

The Shu-Yandu Road, or the Sichuan-Yunnan-Burma-India Road was observed by Zhang Qian who visited Central Asia at the end of the second century. In Daxia (Bactria) Zhang Qian found Sichuan items, and he knew that 'Daxia is located twelve thousand li southwest of China. Now if the kingdom of Yandu is situated several thousand li southeast of Daxia and obtains Shu goods, it seems that Yandu must not be very far away from Shu. He concluded there existed a road connecting southwest China with Daxia via India.[30]

By the first and second century, this road was thriving, making Yongchang (lit., 'Forever Prosperous'), a frontier city in southern Yunnan, an international trading centre. Various goods from Southeast Asia and India were sold there and transferred to inland China. A southern tributary mission in 120 included some musicians and acrobats. The latter could spit fire, decompose their bodies, and switch the heads of horse and oxen. They claimed to be *Haixiren* (people west of the Sea).[31] 'Haixi' in imperial Chinese records usually refers to Rome. And Yu Yinshi concludes that 'it seems beyond doubt that the Southwestern Barbarians must have developed increasingly close economic relations with some of the natives of Burma and India and, through them, Han China also gradually but steadily came into economic intercourse with both Burma and India along this famous trade route.'[32]

Xuanzang (mid-seventh century) and Yijing (late seventh century)—two famous Chinese Buddhist pilgrims—referred to the route between India and Sichuan in some detail. Their records of miles and days were fairly close, indicating that people of that time were familiar with the route. Fan Chuo, a military official who served in Tang China's Annam Protectorate, recorded these roads in the mid-ninth century. Jia Dan, a prime minister in the Tang court in 801 presented the Emperor with books documenting Sino-foreign communications. The sixth of the seven roads linking China with barbarians of the four directions was the Annam-India Road. This route started from Tonkin, via Yunnan, and went through Prome (Sriksetra) to Magadha in north India.

These Chinese sources clearly illustrate dynamic communications between China, mainland Southeast Asia and the Bay of Bengal. It is through this networking that cowrie shells entered China, taking root as money in medieval Yunnan. The Laws of King Mengrai further substantiate the argument that the Chiang Mai-Yunnan road constituted a vital part of the connection. It must be pointed out that there is no evidence of the cowrie shells taking the Melaka or the Sunda strait routes. Questions remain about Mien which was supposed to be another important source of cowrie shells in Yunnan, and we look forward to archaeological and textual discoveries in Myanmar, hopefully in the near future.

It is worth mentioning that Yunnan also connected Nepal and India through Tibet. Known as the Tea Horse Road, the Yunnan-Tibet connection started much earlier than the eighth century when Tibetan people began to drink tea. However, since Yunnan bordered Tibet, Burma, and India, it could take the southward road through Mien and India and then go on to Tibet. While cowrie shells were not used as money in Tibet, other economic and cultural interactions took place along this route, for example, the spread of Buddhist beliefs.

## Reflection: The Cowrie World

In addition to India, medieval Yunnan, and the Chiang Mai kingdom, various sources refer to the wide existence of the cowrie currency in many parts of early Southeast Asia.

Before the early fifteenth century, when barter was prevalent in Southeast Asia, 'precious metals, such as silver or gold, frequently became measures of value. In some instances, rice, lengths of cloths, or imported cowrie shells performed the same function.'[33] Indeed, the Bengal-centred cowrie monetary system had extended to neighbouring Southeast Asian areas as observed by both western and Chinese travellers.

In southeastern Bengal and Assam, smaller transactions were carried out through imported cowries, and in the thirteenth and fourteenth centuries, the Turks began to mint Islamic-style silver coinage while cowries remained the preferred subsidiary currency.[34] Assam possessed a rudimentary cowrie-based monetary system before the fifteenth century. In Arakan and Pegu (lower Burma) white cowries were used as coinage.[35] 'In Martaban fifteen thousand are usually worth one *vica*, which is ten *calains*; when they are cheap sixteen thousand; when they are very dear fourteen thousand, and generally fifteen thousand. A *calaim* is worth one thousand five hundred. For four hundred or five hundred they will give a chicken, and things of that sort for the same price.'[36] Tomè Pires specified that 'The cowries come from the Maldives (*Diva*) Islands, where they make large quantities of towers, and they also come from the islands of *Bagangã* and of Borneo (*Burney*) and they bring them to Malacca and from there they go to Pegu.'[37] In Siam, 'cowries, like those current in Pegu, are current throughout the country for small money, and gold and silver for the larger coins. This money is worth the same as we have said for Pegu.'[38] While the Maldives were the main source for cowries in Siam, white cowries also came from Melaka.[39] In Sukhothai (in northern Thailand) where a large quantity of Maldivian cowries was unearthed, many inscriptions composed between 1292 and 1400 demonstrate cowries as a measure of value in Thai society.[40] Cowries were used for religious dedications, for the purchase of inexpensive goods such as cloth and lamps, but were also used in more expensive deals such as land transactions. In fact, the use of cowrie money in Thailand did not end until the latter part of the nineteenth century.[41]

The situation east of Siam seems very different, as cowrie currency was not found either in Cambodia or in Cochin China. Chinese copper coins dominated local markets in these regions. In Cambodia, 'cashes from China are used for the small money, and in trade, gold and silver [are used]';[42] In Cochin China, 'The money they use for buying food is the cash from China, and for merchandise gold and silver.'[43] And so it was in Java where for small money, local people 'used cash from China.'[44]

While upper mainland Southeast Asia was generally not mentioned, the Pyu Kingdom might have imported cowries, cowries being found at Beikthano.[45] And Laos, although an inland country, was found to use cowries as money during the seventeenth century.[46] This is understandable, since cowries had been used in the neighbouring Chiang Mai kingdom.

Not surprisingly, the Western records cited were in line with what Marco Polo records. The legendary traveller spoke of the cowrie currency in Bengal (as reported to him), Lochac (Siam), and Caugigu (Tongkin, modern Hanoi area).[47] Polo might have been mistaken in the case of Tongkin as no other sources support the use of cowrie currency, but cowries might 'have been used more or less on its northwestern borders.'[48] His report was the earliest mention of the use of cowries in Siam, according to Pelliot,[49] which would have been confirmed by many Chinese observers during the Yuan-Ming period (1279-1644).

As such, by the thirteenth century there existed a cowrie currency world incorporating various societies in South Asia and Southeast Asia including medieval Yunnan. By the sixteenth century, with the arrival of Europeans, the cowrie currency world interacted and overlapped with part of the European world-system, morphing into a global world in which cowrie currency played a key role in the trans-Atlantic slave trade until the nineteenth century. Based on this first global currency and the archaeological discoveries of cowrie shells in pre-historic East Asia, Southeast Asia, India, Central Asia, Mesopotamia, and the Near East, this chapter highlights cowrie shells functioning in a similar way to bronze, silver, silk, tea, or opium in world history.

The cowrie shells and the cowrie monetary system serve as a firm case to challenge national, regional and civilizational approaches or paradigms. Cowrie shells were marine products, but played crucial roles in inland societies and kingdoms such as the Shang Dynasty, Orissa, Chiang Mai, Nanzhao (and later Dali), Mali, and West Africa,[50] whether as ritual value, precious item, commodity-money, or general money. As such, cowries demonstrated the far-reaching and long-lasting influence of the ocean on the landmass, symbolising land-ocean connections and interactions.

A few pioneering scholars such as Coedès once highlighted the role of the sea in Asia's history.[51] James Heimann examined the cowrie trade to illustrate the integration of the Indian Ocean 'world-economy.'[52] Rila Mukherjee produced an inspiring work that elaborates on this watery region of the eastern Indian Ocean, describing it as 'an arena of littoral societies, hybrid polities, religious/commercial practices or connected societies.'[53] Their approaches have been elaborated by Watson Andaya who warns about the risk of a purely land-based perspective, calling attention to 'oceans unbounded.'[54] While promoting a maritime view of history, Bentley not only conceptualized 'sea and ocean basins as frameworks of historical analysis' and discussed their advantages (for studying commercial, biological, and cultural exchanges), but also pointed out the limits and problems (fluctuating spatial and temporal boundaries and relations among maritime regions and with the larger world).[55]

Following their theoretical constructions and empirical analyses, the author would like to propose the term 'cowrie world' that serves as an alternative to purely land-based regional studies. The 'cowrie world' balances an ocean-based analysis paralleling as well as challenging recent paradigms such as Zomia. The physical cowrie world links the large landmass and vast waterworld in which cowrie shells lived, and combines them into an intertwined commercial and cultural world. This world, to a large extent, crossed various boundaries of topography, people, culture, religion, and society.

## NOTES

1. Peng Xinwei, *Zhongguo Huobi Shi* (A History of Chinese Currencies), Shanghai: Shanghai Renmin Chubanshe, 1965; Huang Xiquan, *Xianqin Huobi Tonglun* (A Comprehensive Examination of the Pre-Qin Currencies), Beijing: Zijincheng Chubanshe, 2001; Li Yung-Ti, 'On the Functions of Cowries in the Shang and Western Zhou China,' *Journal of East Asian Archaeology* 5 (2006), pp. 1-26.
2. Ke Peng and Yanshi Zhu are the only scholars who have done a serious scientific research on the origins of cowries used in ancient China. Ke Peng and Yanshi Zhu, *New Research on the Origins of Cowries Used in Ancient China,* Philadelphia: University of Pennsylvania, 1995. The two authors conclude that origins of cowries in ancient China were the Indian Ocean, a rebuttal to the conventional South China Sea hypothesis.
3. Jan Hogendorn and Marion Johnson, *The Shell Money of the Slave Trade,* London: Cambridge University Press, 1986.
4. For Chinese studies on cowrie shells such as those done by Fang Guoyu, Jiang Yingliang, Li Jiadui, and Zhang Bincun, most have been collected into Yang Shouchuan, ed., *Beibi Yanjiu* (Studies on the Cowrie Currency), Kunming: Yunnan University Press, 1997. For non-Chinese studies, see Pelliot, *Notes on Marco Polo*, Paris: Imprimerie nationale, 1959, vol. 1, pp. 531-63; Hans Ulrich Vogel, 'Cowry Cowrie Trade and Its Role in the Economy of Yunnan: From the Ninth to the Mid-Seventeenth Century', *Journal of the Economic and Social History of the Orient*, pt. I, vol. 36, no. 3, 1993, pp. 211-52; pt. II, vol. 36, no. 4, 1993, pp. 309-53; Bin Yang, 'Horses, Silver, Cowries: Yunnan in a Global Perspective.' *Journal of World History*, vol. 15, no. 3, September 2004, pp. 281-322; idem, *Between Winds and Clouds: The Making of Yunnan (Second Century* BCE*-20th Century* AD*),* New York: Columbia University Press, 2008; idem, 'The Rise and Fall of Cowrie Shells: The Asian Story', *Journal of World History*, vol. 22, no. 1, March 2011, pp. 1-26; idem, 'The Bengal Connections in Yunnan', *China Report*, vol. 48, nos. 1 and 2, February and May 2012, pp. 125-46.
5. Yang Shouchuan, 'Beibi Yanjiu: Zhongyuan yu Yunnan yong Haibei

zuo Huobi de Lishi (Studies on Cowrie: Historical Survey on Cowrie as Currency in the Central Plain and in Yunnan)', in *Beibi Yanjiu*.

6. Mich'le Pirazzoli-t'Serstevens, 'Cowrie and Chinese Copper Cash as Prestige Goods in Dian', in Ian Glover, ed., *Southeast Asian Archaeology 1990: Proceedings of the Third Conference of the European Association of Southeast Asian Archaeologists*, Hull: University of Hull, 1992, p. 49.
7. Pelliot, *Notes on Marco Polo*, vol. 1, pp. 531-63.
8. See Bin Yang, 'Horses, Silver, Cowries'; idem., 'The Rise and Fall of Cowrie Shells'; idem, 'The Bengal Connections in Yunnan'.
9. Peng Xinwei, *Zhongguo Huobishi*, 1965.
10. Jiang Yingliang, 'Yunnan yongbei kao (A Study of the Use of Cowrie Shells in Yunnan)', in *Beibi Yanjiu*, pp. 92-3.
11. Li Jiarui, 'Gudai Yunnan Yongbei de Dagai Qingxing (A General Profile of Cowrie Money in Ancient Yunnan)', in *Beibi Yanjiu*, p. 98.
12. Yang Shouchuan, 'Yunnan Yongbei,' pp. 71-2.
13. Vogel, 'Cowrie Trade', pt. I, p. 237.
14. For the Law Code, see Aroonrut Wichienkeeo and Gehan Wijeyewardene, trs and eds, *The Laws of King Mengrai (Mangrayathammasart),* Canberra: Australian National University, 1986.
15. Wichienkeeo and Wijeyewardene, *The Laws of King Mengrai*. '[]' is what the two editors correct or revise. Page numbers are omitted, due to the many entries, while the list of articles makes it easy for readers to locate the concerned article in the book.
16. Wang Dayuan, *Dao yi zhi lue jiao shi*, ed. Su Jiqin, Beijing, 1981; rpt. 2000, p. 352.
17. Ma Huan, *Yingya Shenglan*, pp. 105-6.
18. Huang Xingceng, *Xiyang Chaogong Dianlu*, p. 59.
19. Ibid.
20. Tomè Pires, *The Suma Oriental of Tomè Pires, an Account of the East, from the Red Sea to Japan, Written in Malacca and India in 1512-1515, and The book of Francisco Rodrigues Rutter of a Voyage in the Red Sea, Nautical Rules, Almanack and Maps, Written and Drawn in the East before 1515,* tr. and ed. Armando Cortesao, London: The Hakluyt Society, 1944, p. 103.
21. Pelliot, *Notes on Marco Polo*, pp. 552, 554.
22. Ibid.
23. *Beichi*, is so named, because of the marks inside the edge of the shell that resemble the teeth. See James Legge, tr. and ed., *A Record of Buddhistic Kingdoms being an Account by the Chinese Monk Fâ-Hien*

of his Travels in India and Ceylon (A.D. 399-410)*, Oxford: Clarendon Press, 1886, p. 43 and fn. 2.

24. Namio Egami, 'Migration of Cowrie-Shell Culture in East Asia', *Acta Asiatica*, vol. 26, 1974, p. 36.
25. Dayuan, *Dao yi zhi lue jiao shi*, p. 264.
26. Egami states that it is 'apparently.' See Egami, 'Migration of Cowrie-Shell,' p. 34.
27. Pelliot, *Notes on Marco Polo*, p. 554; Egami, 'Migration of Cowrie-Shell', p. 32.
28. Pelliot, *Notes on Marco Polo*, p. 554.
29. For the Southern Silk Road, Bin, 'Horses, Silver, and Cowries', pp. 281-322, where I used the term 'Southwest Silk Road'. Also see James A. Anderson, 'China's Southwestern Silk Road in World History', *World History Connected,* vol. 6, no. 1, March 2009, pp. 1-7. http://worldhistoryconnected. press.illinois.edu/6.1/anderson.html, accessed 7 June 2016.
30. *Shi Ji* (Records of the Historian), *juan* 123, in *Yunnan Shiliao Congkan* (The Collection of Yunnan Historical Sources), ed. Fang Guoyu, Kunming: Yunnandaxue Chubanshe, 1998, vol. 1.
31. *Houhan Shu* (Record of the Later Han Dynasty), *juan* 86, in *Yunnan Shiliao Congkan,* vol. 1.
32. Yu Yingshi, *Trade and Expansion in Han China: A Study in the Structure of Sino-Barbarian Economic Relations*, Berkeley: University of California Press, 1967, p. 115.
33. Robert S. Wicks, *Money, Markets, and Trade in Early Southeast Asia*, Ithaca: SEAP, Cornell University, 1992, p. 7.
34. Ibid., p. 66.
35. Pires, *The Suma Oriental,* pp. 97-100.
36. Ibid., p. 100.
37. Ibid.
38. Ibid., p. 104.
39. Ibid., p. 108.
40. Wicks, *Money, Markets, and Trade*, pp. 170-82.
41. Ibid., p. 166.
42. Pires, *The Suma Oriental,* p. 114.
43. Ibid., p. 115.
44. Ibid., pp. 170, 181.
45. See Wicks, *Money, Markets, and Trade*, p. 116.
46. Vogel, 'Cowrie Trade', pt. I, p. 230.

47. Pelliot, *Notes on Marco Polo*, vol. 1, p. 552.
48. Ibid.
49. Ibid.
50. Nanzhao-Dali were two sequential kingdoms in medieval Yunnan from the seventh to mid-thirteenth centuries.
51. Coedès, citing Sylvain Levi, emphasized the role of the Indian Ocean: 'the pattern of currents and the pattern of periodic winds that govern navigation have long fostered a system of trade in which the African coast, Arabia, the Persian Gulf, India, Indochina, and the China continually contributed and received their share.' He emphasized the significance of the China Sea in Southeast Asia as the Sea 'has always been a unifying factor rather than an obstacle for the peoples along the rivers.' G. Coedès, *The Indianized States of Southeast Asia*, ed. Walter F. Vella, tr. Susan Brown Cowing, Kuala Lumpur: University of Malaya Press, 1968, pp. 3-4.
52. J. Heimann, 'Small Change and Ballast: Cowrie Trade and Usage as an Example of India Ocean Economic History', *South Asia*, vol. 3, no. 1, 1980, pp. 48-69.
53. Rila Mukherjee, 'The Neglected Sea: The Eastern Indian Ocean in History,' *Journal of the Asiatic Society of Bengal*, vol. XLIX, 2007, no. 3, pp. 1-48; no. 4, pp. 18-45.
54. Barbara Watson Andaya, 'Oceans Unbounded: Transversing Asia across "Area Studies"', *Journal of Asian Studies*, vol. 65, no. 4, November 2006, pp. 669-90.
55. Jerry Bentley, 'Sea and Ocean Basins as Frameworks of Historical Analysis', *Geographical Review*, vol. 89, no. 2, April 1999, pp. 215-25.

## BIBLIOGRAPHY

Andaya, Barbara Watson, 'Oceans Unbounded: Transversing Asia across "Area Studies"', *Journal of Asian Studies*, vol. 65, no. 4, November 2006, pp. 669-90.

Anderson, James A., 'China's South-western Silk Road in World History', *World History Connected*, vol. 6, no. 1, March 2009, pp. 1-7. http://worldhistoryconnected.press.illinois.edu/6.1/anderson.html, accessed 7 June 2016.

Bentley, Jerry, 'Sea and Ocean Basins as Frameworks of Historical Analysis,' *Geographical Review*, vol. 89, no. 2, April 1999, pp. 215-25.

Coedès, G., *The Indianized States of Southeast Asia*, ed. Walter F. Vella, tr. Susan Brown Cowing, Kuala Lumpur: University of Malaya Press, 1968.

Egami, Namio, 'Migration of Cowrie-Shell Culture in East Asia', *Acta Asiatica*, vol. 26, 1974, pp. 1-52.

Fang, Guoyu (ed.), *Yunnan Shiliao Congkan* (The collection of Yunnan historical sources), vol. 1, Kunming: Yunnandaxue Chubanshe, 1998.

Heimann, J., 'Small Change and Ballast: Cowrie Trade and Usage as an Example of India Ocean Economic History', *South Asia*, vol. 3, no. 1, 1980, pp. 48-69.

Hogendorn, Jan and Marion Johnson, *The Shell Money of the Slave Trade*, London: Cambridge University Press, 1986.

*Houhan Shu* (Record of the Later Han Dynasty), *juan* 86, in Fang, *Yunnan Shiliao Congkan*, vol. 1, pp. 29-36.

Huang Xingceng, *Xiyang Chaogong Dianlu Jiaozhu*, Xie Fang annotated, Beijing: Zhonghua shuju, 2000.

Huang Xiquan, *Xianqin Huobi Tonglun* (A Comprehensive Examination of the pre-Qin Currencies), Beijing: Zijincheng Chubanshe, 2001.

Jiang Yingliang, 'Yunnan yongbei kao (A Study of the Use of Cowrie Shells in Yunnan', in Yang, *Beibi Yanjiu*, pp. 81-93.

Ke Peng and Yanshi Zhu, *New Research on the Origins of Cowries Used in Ancient China*, Sino-Platonic Papers, Department of East Asian Languages and Civilizations, University of Pennsylvania, Philadelphia, PA 19104-6305 USA, www.sino-platonic.org, 1995.

Legge, James, tr. and ed., *A Record of Buddhistic Kingdoms Being an Account by the Chinese Monk Fâ-Hien of his Travels in India and Ceylon (A.D. 399-410)*, Oxford: Clarendon Press, 1886.

Li Jiarui, 'Gudai Yunnan Yongbei de Dagai Qingxing (A General Profile of Cowrie Money in Ancient Yunnan)', in Yang, *Beibi Yanjiu*, pp. 94-118.

Li Yung-Ti, 'On the Functions of Cowries in the Shang and Western Zhou China', *Journal of East Asian Archaeology*, vol. 5, 2006, pp. 1-26.

Ma Huan, *Yingya Shenglan* (The Overall Survey of the Ocean's Shores), trans. from the Chinese texts, ed. Feng Chengjun, with intro., notes, and appendices by J.V.G. Mills, Cambridge: Cambridge University Press for the Hakluyt Society, 1970.

Mukherjee, Rila, 'The Neglected Sea: The Eastern Indian Ocean in History,' *Journal of the Asiatic Society of Bengal*, vol. XLIX, 2007, no. 3, pp. 1-48; no. 4, pp. 18-45.

Pelliot, Paul, *Notes on Marco Polo*, vol. 1, Paris: Imprimerie Nationale, 1959.

Peng Xinwei, *Zhongguo Huobi Shi* (A History of Chinese Currencies), Shanghai: Shanghai Renmin Chubanshe, 1965.

Pirazzoli-t'Serstevens, Michèle, 'Cowrie and Chinese Copper Cash as Prestige Goods in Dian', in Ian Glover, ed., *Southeast Asian Archaeology 1990: Proceedings of the Third Conference of the European Association of Southeast Asian Archaeologists*, Hull: University of Hull, 1992, pp. 45-52.

Pires, Tomè, *The Suma Oriental of Tomè Pires: An Account of the East, from the Red Sea to Japan, Written in Malacca and India in 1512-1515, and The Book of Francisco Rodrigues Rutter of a Voyage in the Red Sea, Nautical Rules, Almanack and Maps, Written and Drawn in the East before 1515*, tr. and ed. Armando Cortesao, London: The Hakluyt Society, 1944.

*Shi Ji* (Records of the Historian), *juan* 123, in Fang, *Yunnan Shiliao Congkan*, pp. 10-11.

Vogel, Hans Ulrich, 'Cowry Trade and Its Role in the Economy of Yunnan: From the Ninth to the Mid-Seventeenth Century', *Journal of the Economic and Social History of the Orient*, pt. I, vol. 36, no. 3, 1993, pp. 211-52; pt. II, vol. 36, no. 4, 1993, pp. 309-53.

Wang Dayuan, *Dao yi zhi lue jiao shi*, ed., Su Jiqin, Beijing: Zhonghua Shuju, 1981; rpt. 2000.

Wichienkeeo, Aroonrut and Gehan Wijeyewardene, trs and eds, *The Laws of King Mengrai (Mangrayathammasart)*, Canberra: Australian National University, 1986.

Wicks, Robert S., *Money, Markets, and Trade in Early Southeast Asia*, Ithaca: SEAP, Cornell University, 1992.

Yang Shouchuan, ed., *Beibi Yanjiu* (Studies on the Cowrie Currency), Kunming: Yunnan University Press, 1997.

———, 'Beibi Yanjiu: Zhongyuan yu Yunnan yong Haibei zuo Huobi de Lishi (Studies on Cowrie: Historical Survey on Cowrie as Currency in the Central Plain and in Yunnan)', *Beibi Yanjiu*, pp. 1-27

———, 'Yunnan Yongbei zuo Huobi de Qishi Niandai (The Period When Yunnan began using Cowrie Shells as Money)', in *Beibi Yanjiu*, pp. 65-80.

Yang, Bin, 'Horses, Silver, Cowries: Yunnan in a Global Perspective', *Journal of World History*, 15, 3, September 2004, pp. 281-322.

———, *Between Winds and Clouds: The Making of Yunnan (Second Century* BCE*-20th Century* AD*)*, New York: Columbia University Press, 2008.

________, 'The Rise and Fall of Cowrie Shells: The Asian Story', *Journal of World History*, vol. 22, no. 1, March 2011, pp. 1-26.

________, 'The Bengal Connections in Yunnan', *China Report*, vol. 48, nos. 1 and 2, February and May 2012, pp. 125-46.

Yu Yingshi, *Trade and Expansion in Han China: A Study in the Structure of Sino-Barbarian Economic Relations*, Berkeley: University of California Press, 1967.

8

# Hard Money and 'Cashless' Economies

## Medieval Bengal and the Greater Asian World

John Deyell

> There was in fact no reason other than historical happenstance that money was for so long equated in the Western mind with metal.
>
> Neill Ferguson, *The Ascent of Money*, p. 27

## The Diversity of Pre-modern Monetary Systems

When historians interpret evidence about the past, we have a tendency to extrapolate our own world views onto former ages. This has certainly been the case with Asia's monetary history, much of which was first explored during the Victorian era. Living in that time of 'hard money', when the gold standard predominated, early historians adopted the numismatic assumption that 'money' meant something tangible. So, *ipso facto*, a pre-modern society lacking coinage was interpreted as 'under-monetized', and coin-using societies were assumed to be more economically advanced than those without.

Nowadays of course, in many parts of the world we live in a nearly 'cashless' society where most money is digital, and invisible aside from numerical displays on computer monitors or smart phone screens. So we are more willing to contemplate the existence of past societies that used money extensively, but where coinage was scarce or absent altogether. The evidence has not changed, but our understanding of the role and nature of money has fundamentally altered.[1] The existence of intangible money, in the absence of a written record in the archaeological evidence, is much harder to corroborate than the existence of tangible money, which is confirmed frequently by the unearthing of coin hoards from the past.

There can be no doubt that at base, money is a social convention.[2] Presently this is obscured by the institutional backing of the money in our pockets, but in former times it was clearer that anything that was commonly held to be money, and accepted as money, was in fact money. However as societies became more organizationally complex, money came to be identified with institutions that defined its value and moderated its exchange. In some cases of very simple money, earlier arrangements survived as a monetary niche, as when merchants imported cowry shells from afar and used them in local markets.

In the panel that gave rise to this chapter, we attempted to grapple with a seeming contradiction: how could some great empires and active kingdoms in the early medieval Asian world rely on prolific coinage, while others, often their neighbours, function quite effectively with no coinage at all?[3] Since the historiography is imbalanced, long favouring research on the societies that used coinage, by way of rebalancing we must consider in greater detail the case of societies that functioned without it. A valid exercise in itself, it begs the question of how the 'hard money' economies and the 'cashless' economies interacted. So a second theme of this chapter is the exploration of how 'international trade' (if we can be excused the anachronism) was conducted between contrasting economic systems.

The task is made somewhat easier thanks to the surge of fairly recent publications exploring different aspects of the historical development of money, in the broader world.[4] While scholarly opinion is yet to agree on a new 'standard model' for pre-modern monetary systems, much former misunderstanding and error has been cleared away. One such discredited myth masquerading as historical analysis was the uncritical adoption by some economic historians of the Aristotelian fable about the universal use of barter in the ancient world, and its displacement by the invention of coinage and the subsequent development of markets.[5] This opinion is regrettably still found in books surveying the history of money.[6] It has been firmly refuted by archaeologists and by anthropologists examining the economies of neolithic tribes surviving into the modern world. Both find that the earliest forms of financial relations can be characterized as forms of *debt*, be they social debt (mutual obligations), purchase debt (owed for goods or services received), punitive debt (fines for lawbreaking), or tax debt (contributions to support the community). They also found that recognizable markets long predated the development of coinage: '"the market" . . . after all, has existed since time immemorial.'[7]

Without delving too deeply into the swiftly expanding historiography of this field, suffice to say that it is now understood that debt gave rise to money, and money gave rise to coinage. This is clearest in ancient Mesopotamia, where plentiful written records in the form of archives of cuneiform tablets have been recovered and deciphered. These records describe the workings of temple and royal treasuries and storehouses, which accepted agricultural products, precious items and metals on deposit and issued receipts for their redemption. The value of these goods was assessed and recorded in terms of money of account, based variously on cattle, grain and precious metals. Such receipts recorded domestic and commercial transactions such as the purchase or sale of land or slaves, the exchange of goods or other business transactions, or the negotiation of marriage contracts. The state had a facilitative role by establishing common standards in weights and measures, but otherwise the cuneiform documents describe a market economy in which supply and demand created a system of value and exchange, moderated (lightly or heavily, depending on circumstances) by trusted royal and religious institutions.[8] 'What can be safely stated is that . . . the boundaries between public and private were rarely clear cut. . . . He could be a trader who travels with his merchandise, or a functionary whose task is to facilitate trade – as banker or as merchant, or a moneylender who gives out commercial loans.'[9]

Mesopotamia was not unique in this system; in agricultural and urban societies as far back as archaeologists can see, debt was denominated and cleared in money of account, often expressed in measures of weight. Account balancing only occasionally required the transfer of physical money or its commodity analogues. This proved practical because farmers and city-dwellers were by and large sedentary people who conducted their economic affairs through stable and durable institutions. Around these institutions, grew communities of specialists who produced or traded value-added goods, exchanging these far and wide in the search for key commodities not available locally. Such commercial communities developed symbiotic relationships with the religious and state organs with which they interfaced; indeed, some of these ventures have been characterized as private banks. This is seen in India as well during the late first millennium BCE. In these circumstances, they were most efficiently served by written debt and credit transactions.

Some small daily interactions did not merit such formal arrangements, as when city folk and farmers dealt with each other at markets. Often small counters like sea shells, beans, or nuts served admirably to keep track of the balance of exchange, much like chips in a game. Cowries or other tiny shells seem to have been used as small money in many societies in both the Old World and the New. But large transactions were recorded. Indeed, such an emphasis on intangible money may well be a defining characteristic of the economy of settled societies.

In contrast, hunter/gatherer and nomadic societies were structured around the capacity to pick up and move all their worldly belongings on short notice, and hence prized the compact and the portable. In their transactions with others of their kind or with settled societies they preferred to make exchanges and clear debts in tangible or physical money. In the Bronze Age, bits and pieces of metal like gold or silver were used. When they encountered coinage sometime after its invention in the sixth or fifth centuries BCE, the wandering peoples of the steppes adopted it wholeheartedly. By the time they entered the historical record, the ephemeral hordes and tribes of Asia's nomadic horsemen by preference conducted war and trade through the medium of coins.

Others who valued portable forms of wealth were long-distance traders operating along caravan roads and maritime routes. In an era when space and carrying capacity were at a premium, traders favoured small, light, high-value merchandise. Foremost amongst these would be precious metals, often in the form of coins, which were resistant to the ravages of dust storms and oceanic weather alike. So nomads and traders formed a symbiotic relationship, sometimes (although not always) defined by the use of coinage in their exchanges.[10]

So to recapitulate this survey of early money: it is recognized that money was a pervasive tool of settled societies, closely associated with those societies' institutions and commercial communities.[11] Coinage was convenient but not at all essential to the orderly administration of debt and credit in such institutional settings. It was, however, of high utility where movement or portability was at a premium.

Once coinage was adopted by an administration, its use became over time embedded in its institutional structure, and adherence to the coinage norm became remarkably tenacious. We might note in this respect the Hellenistic system that introduced silver coinage into the conquered Achaemenid realm, which as inscriptions inform us, had previously no need for coinage in its central provinces nor in its revenue system.[12] Yet once adopted, successive Iranian administrations of the Seleucids, Parthians, Sasanians, Abbasids, Seljuks, Ilkhanids, Timurids, etc., continued to function using silver coinage almost exclusively. So although complex administrations could administer their monetary functions over great distances and long periods of time without reference to coinage, once coinage was introduced it tended to continue in use.

## The Development of Money, and Coins, in India

Unlike in contemporary Mesopotamia, India's early Indus Civilization of the third and second millennia BCE, has not left a body of original documentation. Or rather it has, but we can't read it. Its writing is for the most part restricted to short inscriptions on seals, that have so far eluded decipherment. So the question of money development or use in bronze-age India lacks both evidence and attention.[13] Even fairly recent surveys of Harappan civilization fail to address whether money existed.[14]

In the last decade there has been considerable archaeological investigation of the sources and uses of metal and non-metallic materials in Harappa, Mohenjo-daro and elsewhere in northwest India during that period.[15] While there is considerable evidence for mining, long-distance trade and metal refining and fabricating, there is no specific evidence for the existence of money in the conduct of these activities. No doubt the existence of number systems and accounting can be inferred, but not money use *per se*. Likewise, there is evidence for a jewellery industry (gold and carnelian beads, touch-stones, etc.), but nothing that would establish whether jewellers exercised a financial function.[16]

Later, during India's 'second urbanization' (of the Gangetic valley), scholars have determined that a number of early religious works contain words that might refer to money generally, or even to coins. An oft-quoted passage in the *Rgveda* (*c.* second millennium BCE) mentions '*manas* of gold', indicating the existence of a system for the measurement of precious metals, if not a monetary system.[17] Likewise, the *Atharvaveda* (eleventh century BCE) contains many mentions of precious metals in various forms, but in an equivocal context that may or may not indicate their use as money or coins.[18] Some scholars feel the evidence is adequate to ascribe money use to this period: 'In the Vedic literature references are to be found to the use of metal in payments. ...there is no reason to doubt that these texts are referring to the use of precious metal as money.'[19]

It appears that in India, in comparison to Mesopotamia, the first historical mentions of money use are not a great deal earlier than the first notices of coined money. So the next step in this analysis is to consider the circumstances of the invention of coinage more broadly, as well as its first its appearance in India.

It is well known that the idea for coinage arose in Greece, India, and China at roughly the same time, and there has been speculation as to why this might be so. A currently much-discussed proposal by Graeber and others, relates the invention of coinage to the disruption of settled societies by periods of intrusive war and unrest, citing the distinct preference of soldiers for portable wealth.[20] This explanation however has its own problems, since it can hardly be claimed that warfare on a massive scale was an innovation of the sixth century BCE.

Rather more promising is a line of inquiry that notes that this period was one of social unrest and dislocation coincidentally in the Aegean, India and China.[21] The first coinage in Athens, for example, is associated with the pro-commoner demagoguery of 'tyrants', who attempted to counter the entrenched power of the ruling elite by freeing credit from the grasp of their institutions. 'Thus we might offer an alternative narrative behind the development of various money forms in Greece: an ongoing struggle over... who controlled the highest spheres of exchange, between the traditional elite and the emerging city-state.'[22] The anonymity of coinage proved to be a democratic quality.

In contrast, the establishment of the renowned copper cash as a universal Chinese currency rather than local curiosity is ascribed to the 'Warring States' period (*c.* 600 BE), when the money-form, and armies of one regional state slowly prevailed over others.[23] Here we may perhaps give the disruption thesis some leeway.

Roughly the same period in north India has been described as one of restlessness with the established cosmology, and the birth of new ideas.[24] The radical social-leavening messages of the Buddha and his Jain counterpart Mahavira, can be seen in a similar light as the Greek reform efforts. In such an environment, it is argued, it is no accident that coinage arose to allow people to undertake their economic affairs free of the constraints, controls, and limitations of the status quo.

While such theories would require closer examination to gain wider acceptance, they do provide us with an intriguing challenge: how can we explain the invention of coinage in terms of the dynamics of the societies in which they arose? Undoubtedly that which seems a compelling argument from the distance of 2500 years may need considerable refining and adjustment when looked at more closely. Still, the tenor of this line of inquiry seems promising.

In India, it is generally agreed that coinage first arose among the *janapadas*, i.e. the tribal republics and elective monarchies of north India, sometime about the sixth century BCE. To be precise, the area where such coinages are found is more or less congruent with the presumed territories of certain *janapadas*; the question of who issued them is less clear. The *janapada* coinage consisted of flat silver ingots of uniform metal content that were stamped with so-called 'punchmarks' or attestation marks. [25] A little later, copper coins, formed by both casting and striking, were issued by *negamas* or guilds, as well as by small tribal kingdoms. No gold coins are known from this early period.

The idea of silver punchmarked coins was then appropriated by Magadha and was one of the administrative tools used to leverage their local kingdom into the first pan-Indian empire. Mauryan and Sunga silver *karshapanas* are found in virtually every corner of the Indian subcontinent.[26] With the passing of the Mauryan/Sunga state, however, its institutions also passed, and the punchmarked coin was only sporadically taken up thereafter, most notably in various peripheral and secondary kingdoms of the south, and then only in gold, the preferred local metal.

So the Mauryan *karshapana* model failed to take root more broadly, and with the passing of empire, few if any successor kingdoms continued to follow this coining tradition. This is an enigma that has not, to my knowledge, been properly explained. Since the *Arthashastra* asserts that the *karshapana* coinage was closely linked with the administration and army in Mauryan polity,[27] we can only conclude that this governance model sat lightly over most of the subcontinent and faded quickly with the re-emergence of local norms.

The second wave of coinage adoption in India can be traced to the influence of erstwhile pastoral nomads of Central Asia. The settled agricultural regions of northwest India suffered a constant intrusion of lower-culture pastoralist or recently post-nomadic peoples, namely the Sakas, Kushans, Kidarites, Hephthalites, and Hunas. These people had a predilection for portable wealth, and keenly took up the idea of coinage from the kingdoms they had overwhelmed in their long journey of conquest from Central Asia into India. Although not numerous, they militarily overwhelmed the settled peoples they found in their path, forming new ruling elites.

Into an area with no tradition of gold coins, a firmly-laid tradition of silver punch-marked *karshapana* coins, as well as a plethora of local cast copper coins, the successive invaders brought new coinage norms. The Sakas and Pahlavas brought the Indo-Greek style silver coinage (second to first centuries BCE); the Kushans brought double die-struck heavy gold and copper coins (second to third centuries CE), and their Saka satrapal subordinates extended their silver *dramma* (i.e. *drachm*) coinage throughout Malwa and Gujarat (third to fourth centuries).

The net effect over time was to thoroughly embed the idea of coinage in the cultural ethos of northwest India, as far east as Mathura, Malwa, and the upper Gangetic plains. So much so that when the Bihar-based Gupta kingdom extended its boundaries throughout Madhyadesha in fourth to fifth century, they adopted *holus-bolus* the Kushan gold *dinara* coinage; and when they further extended their boundaries into Malwa and Gujarat in the fifth century, they adopted the Western Kshatrapa silver *dramma* coinage.

Among the many post-nomadic invaders were one particular tribal group, the Gujjars, who trailed into India in the wake of more powerful invasions (sixth century) and who were initially not particularly successful in the new lands. After taking their pastoral subsistence through Punjab, Sind and Gujarat, they settled in eastern Rajasthan in the seventh century. Wherever they went, they brought the tradition of Sasanian-style silver coins with them, evolving their coinage style and design over time as they took up residence in different localities. One family amongst them took advantage of political opportunity, forming the Pratihara dynasty of Kanauj, expanding their suzerainty eastwards and southwards until they came to the frontiers of the Pala rulers of Bengal and the Rashtrakuta rulers of the Deccan in the eighth to ninth century. They expanded greatly the scope and scale of their (by now) Indo-Sasanian silver coinage, until it became the predominant money form of Hindustan in the eighth through tenth centuries.

Map 8.1, shows the pattern of coin hoard findings of silver *drammas* attributed to Pratihara emperor Bhoja Deva, issued in the ninth century.[28] The more hoards found, the darker the shading. These coins would fall into our category of institutionally-managed money, and more particularly issued by an institution of state. Interestingly, their loosely-defined political boundaries with the Palas and Rashtrakutas became as well a monetary boundary, marking the furthest extent of double-die struck coinage as the dominant money form in India at the time.

At this point I hasten to add that there was one other money-

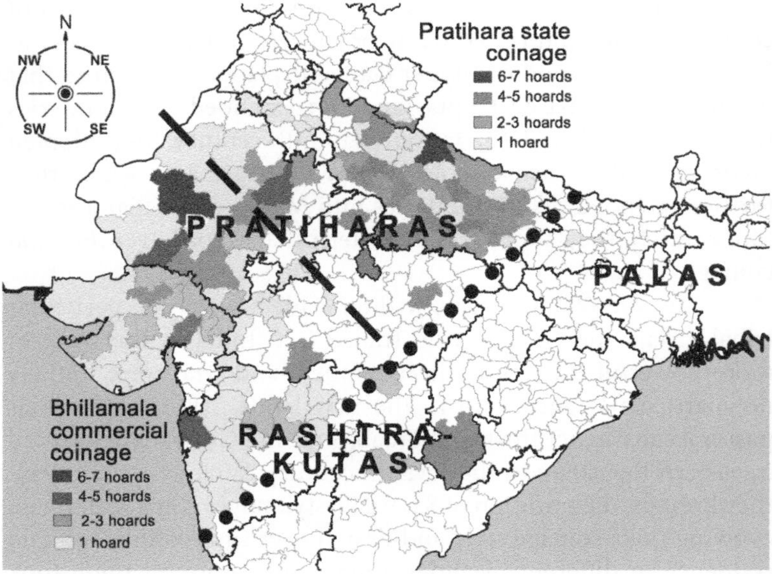


Map 8.1: The distribution of 'state coinage' of the Gurjara-Pratihara empire, *c.* 825 CE (northeast of the dashed line), compared to the distribution of 'commercial coinage' of the Bhillamala merchants in the tenth-eleventh centuries (southwest of the dashed line). The dotted line shows the approximate boundary between the 'hard cash' region (northwest) and the 'cashless' region (southeast). This is also roughly the boundary between wheat- and rice-growing regions.

*Source:* The author, based on official treasure trove reports. The map shows modern administrative boundaries.

form within this tradition, which had a significant impact, and which sits on the commercial community side of the ledger. Map 8.1 also shows the pattern of coin hoard findings of anonymous silver *drammas* (that is, lacking any inscription), called 'Gadhaiya', a Vaisya caste name, attributed to the merchants of Bhillamala or Bhinmal or Srimal in southern Rajasthan/northern Gujarat.[29] Again, the more hoards found, the darker the shading. The map shows the remarkable growth and far-ranging distribution of these *drammas*. Evidently produced by a trading community of that city for their own commercial purposes, it came to be the dominant coinage form of Gujarat and the northern Konkan, circulating well into interior Maharashtra. This despite the fact that those territories were under different political jurisdictions, the Chavadas, Silaharas and Rashtrakutas, respectively. The agents of circulation were the Bhillamala traders, and Ranabir Chakravarti has chronicled the means by which both the traders and their currency insinuated themselves into the local environment of western Maharashtra.[30]

However, this second example of a coinage realm is an exception to the rule, and otherwise the coinage frontier between northwest India and southeast India in the eighth through tenth centuries was fairly well defined (shown by the dotted line in Map 8.1).

## Uncoined Money: The Cowry

At this point it is necessary to pick up the thread mentioned earlier, about the monetary niche of simple money, and specifically the cowry. The role of the cowry in Indian monetary systems has long been recognized, indeed was highlighted in the exchange of views between B.D. Chattopadhyaya and the late R.S. Sharma.[31] However, the tenor of the discussion has verged on the dismissive: cowries are usually pegged as a low-level money serving minor market functions. The truth, I suspect, is quite the opposite. Susmita Basu Majumdar has been overseeing a project to determine the full range of cowry use throughout India, by drawing on excavated material, epigraphic citations, a long historiography, and most importantly by correlating the range of cowry production and use throughout the Indian Ocean and South China Sea. The preliminary findings are that cowries were used to a much greater extent and over a wider tract of Indian territory than has been generally recognized in the literature.[32] One reason for this is a 'blind spot' in archaeological methodology; at many sites cowries have been treated like any other overburden, to be cleared away before the serious work has begun. At other sites, where significant caches of cowries have been found in stratigraphic horizons, they have been left out of reports, and even excavation notes, as not meriting notice.

Figure 8.1 shows a Treasure Trove hoard in the Lucknow Museum, unreported and unpublished. As might be expected, the cowries were in large numbers, as befits a modestly-valued money form.

In contrast to the famine of official notices, the overwhelming use of cowries in times past is a staple of oral history and figures of speech throughout India. Even today, cashier's tills in older establishments will sometimes have a few cowries tucked away in

Fig. 8.1: Treasure Trove Hoard of Cowry Shells in the State Museum, Lucknow. Photo courtesy Prof. Pratipal Bhatia.

the corner for good luck. And of course the ritual of cremation still involves payment of cowries to those officiating and serving. Sanjay Garg has published letters in the National Archives from the District Collectors of Sylhet to the Honourable East India Company, pointing out that they received the district's annual revenue demand wholly in cowries, and undertook considerable expense to process, store, and convey the cowries to the seat of government.[33]

Indeed, this level of transaction can be linked to state systems. Sayantani Pal in her contribution to this volume notes the Sena copperplates mention a unit of account called the *kapardika purana*, that is a notional value of 32 *ratis* silver to be actually paid in cowries. Likewise Kalhana's *Rajatarangini* explains in some detail the functioning of Kashmir's state bureaucracy on the basis of paddy, cowries, and copper coins.[34]

While there are many sources of cowries in the Indian Ocean and the China Sea, Indian markets since ancient times have preferred almost exclusively the small smooth white cowry produced in the Maldive Islands. Hogendorn has shown that it is the special condition of high average water temperature and high-angle solar radiation in the Maldives that produce the smallest cowries. [35] There is a large and growing literature on the cowry trade between various Indian regions and the Maldives, which need only be referenced here.[36]

Blanchard has shown that the Indian Ocean experienced sustained periods of climatic change, when wind systems and ocean currents departed from the norm.[37] The Maldivian cowry was extremely sensitive to variations in temperature and salinity, and although there have not as yet been detailed studies of the phenomenon, it is clear that production must have varied considerably over decades and centuries, depending on climatic and oceanic conditions.

There were two aspects to this variation. The first were global climatic long cycles, such as the Medieval Warm Period of the seventh to tenth centuries (that enabled Nordic colonization of Greenland), or the 'Little Ice Age' of the seventeenth and eighteenth centuries (that froze the Thames and Dutch canals each winter). The Indian Ocean effects of these global changes have been usefully graphed by Beaujard.[38]

The second was the so-called Indian Ocean Dipole, a shorter-term phenomenon influencing current direction and ocean surface temperatures. The literature on this phenomenon, dating back only to the 1990s, does not yet seem to have any historical precision, at least as concerns the pre-modern period.[39] The Dipole is likely, however, to have been a factor in short-term cowry supply, and may have been one reason for the wild swing in market prices, noted by Ibn Batuta.[40]

Given these two phenomena, however, it is safe to assume considerable variations in cowry shell production during the period of this study, which would influence the availability of Maldivian monetary cowries throughout the Indian Ocean. As climatic modelling is further refined, and a body of climate history evidence is accumulated from various techniques like coral sampling, it is to be hoped that the economic impact of cowry production variations will be better traced.

Recently, Thomas Sargent has drawn attention to the difficulty of servicing all levels of an industrial society with efficient money, which he aptly called the 'big problem of small change'.[41] With cowries, it would seem that India at various stages of its history, has effectively dealt with the problem, even creating linkages with the macro level of state finance.

To state the obvious, cowries were imported and put into circulation by non-state actors. Commercial elements sought out the cowries at their source in the Maldives, landed them at Indian ports, and sold them into the market. Market demand caused the cowries to be carried far inland, to be used widely in the Gangetic plains and even at one point in landlocked mountainous Yunnan (an aspect discussed more fully in the contribution by Bin Yang, elsewhere in this volume). While Sanskrit texts cite a fixed value for the cowries vis-à-vis other money forms, in fact they varied widely in their local value depending on supply and demand and distance from the sea. Earlier the role of institutions in assuring an operative money was discussed; here is a concrete example of the associated phenomenon, the role of communities.

## Applying the Monetary Model to Bengal

Our knowledge of early medieval Bengal's monetary system derives from the archaeological record, notably excavation reports, copper plate inscriptions and treasure trove hoards; as well as the Sanskrit literature and travellers' accounts. Excavation (Mahasthangarh, Wari-Bateshwar, Chandraketugarh, etc.) has uncovered evidence of widespread coin use in the ancient period from the Mauryans to the Guptas but nothing after the Gaudas and later Guptas (e.g. early seventh century). As B.N. Mukherjee phrased it, 'No metallic money was coined in the major portion of the Pala or Sena kingdom',[42] not a diminution of local coin manufacture and use but its disappearance altogether. Cowries aplenty, but (barring rare ceremonial issues), no coins whatever in Pala or Sena Bengal, from ca. 650 to 1200.[43]

Sayantani Pal shows in this volume that studies of the land-grant copper plates vividly demonstrate the transformation of the monetary system, moving from prices in (Gupta) gold *dinaras*, to a money of account, the *kapardika purana*. It seems that this money of account performed most of the classically understood functions of money: as Wicks remarks, 'The solution adopted by the Senas was to utilize the cowrie as a standard of value, as it had performed as a measure of value and medium of exchange in the region since at least Gupta times.'[44]

It is not that the money supply contracted; what is witnessed in Pala/Sena Bengal was not a partially functioning system servicing only quotidian transactions. The confusion might arise because of the contrast with the preceding Gupta period, in which gold *dinaras*, silver *drammas*, copper coins and cowries all seem to have had a role in the economy. While scholars of the period do not address the issue, it is clear that the Gupta system was highly stratified denominationally: gold, silver and copper serviced different levels of transactions. Gold coins are cited in the price of land transfers, but, as Faxien noted, 'In buying and selling commodities they use cowries'[45] (or, an alternative translation), 'As a medium of exchange they use cowry shells'.[46] Perhaps inevitably for a Buddhist monk of modest means, he failed to remark the use of metal coins.

Such denominational stratification was noticeable even in the transition from the Gupta coinage system to the Pala money of account system. In Pundravardhana (northwest Bengal) in 478, land was paid for with *dinaras* provided by provincial officials,[47] i.e. in Gupta gold coins. About a century later in northern Bengal, a village yielding a tax of 45 *karshapanas* (over an unspecified period of years) was sold for the price of 1000 *churnikas*.[48] The *karshapana* was the same as the *purana*, that is a Mauryan silver punchmarked coin, last issued in that region about the third century BCE.[49] Hence it was unlikely to be still in physical circulation; it must have become an accounting unit, worth according to D.C. Sircar, 1,280 cowries in actual cash.[50] The *churnika*, according to B.D. Chattopadhayaya, was a monetary measure comprising a thousand cowries.[51] So already the *dinara* (initially an actual coin, but increasingly an accounting measure), was starting to be superseded by lesser-value units of obsolete silver and actual circulating cowry shells. Finally, as Sayantani Pal has shown, the two merged into a money of account called the *kapardika purana*.

The money of the Palas and Senas as reflected in land grants is fully explored elsewhere in this volume, and will be taken here as read. Suffice to say, a broad variety of transactions were accounted in a common unit, but cleared, when necessary, in bags of cowries. There can be no doubt that, although legal texts mention fixed rates of exchange, the market price of cowries (the relationship of physical cowries to units of account) must have varied considerably over time and according to the locality of the transaction. In this, merchants and bankers acted as providers of a medium of exchange which underlay the official standard of value.

Although land grant records make up the bulk of our evidence for the operation of this 'money of account' monetary system, that was not the only economic sector mentioned in the copperplates. Ranabir Chakravarti notes that the inscriptions of the Palas and Senas 'invariably refer to the cavalry'. He adds, 'It is well known that fine war horses were never bred in Bengal and Bihar.' They were 'presented as tribute to the Pala monarch by many rulers of the northern quarter.'[52] This helps illuminate a further aspect of the 'cashless' system: some critical elements of supply like horses, were received in kind. In effect, they were on the revenue side of the ledger rather than the expenditure side, and the need for 'hard cash' (in this sector at least) was averted.

This brings us full circle to the question of the economic structure of the Pala, Sena (and perhaps Rashtrakuta) realms. It is satisfactorily established that advanced agriculturally-based civilizations developed complex political and administrative structures, fully capable of governing considerable tracts of country, using an institutional approach to money for purposes of revenue and taxation, expenditure, salaries, and military expenses. To give this greater detail, this volume has investigated the evidence for monies of account, especially references to obsolete or alien money forms in the land records and grants of the period.

In the end the question hinges on the economic functioning of a kingdom of imperial status that felt no need for high-value gold coinage. Given our comments above on denominational stratification, and given the fact that most other transactions were well serviced by the combination of moneys of account and cowries, the question is reduced to the relationship of the Pala regime to its powerful functionaries. The copperplates refer to an impressively articulated hierarchy of administrators from the provincial level down to the village level. What might have been the financial and material relations between these persons and the Pala/Sena king, remains a fascinating and challenging study for the future.

This raises the other question, of course, of how such a system responded to situations where either hard money (coins) or precious metals were required? The supply of horses was not the only import trade necessary for the maintenance of Pala and Sena power. Many other commodities that were needed for both military and elite life, were obtainable only through trade channels over long distances. How were they obtained? The following section will consider this conundrum.

## How did a 'Cashless' Economy Conduct its Trade?

In the early medieval period, Bengal experienced both the expansion and densification of its overland and maritime connections. On its northern border lay the powerful Tibetan kingdom; in the high mountains bounding the great rivers just beyond its eastern frontier lay in succession the Nanzhao and Dali kingdoms (Yunnan); to its immediate southeast in succession were the kingdoms of Sri Kshetra, Tagaung and Bagan (Myanmar); and beyond all these lay the great Tang empire (China). In the Bay of Bengal, shipping routes linked Bengal to Arakan, Srivijaya (Indonesia), Champa (Vietnam), and southern Chinese ports. Slightly later, Bengal enjoyed maritime communication with the Khmer empire (Thailand and Cambodia). These myriad channels brought Bengal into contact with Persian and Arab merchants, Srivijayan embassies, Chinese merchants and pilgrims. It also spread Bengali culture and religious orientations throughout Indonesia and Indochina.

In contrast, the later medieval period was one of marked change for Bengal, both domestically and internationally. The government passed from the Senas into the hands of Turks of Central Asian origin. To bolster their rule these newcomers encouraged the immigration of large numbers of Persian, Khurasani, and Afghan cavalrymen, soldiers, administrators, religious leaders and jurists. This brought not only a new legal and revenue structure, but also changed the expectation of the elite as to the form and function of the kingdom's monetary system.

In this later period, many of the erstwhile kingdoms on Bengal's borders were absorbed into the expanding Yuan empire, directly or through imposition of subsidiary status. Later still, Ming fleets reached Bengal and Chinese seafarers and merchants supplanted the Arabs in the Bay of Bengal. Bengali merchants settled in number in the ports of northern Sumatra and the Malacca Straits. By the end of the late medieval period, the Portuguese had seized Melaka and European merchants started to have a greater impact. Indeed, the arrival of the Europeans heralded the transition from the medieval to the early modern eras.

Prior to the thirteenth century, however, the Pala/Sena 'cashless' economy thrived, which raises the question of how it interfaced with the maritime trading world. While there is some evidence for the activities of Bengali traders themselves, they seem to have been noticed mainly in the later medieval period, rather than earlier. Most mentions of ocean-going traders in the early medieval period concern 'foreigners' rather than Bengalis. Of course, the pattern of trade in the Indian Ocean changed considerably over time. These changes were not so much in the principal products that were traded but rather in trade routes and the merchants who undertook the trading.[53]

In the ninth century, Arab merchants ventured in their ships all the way to China and had a considerable presence in Chinese ports. The merchant Sulaiman, who visited 'Canfu' (the port of Xifu, the present Hangzhou), before 851, noted that 'Arabs' had frequented the port prior to Islam, and that by his time, Iraqis were active. A mosque had been built and Muslims were allowed to dispense their own justice.[54]

In the eleventh century, the Cholas of southern India managed to encompass completely the centre of this oceanic axis, by extending their naval might in support of their commercial guilds, from the Maldives in the west to the Malay Peninsula, Sumatra and Java in the east.[55] Radhika Seshan explores this southern India phenomenon in her contribution.

By the thirteenth century the Chinese themselves brought their goods as far as India's Malabar coast, where Arab merchants made their purchases for onward shipment to the Red Sea.[56] So there became in effect two different trading spheres in the Indian Ocean: that operating from east Africa, the Red Sea and the Persian Gulf to India's west coast ports, and that operating from China, Java/Sumatra and Pegu to India's east coast ports, Bengal, Sri Lanka and India's southern tip.[57]

The traders' memoirs, to the extent they survive, tell of their enforced stay in Indian ports following the conclusion of their business, while they waited for favourable winds to continue their journeys or return whence they came. Over time it was found expedient to settle in the ports themselves, in order to make best use of local 'down-time'. [58]

So for example, in the early medieval period, permanent Arab communities grew both in Gujarat (the Bohras) and in northern Malabar (the Mapillas).[59] Both communities survive to the present day; the former are still noted as business-oriented. Chittagong historians mention an Arab presence, confirmed by Sulaiman, that has echoes in the present day local dialect.[60] According to Qanungo, 'The *Arakanese Chronicles* trace the Muslim contact with this region back to as early as the eighth century AD.'[61] Not all the Arab traders reaching India were Muslim: Arabic-speaking Jewish traders based in Fustat (Cairo) and Aden established themselves in the Malabar coastal ports late in the first millennium, and had a well-established trade by the dawn of the thirteenth century.[62] From Sasanian times onwards, Iraqi Christians became active in the trade between the Persian Gulf and southern India. The Christian community of Socotra near the mouth of the Red Sea was likewise engaged. Malekandathil notes, 'When the foreign Christians from West Asia were involved in the overseas trade of Quilon, the indigenous Christians engaged in spice production in the hinterland. . . .'[63]

These communities, and others, highlight the tremendous diversity of the Indian Ocean merchants as a class, and make evident the complexity of the customs, attitudes, and value systems that shaped their operations. More specifically, merchants carried with them important assumptions about money. As an example, merchants from Song China (ninth through twelfth centuries) were accustomed to a monetary system nominally accounted in strings of copper cash, but where paper money served as the circulating medium.[64] By the late thirteenth century, succeeding merchants from Yuan China came from a similar environment (copper, paper money), but in which the Mongol predilection for silver bullion was becoming institutionalized.[65] Fifteenth-century Ming China initially continued this monetary approach, relying on copper cash, paper money and silver bullion from new mining ventures. However, by 1430 the minting of copper cash was suspended. Chinese merchants would thereafter have a predilection for silver.[66]

Likewise, from the tenth to the thirteenth centuries, Arab and Jewish merchants from Aden were accustomed to Yemeni 'Maliki' gold dinars; while from the late thirteenth century onwards they customarily used Egyptian Mamluk gold *dinars*, silver *dirhams* that were highly debased, and copious copper *falus*.[67] In Yemen, these traders encountered the small Rasulid silver *dirhams*, produced from a number of mints until the turn of the fifteenth century.[68] For the Indian ocean trade, these coins were supplemented by Venetian gold *ducats* received in the markets of Alexandria from Europeans.

## The Changing Impact of Indian Ocean Traders on Money

However, it cannot be said that this predilection for familiar trade coinage had an equal impact on the Indian states that were linked into these Indian Ocean trading networks, especially in the case of Bengal. Rila Mukherjee has highlighted both temporal and spatial aspects to this asymmetry: Bengal's maritime trade connections temporarily declined in the late-first, early-second millennia; and throughout the medieval period, Bengal was relatively less attractive to Indian Ocean traders than India's west coast and Sri Lanka. As Mukherjee aptly remarked, 'No Bengal port transformed into [an] emporium,' which she defined as 'a locus or node in a longer network of long distance maritime trade.'[69]

Partly, this was a simple recognition of a geographic imperative: Bengal was far off the main trade axis of China – Southeast Asia – Sri Lanka/Malabar – West Asia. The main entrepôts of this long maritime highway might change over a millennium (Hangzhou to Yangzhou; Srivijaya to Melaka; Cochin to Calicut; Aden to Hormuz), but the economic imperative of the shortest route reigned supreme (Map 8.2).

This asymmetry is reflected in an imbalance in the volume of textual evidence left by the traders themselves. It is modest, even

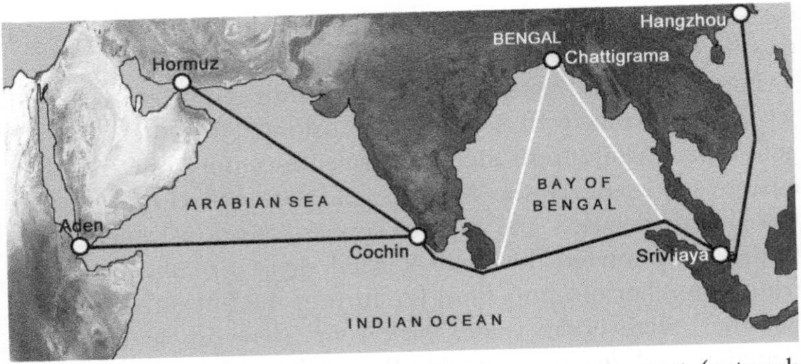


Map 8.2: Medieval Indian Ocean trade routes east to west (network schematic). The main routes are in black; the connections to Bengal in white. Overlay: the author. Underlay: © Google Maps (through its 'fair use' policy).

sparse, for Bengal. In contrast, it is increasingly large and detailed for India's west coast from the ninth century onwards, reaching a crescendo in the fifteenth century just prior to the arrival of the Portuguese.

So, for example, in the pre-1200 period, we have accounts of India's west coast left by disparate trading communities such as the Iraqi Christians, Persian Muslims, and Arab Jews (mentioned above). In the post-1200 period, accounts of commerce on India's west coast were left by an expanding group of travellers representative of the great diversity of international travel in that age. A sampling of those most readily accessible include the Yuan Chinese diplomatic mission in 1281;[70] the Venetian Marco Polo in 1292;[71] the Moroccan Ibn Batuta in 1342;[72] the Ming Chinese Ma Huan in the 1420s;[73] the Venetian Nicolo di Conti in the 1430s;[74] the Ilkhanid ambassador Abdur-Razzak Samarqandi in 1442;[75] the Russian Athanasius Nikitin in 1470;[76] the Genovese di Santo Stefano in 1499;[77] and the Portuguese Tome Pires in 1512-15.[78]

Most of these showed a keen awareness of the precious metals trade and the foreign and local coinages circulating in the Indian markets of their day. Marco Polo noted of Cambay in Gujarat, that 'Merchants come here with many ships and cargoes, but what they chiefly bring is gold, silver and copper.'[79] He said of Thana in the

Konkan, 'The merchants in their ships also import . . . gold, silver, copper.'[80] Visiting the kingdom of Malabar, he said 'The ships that come from the east bring copper in ballast. They also bring hither . . . gold and silver, . . . for which there is a demand here.'[81]

Slightly later, Ibn Batuta wrote, 'We travelled to the city of Calicut, one of the chief harbours of the country of Malabar where people from China, Jawa [Sumatra], Saylan [Ceylon], Mahal [Maldives], Yemen and Fars [Persia] come, and here gather merchants from all quarters of the globe. And the harbour of Calicut is one of the largest in the world... in which there were then thirteen ships of China. ...The China Sea is navigated only by the Chinese ships...'[82]

Ma Huan, who accompanied Ming admiral Zheng He's flotilla in the first half of the fifteenth century, carefully noted the monetary particulars of the three cities the Chinese most frequented:

> The country of little Ko-lan [Quilon]: ...The king uses gold to cast coins; each coin weighs one *fen* on our official steelyard; in general use."[83]
>
> The country of Ko-chih [Cochin]: The king uses gold of ninety per cent [fineness] to cast coins for current use; they are called fa-nan [*fanam*].[84]
>
> The country of Ku-li [Calicut]: 'The king uses gold of sixty per cent [fineness] to cast a coin for current use; it is named a pa-nan [*fanam*]. He also makes a coin of silver . . . used for petty transactions.[85]

The Ilkhanid ambassador to Vijayanagar left a vivid description of that state's monetary system: In this country, they have three kinds of money, made of gold mixed with alloy. . . . They cast in pure silver a coin. . . . A copper coin . . . is called *jital*.[86]

Late in the fifteenth century, Hieronimo di Santo Stefano noted, 'I arrived . . . at Cambay. Here I found some Moorish merchants of Alexandria and Damascus, by whom I was assisted with money for my expenses."[87]

As these few quotations vividly show, the foreign merchants themselves both serviced (by their import and sale of coinage metals) and helped shape (by their importation of foreign coins and their participation in the local exchange markets), the monetary systems of the various kingdoms of India's west coast in the later medieval period.

In contrast, the frequency and intensity of coverage of India's east coast, including Bengal, is modest for the first millennium and not a great deal more plentiful until the fourteenth century. In the earlier period, the accounts of Bengal are mostly left by Chinese Buddhist pilgrims like Yijing *c.* 671-95;[88] Arab merchants like Sulaiman about 850;[89] and an unnamed emissary of the Javan king Balaputradeva also ca. 850.[90] In the later medieval period, aside from visits by Ibn Batuta and Ma Huan (mentioned above), very little seaborne visitation is recorded until the Portuguese period in the 1500s, when the tempo of written accounts of Bengal rose sharply.

Given these realities of the structure of maritime trade in the Indian Ocean, it would seem that during the early medieval Pala-Sena period, there was little opportunity for foreign merchants to make demands of, or even to interface with, the 'cashless' monetary system of Bengal. The maritime trade we are aware of, reinforced this system through the import of cowry shells from the Maldive Islands, in a rice/shell countertrade.

Exceptionally, as Suchandra Ghosh has pointed out in this volume, the extreme southeast of Bengal, beyond Pala or Sena authority, did operate a gold and silver coinage-based economy in the mid–first millennium. This Samatata and Harikela coinage was contemporary with (and influenced by) similar coinage-based systems of the Chandras in Arakan, the Pyus and Mons in Burma, Dvaravati in Thailand and the early Khmer in Cambodia.[91]

Earlier in this volume, Rila Mukherjee has highlighted a striking convergence of monetary usages later in the first millennium: the adoption of 'cashless' monetary systems by the successive Pala and Sena realms in Bengal (from the ninth century), by Bagan in Burma (also ninth century), and the Khmer of Thailand and Cambodia (about the ninth century).[92] Some commentators have taken this as evidence of the general disappearance of silver in the trade of the eastern Indian Ocean. However there is a danger of circular reasoning here. A closer look suggests that the lack of coins was due to conscious monetary policy rather than a response to a commercial precious metals shortfall. Bagan, for example, continued to rely heavily on silver in its exchange transactions, but not in a coined form.[93]

It is noticeable that these three empires were all dependent on the revenues from rice-based agriculture, and all used paddy prominently (but not exclusively) in their settling of accounts. One wonders whether the great monetary cycle had gone full circle: these settled agricultural societies increasingly relied on institutional forms of money, at a time (ninth-tenth century) when Islam was being borne across the seas by Arab traders. The foreign business communities brought with them a commercial system that relied not on great indigenous institutions of royal and official patronage, but on their freely-exchangeable gold *dinars*, silver *dirhams* and copper *fals*. Did the rulers of Bengal, Bagan and Angkor seek to neutralize this new influence by avoiding coinage altogether, in an attempt to bring foreign merchants within the sway of their domestic power? It is well beyond the scope of this modest chapter to investigate in any detail the political and economic drivers leading to such a significant shift in governance models. Suffice to say that there is every possibility that the exchange of information within the Buddhist world extended well beyond religious precepts into the minutiae of rulership norms. As guardian of Buddhism's holy places in the ninth and tenth century, Bengal may have influenced other great Buddhist states in the realm of money and governance. Alternately, it could have been the recipient of those ideas from further southeast. Only a more vigorous consideration of the historiography and the available evidence can address this intriguing coincidence.

## Bengal's Transition from 'Cashless' to Coin

Following the establishment of the Bengal Sultanate in 1206, a silver coin was introduced to complement the cowries in circulation. Early attempts at a gold currency were abandoned about 1220, and copper coinage was never issued as cowries filled this need satisfactorily.

By 1500, Bengal's silver coin had displaced the cowry as the major form of circulating medium. Sutapa Sinha's contribution to this volume examines the long evolution and growth of the Sultanate's monetary system. During the transition, Ma Huan recorded the fifteenth century Chinese treasure fleets:

The country of Pang-ko-la [Bangala or Bengal]: Setting sail from the country of Sumen-ta-la [Samudra in northern Sumatra] . . . you come first to Che-ti-chiang [Chittagong].[94]

The king of the country uses silver to cast a coin named t'ang-ch'ieh [*tanka*]; . . . in every purchase and sale they all use this coin for calculating prices in petty transactions. The cowrie goes by the foreign name of k'ao-li [*kauri*], in trading they calculate in units.[95]

Later medieval Bengal depended equally on horse cavalry, elephants, and a riverine navy to maintain its independence and influence over neighbouring states. Through a succession of ports in the ever-shifting delta river system, notably Sonargaon and Chittagong, Bengal maintained maritime links with Arakan and Pegu in Burma and Melaka on the Malaya peninsula.

This enabled it to maintain a relatively constant supply of silver bullion from inland sources in Yunnan and upper Burma via Pegu and Arakan.[96] This silver was clearly not imported in the form of coinage, since contemporary Bagan relied on a money of account, the *klyap*, settled in silver ingots or other commodities.[97] In effect, by the dawn of the modern age, their monetary situations had reversed: early on, Burma went from a coin-using system to a 'cashless' economy; somewhat later, Bengal went from a 'cashless' to a coinage system. The relative dynamics of these transitions, rooted in the relationship of rulership to revenue, would make an interesting study on its own.

It must not be imagined, however, that the long slow monetary evolution of Bengal's money from 'cashless' to coinage, was a smooth one; the supply of silver was subject to much variance over time. It is known that Yunnan's mines experienced periods of strong production as well as periods of relative decline, between the thirteenth and sixteenth centuries.[98] As well, the demand of other centres like China for silver, went through episodes that impacted on the availability of Yunnanese silver for trade to the west.[99]

Closely interlinked with the bullion trade was the horse trade (mentioned above in respect to the early medieval Pala realm). Unlike the contemporary Sultanates in the fourteenth and fifteenth centuries which were able to import Khurasani horses overland

(Delhi Sultanate) or to import Arabian horses by sea (Gujarat, Bahmanids and Vijayanagara), Bengal had no such West Asian trade links. However, the mountain ponies of Yunnan and Tibet proved surprisingly fit as cavalry mounts, and a brisk trade grew up.[100] This Bengal-Tibet trade is examined in detail by M.N. Rajesh elsewhere in this book.

Indeed, the Chinese name for the northern trade route from Yunnan via Tibet to Bengal, was *Dian-Zang cha-ma gudao* or 'Yunnan-Tibet Tea-Horse Ancient Road'. The western road out of Yunnan was the *Dian-Mian-Yin gudao*, or 'Yunnan-Burma-India ancient road', along which both gold and silver bullion travelled from mines to market.[101]

So robust was this trade that Bengal Sultans sent these horses onwards to the Chinese emperor as gifts accompanying their embassies.[102]

In the later medieval period, the cowry trade, still in the hands of private merchants, continued to thrive. In the 1340s, Ibn Batuta visited the islands and recorded,

> All transactions take place in this country by means of the cowrie. One hundred thousand [cowries] are called *bustu*. They are used for buying and selling at the rate of four *bustus* for one gold dinar. Sometimes the cowries depreciate, and in that case even ten bustus can be had for one dinar. They are sold to the inhabitants of Bengal for rice, because the cowries are also current in Bengal.[103]

The frequency of use of this sea route was confirmed by Ibn Batuta himself, who sailed directly from the Maldives to Bengal, making landfall at the port of Chittagong, and visiting the upriver cities of Sylhet and Sonargaon.[104]

It is beyond the scope of this chapter to look in any detail at the temporal cycles of precious metal plenty and shortage in the various nodes of the Indian Ocean trade. However, there are some obvious synchronicities that are interesting. One of these is the 'bullion famine' of the first half of the fifteenth century. Haider pointed out that the acute shortage of silver in European countries noted by Spufford, Day, Munro and others for the period prior to 1460, was concurrent with a monetary silver shortage in Gujarat and Delhi.[105]

In fact the phenomenon was more widespread, with one significant exception. Studies of coin quantities in the numismatic trade, rather than in institutional collections, show that in Delhi, Jaunpur, Gujarat, and the Bahmani kingdom, there was little silver coinage between 1400 and 1450, while the same was true for Malwa in 1400-40. The sole exception was Bengal, where the plentiful issues of silver *tankas* continued unabated in the 1400-1450 period.[106]

Now Atwell has shown in a striking graph that in contemporary China, the early Ming encouragement of silver remittances from 1403 onwards, bore fruit as early as 1410, with silver receipts rising to a quarter million *taels* per annum for the following decades. He also shows that the level of remittances collapsed in the late 1440s.[107] Was this linked to developments further west? Atwell notes, '. . . governments from London to Cairo were complaining bitterly about a 'flight of bullion to the East' . . . silver coins were becoming increasingly difficult to find in parts of northern India and Java. . . . Yet silver appears to have been readily available along the major overland and maritime trade routes to China.'[108]

From our analysis above, it will be immediately recognized that what is under discussion here is the flow of *Levantine* bullion eastward to India and ultimately to China. It is noticeable that the great Ming 'treasure ship' voyages of the period 1405-33 frequented Malabar and Aden earlier and more frequently than Bengal.[109] Bengal suffered no 'silver famine' during this period, which means that it was likely not dependent on silver from the western Indian Ocean. Its Bay of Bengal sources, ultimately from Yunnan and Burma, remained intact throughout the first half of the fifteenth century. This highlights once more, the different nature of the maritime trade on India's western and eastern coasts.

It appears, then, that, while the monetary system of the Palas and Senas was dependent on only one aspect of Indian Ocean commerce (the cowry trade), the cowry- and coinage-based monetary system of the succeeding Bengal Sultanate was closely linked into the upper Bay of Bengal silver trade. It was not, however, as deeply influenced by the many communities of Indian

Ocean traders as were the contemporary kingdoms of India's west coast.

## The Triumph of Cash

The above discussion has demonstrated the vitality of Bengal's 'cashless' system in the early medieval period, but also highlighted the gradual supplanting of this system by a 'hard cash' alternative in the later medieval period. It has to be recognized that this transition occurred over a broader canvas than we have painted here: by the mid fourteenth century, under the influence of the expanding Delhi Sultanate, most of India had adopted a monetary system based on coinage. This in turn influenced the patterns of the coinage metal trade, both overland and maritime. The question of trade volumes, however, does not rest alone on coinage and metals; as noted earlier, the 'sinews of war' included horses for the rapidly expanding cavalry of expanding and defending kingdoms alike.

The result was that, in the period 1200-1500, bullion and horses were India's two most consistently-demanded goods in both overland and maritime trade (as opposed to the spices and textiles that were the principal focus for foreign traders). Indeed, they were often closely intertwined. Being related to military power and hence ultimately to political power, the trade in both can usefully be differentiated from the universal trade in luxury products for urban elites. It must be recognized, however, that there were sharp shocks to the trading system over time, and marked divergences in established trading patterns, favouring new routes, suppliers and merchant networks.

The demand for monetary commodities was created by the internal logic and dynamics of each monetary system, the structure of which can fairly be said to have been oriented to domestic political, social and economic concerns. So cowries were in high demand throughout the period of this study in Orissa and Bengal, and perhaps in the twelfth century in Gujarat, and not necessarily anywhere else.

Likewise, in addition to the demands of the manufacturing trades for copper, and the demands of the jewellery trade for silver and gold, the monetary systems of the various kingdoms of India each created specific demands for monetary metals. Most significantly from our perspective, in the later medieval period, the progressive adoption of a dual-denomination but monometallic monetary system (i.e. cowries and silver coins), caused Bengal to place significant demands on the silver trade of the northern Bay of Bengal hinterland, as well as seaborne trade to and from the southeast. This in turn led to a considerable exchange with inland Yunnan, as has been investigated in some detail by Bin Yang in this volume and other publications.

As we have seen, for the rest of India, the supply by overseas traders of these metals was geographically and temporally differentiated. Copper was in great demand all along India's west coast in the late medieval period, being the basis of low-value coinage in the Delhi, Gujarat, and Bahmani sultanates. In the latter kingdom, the issue of copper coinage was prodigious. Traders from Aden as well as China brought copper as ballast, to be sold profitably into the markets in port cities. In contrast, in Bengal there was no demand at all for copper for monetary purposes, prior to 1538.

Likewise, gold was mined in southern India, and for this reason was the mainstay of the monetary systems of southern kingdoms both before and during the period of our study. However, it would appear local supply was never adequate to meet demand, so foreign traders found it profitable to import gold, especially into Malabar ports; this is mentioned many times in traders' accounts. Foreign gold coins did not circulate as money in Indian kingdoms; where they have been found in hoards, it is evident that they were imported as bullion, having become obsolete or undervalued in their places of issue.

In the early medieval period, silver had been predominant in the Gurjara-Pratihara realms of north and west India, while Gujarati trading communities created base silver coinages that circulated far into the Deccan. The Rashtrakutas had virtually no coined money; the whys and wherefores of their monetary system have yet to be researched in detail. Further south, south Indian regimes used gold coinages; the Cholas were the first south Indian dynasty to support the use of gold, silver and copper simultaneously.

In the later medieval period, silver remained by far the dominant precious metal in north India and the Deccan. But there were very different paths that silver took to satisfy this demand. Merchants from the Red Sea and the Persian Gulf brought silver whenever they could; there was a voracious appetite for it in Cambay, which serviced the monetary systems of Delhi, Gujarat and Malwa. In addition to raw bullion, there is evidence that Rasulid coins were brought from Yemen, and Ilkhanid coins from Persia and Iraq. Again, these did not circulate in India, but were tendered at the mints for conversion to local coin, as we learned from the memoirs of the Delhi mint assayer.

The pattern in eastern India, notably Bengal, was quite different. Here, merchants brought silver bullion from Melaka, Pegu and Arakan into Bengal's ports, where there was an insatiable demand for monetary purposes, growing stronger from the thirteenth to the sixteenth centuries. The ultimate sources of this metal were the mines of Yunnan and upper Burma, but the proportion of silver that entered India overland was probably less that that carried by maritime trade.

During this period, foreign traders, and writers who used traders as their sources, remarked on the tendency of gold and silver to gravitate to India, but not re-merge. Haider notes, The Il-Khanid historian, Wassaf, while describing the characteristic features of India . . . in the early fourteenth century, marvelled at the Indian exports . . . which were traded against gold and silver. . . . He also added that this stock of precious metals acquired through trade was never exported out of the country.[110]

In this way, the emerging coinage-based monetary systems of India established a new symbiosis with the trading patterns of the greater Indian Ocean World. The stage was set for the arrival of the Portuguese and other European traders, and the irruption of New World Silver into the Indian Ocean.

## Conclusion

In summary, we might say that money in any society is a social convention, but in advanced societies it is also an institutional arrangement to measure and to settle debt. Debt is a form of obligation, but not the only one; other obligations include those of family, community, and state. In ancient and medieval times, service to the state was a highly ritualized and institutionalized obligation. One way of satisfying this obligation, that is one amongst many, was to tender money in the form of taxes, cesses or duties.

When stable institutions of some longevity, reputation and stability were involved, such as temples, monasteries, merchant guilds, or ministries of kingdoms, the clearance of debt could and did often involve book-keeping entries or their analogues. In other circumstances, tangible money such as cowries or coins might be involved, depending on the nature and scale of the transaction. A predilection for the use of coin was characteristic of certain forms of statecraft, or rather of statecraft as practiced by ruling elites of a certain background.

Prior to 1200, many of the major empires and kingdoms of India derived the majority of their state revenue from agricultural taxes, and often relied on intangible moneys of account to administer this system. Notable amongst these in terms of scale and economic power, was Bengal successively under the Palas and Senas (eighth to late twelfth centuries). In these monetary systems, tangible circulating media, where they existed, often comprised huge quantities of cowries, alone or in combination with modest amounts of bullion. Coinages of precious metals, where they existed, were often closely related to trade, its financing and its taxation, or military pay and provisioning.

This monetary orientation helps to illuminate the otherwise murky question of why some states such as the Pratiharas had a proliferate coinage, while other contemporary states such as the Palas, Senas, and Rashtrakutas did not. If we take money more broadly as a marker of economic activity, rather than coinage, we remove some of the ambiguity around this question. Interestingly, we have remarked that from the ninth century, the great agricultural kingdoms of Bagan and the Khmers also managed without coinage.[111] The intriguing possibility was raised that this 'institutional money' approach was part of a response by local rulers to counter the rising influence of the Arab trading network and its reliance on Islamic coinage forms.

Increasingly after 1200, as the Central Asian model of centralized state formation expanded in India, this indigenous mixed monetary system was replaced by a coin-based one (confusingly characterized by the historians as monetization). Hence the Indian demand for coinage metals rose progressively and sharply from the thirteenth to the sixteenth centuries. There were, of course, many variations in this trend, some of which were identified in this chapter.

Finally, we have noted that even with relatively preliminary data it is possible to detect patterns of synchronicity between the Indian Ocean bullion trade's eastern and western termini, moderated by the interposition between east and west of India's demand. This line of investigation seems to hold great promise.

## NOTES

1. See e.g. Jonathon Chiu and Tsz-Nga Wong, 'On the Essentiality of E-Money', Bank of Canada Staff Working Paper 2015-43, pp. 1-69.
2. 'Money is any asset that is widely accepted as a means of making payments or settling debts' – Bank of Canada, *Backgrounder: Money,* July 2012, p. 1.
3. 'Writing World History II: A Monetary History of Early Medieval Greater Bengal', Institut de Chandernagor, West Bengal, 27 February-1 March 2014. I am grateful to Prof. Rila Mukherjee, at that time Director of the Institut, for arranging and hosting this panel.
4. To name but a few: Joe Cribb, 'Money as Metaphor I (the Origins of Money and Coinage)', *Numismatic Chronicle,* vol. 165, pp. 417-38; Neill Ferguson, *The Ascent of Money,* New York: Penguin, 2008; David Graeber, *Debt: The First 5,000 Years*, Brooklyn: Melville House, 2011.
5. Given theoretical credence by Ludwig von Mises, *The Theory of Money and Credit,* Indianapolis: Liberty Fund, 1980, pp. 44-5.

6. 'Despite their lack of knowledge of money, it was very near the walls of Troy that money was born. It was here . . . that humans first produced coins.' Jack Weatherford, *The History of Money*, New York: Crown Publishers, 1997, p. 29.
7. Gareth Dale, '"Marketless Trading in Hammurabi's Time": A Re-Appraisal', *Journal of the Economic and Social History of the Orient*, vol. 56, 2013, p. 180.
8. Joe Cribb, 'The Origins of Money, Evidence from the Ancient Near East and Egypt', in Guido Crapanzano (ed.), *La Banca Premonitale.* Milan, 2004, pp. 4-13; Glyn Davies, *A History of Money from Ancient Times to the Present Day*, Cardiff: University of Wales Press, 2006, pp. 50-1. Dale, 'The Origins of Money', makes the case that while these were markets which utilized money, they were not capitalist in that there was no investment oriented to gaining profits.
9. Dale, 'The Origins of Money', pp. 168-9.
10. Although the documents of the Cairo Geniza make it clear that overseas merchants in the medieval Indian Ocean carried debts between them 'on the books', for considerable periods before clearing accounts by means of coinage payment. S.D. Goitein and M.A. Friedman, *India Traders of the Middle Ages: Documents from the Cairo Geniza*, Leiden: Brill, 2008; rpt. 2011.
11. '"Money," said Keynes in his *Treatise*, "like certain other essential elements in civilisation, is a far more ancient institution than we were taught to believe some few years ago. Its origins are lost in the mists when the ice was melting, and may well stretch back into . . . some Eden of Central Asia (1930, 1, 13)". It was from this lost Eden that money and banking . . . originated.' Davies, *A History of Money*, p. 49.
12. The Achaemenid silver coinage was limited to Ionia in West Asia. In the empire's centre, the first coinage was struck by Alexander who produced silver tetradrachms throughout the former Achaemenid realm, as did the successor Seleucid regime. However, as Dale notes, 'Some Assyriologists claim that silver, as far back as the third millennium, assumed the mantle of the principal definition of economic value, and that it was regularly exchanged for other commodities—and not only in long-distance or high-value trade. . . . Silver was employed for pensatory payments (payments by weight) and in the incurrence and discharge of debts, but was never coined.' Dale, 'The Origins of Money', p. 170.
13. An exception would be D.D. Kosambi, 'On the Origin and Develop-

ment of Silver Coinage in India', *Current Science*, no. 9, Sept. 1941, pp. 395-400, reprinted in D.D. Kosambi, *Indian Numismatics*, New Delhi: Orient Longman, 1981, pp. 85-94.
14. Romila Thapar, *Early India from the Origins to AD 1300*, New Delhi: Penguin Books, 2003, pp. 79-88.
15. Randall Law, *Inter-Regional Interaction and Urbanism in the Ancient Indus Valley*. Kyoto: Research Institute for Humanity and Nature, 2011.
16. Ibid., pp. 77-8.
17. Kosambi, 'On the Origin', p. 86.
18. Rajni Nanda, *The Early History of Gold in India*, New Delhi: Munshiram Manoharlal, 1992, pp. 118-20.
19. Joe Cribb, *The Indian Coinage Tradition: Origins, Continuity & Change*. Nashik: IIRNS Publications, 2005, p. 60.
20. Graeber, *Debt: The First 5,000 Years*, pp. 228-37.
21. Robert Tye, 'Gyges' Magic Ring? The Origin of Coinages and Open Societies', pamphlet published by the author, York, 2013. Available on www.academia.edu
22. Leslie Kurke, *Coins, Bodies, Games and Gold: The Politics of Meaning in Archaic Greece*, Princeton: Princeton University Press, 1999, p. 12. More fully discussed on pp. 6-23, 314.
23. Richard von Glahn, *The Economic History of China, from Antiquity to the Nineteenth Century*. Cambridge: Cambridge University Press, 2016, pp. 62-4.
24. Ranabir Chakravarti, *Exploring Early India up to c. AD 1300*, New Delhi: Macmillan, 2010, pp. 109-14.
25. Parmeshwari Lal Gupta, *Coins*, New Delhi: National Book Trust, 1969 (numerous reprints to 2016), p. 10.
26. P.L. Gupta and T.R. Hardaker, *Punchmarked Coins of the Indian Subcontinent: Magadha-Mauryan Series*, revd. edn., Mumbai: IIRNS Publications, 2014, Map 3, p. 16.
27. Kautilya, *Arthashastra*. R. Shamasastry (tr.), Bangalore: Government Press, 1915, Book II, *The Duties of Government Superintendents*.
28. John S. Deyell, *Living Without Silver: The Monetary History of Early Medieval North India*, New Delhi: Oxford University Press, 1990; rpt. 1999, pp. 26-8. More recently, see K.K. Maheshwari, *Imitations in Continuity: Tracking the Silver Coinage of Early Medieval India*. Mumbai: IIRNS Publications, 2010, pp. 255-76.
29. Deyell, *Living Without Silver*, pp. 112-24; Maheshwari, *Imitations in Continuity*, pp. 77-97.

30. Ranabir Chakravarti, 'Trade at Mandapikas in Early Medieval North India', in D.N. Jha (ed.), *Society and Ideology in India: Essays in Honour of Prof. R.S. Sharma,* New Delhi: Manohar, 2006. Reprinted in Ranabir Chakravarti, *Trade and Traders in Early Indian Society*, New Delhi: Manohar, 2002, rpt. 2007.
31. B.D. Chattopadhyaya, 'Currency in Early Bengal', *Journal of Indian History*, vol. 55, 1977, pp. 41-60; R.S. Sharma, *Early Medieval Indian Society: A Study in Feudalism,* New Delhi: Orient Longman, 2003, pp. 127-8.
32. Susmita Basu Majumdar and Sharmishtha Chatterjee, 'Cowries in Eastern India: Understanding Their Role as Ritual Objects and Money', *Journal of Bengal Art*, vol. 19, 2014, pp. 39-56.
33. Sanjay Garg, 'Non-metallic Currencies of India in Indian Ocean Trade and Economies', in Himanshu Prabha Ray and Edward A. Alpers (eds), *Cross Currents and Community Networks: The History of the Indian Ocean World,* New Delhi: Oxford University Press, 2007, pp. 252-3.
34. Alexander Cunningham, *Coins of Medieval India,* London: Trubner & Sons, 1894, pp. 30-5; Aurel Stein (ed.), Kalhana's *Rājataranginī*, London: Constable, 1900, vol. II, pp. 308-28; S.C. Ray, 'Medium of Exchange in Ancient Kasmira: A Reflection of Contemporary Economic Life', *Journal of the Numismatic Society of India,* vol. XVIII, 1956, pp. 71-5.
35. Jan Hogendorn and Marion Johnson, *The Shell Money of the Slave Trade*, Cambridge, 1986, p. 11.
36. For a fuller bibliography on the monetary role of cowry shells, see John S. Deyell, 'Monetary and Financial Webs: The Regional and International Influence of Pre-modern Bengali Coinage', in Rila Mukherjee (ed.), *Pelagic Passageways: The Northern Bay of Bengal World Before Colonialism*, New Delhi, Primus, 2011, fn 3, p. 305. Most recent is Bin Yang, 'The Rise and Fall of Cowrie Shells: The Asian Story', *Journal of World History*, vol. 22-1, March 2011, pp. 1-26.
37. Ian Blanchard, 'The World of Islam: An Economic and Environmental Analysis', Ch. 3 in *Mining, Metallurgy and Minting,* Stuttgart: Steiner, 2001, pp. 37-102.
38. Philippe Beaujard, *Les mondes de l'océan Indien*, Paris: Armand Colin, 2012, tome 2, Ep. 2: 'Les flux économiques dans le système-monde afro-eurasien (1^er^ – 18^e^ siècles)', p. 574.
39. Li Chongyin, 'The Influence of the Indian Ocean Dipole on Atmo-

spheric Circulation and Climate', *Advances in Atmospheric Sciences*, vol. 18-5, September 2001, pp. 831-43; Nerilie J. Abram et al., 'Seasonal Characteristics of the Indian Ocean Dipole, during the Holocene Epoch', *Nature*, vol. 445, 18 January 2007, pp. 299-302; Nerilie J. Abram et al., 'Evolution of the Southern Annular Mode, during the Past Millennium', *Nature Climate Change*, vol. 4, July 2014, pp. 564-9.

40. Mahdi Husain, tr., *The Rehla of Ibn Batuta*, Baroda: Oriental Institute, 1976, p. 201.
41. Thomas J. Sargent and François R. Velde, *The Big Problem of Small Change*, Princeton: Princeton University Press, 2002.
42. B.N. Mukherjee, *Coins and Currency Systems of Post-Gupta Bengal (c. AD 550-700)*, New Delhi: Munshiram Manoharlal, 1995, p. 54.
43. The Pala realm comprised modern Bihar, West Bengal, and Bangladesh west of the Brahmaputra River. The Part of Modern Bangladesh east of the Meghna River was called variously Samatata or Harikela, and was a distinct monetary realm throughout this period. This is more fully discussed by Suchandra Ghosh in this volume.
44. Robert S. Wicks, *Money, Markets and Trade in Early Southeast Asia: The Development of Indigenous Monetary Systems to AD 1400*, Ithaca: Cornell University, 1992, pp. 99-100.
45. Faxien (Fa-Hsien), *A Record of Buddhistic Kingdoms*, James Legge, tr., Oxford: Clarendon Press, 1886, p. 43.
46. Faxien (Fa-Hsien), *Record of the Buddhist Kingdoms*, Herbert A. Giles, tr., London: Trübner & Co., 1877, p. 30.
47. According to the Kuddalakhata copperplate, Gupta Year 159. Arlo Griffiths, 'New Documents for the Early History of Pundravardhana: Copperplate Inscriptions from the Late Gupta and Early Post-Gupta Periods', *Pratna Samiksha: A Journal of Archaeology*, New Series, vol. 6, 2016, p. 23. I am grateful to Rila Mukherjee for providing this article.
48. According to the Mastakasvabhadra copperplate, Pradyumnabandhu Year 5. Ibid., p. 32.
49. B.N. Mukherjee, *Coins and Currency System of Early Bengal up to c. 300 A.D.*, Calcutta: Progressive Publishers, 2000, p. 15. More recently, see S.K. Bose and Noman Nasir, *Early Coins of Bengal (c. 2nd Century BC–10th Century AD)*, Kolkata: Mira Bose, 2016, p. 28.
50. D.C. Sircar, 'Coins in the Inscriptions of the Pālas and Senas in

Eastern India', *Journal of the Numismatic Society of India*, vol. 36, 1974, pp. 74-5.

51. B.D. Chattopadhyaya, 'Currency in Early Bengal', *Journal of Indian History*, vol. 55-5, 1977, pp. 41-60.
52. Ranabir Chakravarti, 'Early Medieval Bengal and the Trade in Horses: A Note', *Journal of the Economic and Social History of the Orient*, Leiden: Brill, vol. 42-2, 1999, pp. 197-8.
53. Sen notes that 'From the eighth century onwards, the maritime routes between India and China . . . became more popular than the overland routes.' He attributes this to disturbances in Central Asia, improvements in shipbuilding techniques and navigational understanding. Tansen Sen, *Buddhism, Diplomacy and Trade: The Realignment of Sino-Indian Relations 600-1400*, New Delhi: Manohar, 2003; rpt. 2004, p. 176.
54. Eusebius Renaudot, tr., *Ancient Accounts of India and China*, London: Harding, 1733, p. 7. A more recent translation is Gabriel Ferrand, tr., *Voyage du marchand arabe Sulaymân en Inde et en Chine, rédigé en 851, suivi de remarques par Abû Zayd Hasan (vers 916)*, Paris: Brossard, 1922, p. 38. A recent analysis is provided by Alain George, 'Direct Sea Trade Between Early Islamic Iraq and Tang China: From the Exchange of Goods to the Transmission of Ideas', *Journal of the Royal Asiatic Society*, Series 3, vol. 25-4, 2015, pp. 579-624.
55. Hermann Kulke, K. Kesavapany and Vijay Sakhuja, *Nagapattinam to Suvarnadwipa: Reflections on the Chola Naval Expeditions to Southeast Asia*, New Delhi: Manohar, 2010; Kenneth Hall, *Networks of Trade: Polity and Societal Integration in Chola-Era South India, c. 875-1400*, New Delhi: Primus, 2014.
56. Sen notes, '. . . the aggressive policies of the Yuan Court . . . (1260-1294) facilitated the creation of Chinese maritime networks to southern Asia, consisting of intertwined private trade, governmental and shipping segments. Consequently, for the first time in the history of India-China relations, court officials, traders and ships from China made recurrent trips to the coastal regions of India.' Tansen Sen, 'The Formation of Chinese Maritime Networks to Southern Asia, 1200-1450', *Journal of the Economic and Social History of the Orient*, vol. 49-4, 2006, p. 422. Marco Polo noted this in 1292: Henry Yule, tr. and ed., *The Book of Ser Marco Polo the Venetian, Concerning the Kingdoms and Marvels of the East*, vol. II, London: Murray, 1871, p. 312.
57. 'From the twelfth century or slightly later we have three segments:

the Arabian Sea, the Bay of Bengal, and the South China Sea. Chinese and Indians went to Melaka, Persians and Arabs only to India.' Michael Pearson, *The Indian Ocean,* London: Routledge, 2003; rpt. 2010, p. 88.

58. 'Since merchants and shippers often had to wait many months for the monsoon winds to shift before resuming their sailing, foreign merchants tended to settle in semi-permanent communities. Ethnically these enclaves were quite diverse, consisting of Gujaratis, Bengalis, Malays, Chinese, Persians and Arabs, though most tended to share a common religious identity as Muslims.' Richard M. Eaton, 'Multiple lenses: Differing Perspectives of Fifteenth-century Calicut', Ch. 3 in *Essays on Islam and Indian History*, New Delhi: Oxford, 2001, p. 79.
59. Genevieve Bouchon and Denys Lombard, 'The Indian Ocean in the Fifteenth Century', Ch. 3 in Ashin Das Gupta and Michael N. Pearson, *India and the Indian Ocean, 1500-1800*, Calcutta: Oxford, 1987, pp. 62-4.
60. '. . . the evidence of coins and chronicles, vocabulary and the place names, ethnology, travelling accounts clearly indicate the relation between Chittagong and the Arab ports as early as the eighth century . . .', S.B. Qanungo, *A History of Chittagong*, vol. I, Chittagong: Signet Library, 1988, p. 110.
61. Ibid., p. 111.
62. 'Letters and Documents on the India Trade in Medieval Times: A Preview', in Goitein and Friedman, *India Traders of the Middle Ages*, pp. 3-25.
63. Pius Malekandathil, *Maritime India: Trade, Religion and Polity in the Indian Ocean*, New Delhi: Primus, 2010; rpt. 2013, p. 44.
64. Richard von Glahn, 'Monies of Account and Monetary Transition in China, 12th-14th Centuries', *Journal of the Economic and Social History of the Orient*, vol. 53, 2010, pp. 463-505 examines both the Song and Yuan monetary systems in some depth.
65. Akinobu Kuroda, 'The Eurasian Silver Century, 1276-1359: Commensurability and Multiplicity', *Journal of Global History*, vol. 4, 2009, pp. 252-3.
66. William S. Attwell, 'Time, Money, and the Weather: Ming China and the "Great Depression" of the Mid-Fifteenth Century', *The Journal of Asian Studies*, vol. 61-1, February 2002, p. 86. Also Richard von Glahn, 'Chinese Coins and Changes in Monetary Preferences in Maritime East Asia in the Fifteenth-Seventeenth Centuries', *Journal*

*of the Economic and Social History of the Orient*, vol. 57, 2014, p. 630.
67. Stephen Album, 'Mamluk', in *Checklist of Islamic Coins*, Santa Rosa: The Author, 2011, pp. 111-16.
68. 'Rasulid', in ibid., pp. 123-4.
69. Mukherjee, *Pelagic Passageways*, p. 35.
70. Sen, 'The formation of Chinese Maritime Networks', p. 425.
71. Yule, *The Book of Ser Marco Polo.*
72. Husain, *The Rehla of Ibn Battuta.*
73. Ma Huan, *Ying-yai sheng-lan, 'The Overall Survey of the Ocean's Shores*, J.V.G. Mills, tr., Cambridge: Hakluyt Society, 1970.
74. 'The Travels of Nicolo Conti in the East in the Early Part of the Fifteenth Century', pt. 2 of R.H. Major, ed., *India in the Fifteenth Century, Being a Collection of Narratives of Voyages to India.* London: Hakluyt Society, 1858; rpt. Delhi: Asian Educational Services, 1992.
75. 'Narrative of the journey of Abd-er-Razzak', pt. 1 of R.H. Major, *India in the Fifteenth Century.*
76. Count Wielhorsky, 'The Travels of Athanasius Nikitin of Twer', pt. 3 of R.H. Major, *India in the Fifteenth Century.*
77. 'Account of the Journey of Hieronimo di Santo Stefano', pt. 4 of R.H. Major, *India in the Fifteenth Century.*
78. Armando Cortesao, ed., *The Suma Oriental of Tome Pires*, London: Hakluyt Society, 1944; rpt., Delhi: Asian Educational Services, 1992.
79. Yule, *The Book of Ser Marco Polo*, p. 332.
80. Ibid., p. 330.
81. Ibid., p. 425.
82. Ibid., pp. 188-9.
83. Ma Huan, Ying-yai sheng-lan, p. 130.
84. Ibid., p. 136.
85. Ibid., p. 141.
86. Major, 'Abd-er-Razzak', p. 26.
87. Major, 'Hieronimo di Santo Stefano', p. 9.
88. Yijing, *Da Tang Xiyu qiufa gaoseng zhuan*, Latika Lahiri, tr., *Chinese Monks in India: Biography of Eminent Monks Who Went to the Western World in Search of the Law during the Great Tang Dynasty*, Delhi: Motilal Banarsidass, 1986.
89. Renaudot, *Ancient Accounts of India and China.*
90. Bhagwant Sahai, 'The Nalanda Copper-Plate Inscription of Devapala', *The Inscriptions of Bihar*, Delhi: Ramanand Vidya Bhavan, 1983, p. 87.
91. Nicholas G. Rhodes, 'Trade in Southeast Bengal in the First Millennium', Wicks, *Money, Markets and Trade*, p. 302, Map 9.2.

92. Wicks, *Money, Markets and Trade*, p. 4. Kenneth Hall, 'Coinage, Trade and Economy in Early South India and its Southeast Asian Neighbours', *Indian Economic and Social History Review*, 36-4, 1999, p. 448.
93. Ibid., p. 4.
94. Ma Huan, *Ying-yai sheng-lan*, p. 159.
95. Ibid., p. 161.
96. Pranab K. Chattopadhyay, 'In Search of Silver: Southeast Asian Sources for the Coinage of Bengal', in Gouriswar Bhattacharya et al., eds., *Kalhar: Studies in Art, Iconography, Architecture and Archaeology of India and Bangladesh*, Delhi: Kaveri Books, 2007, pp. 296-305. John S. Deyell, 'The China Connection: Problems of Silver Supply in Medieval Bengal', in John F. Richards, ed., *Precious Metals in the Later Medieval and Early Modern Worlds*, Durham: Carolina Academic Press, 1983, pp. 207-27. Reprinted in Sanjay Subrahmanyam, ed., *Money and the Market in India 1100-1700*, New Delhi: Oxford University Press, 1994, pp. 112-36; idem, 'Sources of Silver', in 'Cowries and Coins: The Dual Monetary System of the Bengal Sultanate', *Indian Economic and Social History Review*, Delhi, vol. 47-1, January-March 2010, pp. 88-91, Bin Yang, 'The Bay of Bengal Connections to Yunnan', in Mukherjee (ed.), *Pelagic Passageways*, pp. 317-42.
97. Hall, 'Coinage Trade and Economy', pp. 449-50.
98. For example. von Glahn notes a collapse of silver production prior to the 1430s: Richard von Glahn, *Fountain of Fortune: Money and Monetary Policy in China, 1000-1700*, London: University of California, 1996, pp. 83, 113. Later the mines must have recovered; Bin Yang notes a doubling of silver mining taxes between 1458 and 1460: *Between Wind and Clouds: The Making of Yunnan (Second Century* BCE *to Twentieth Century* CE*)*, New York: Columbia University Press, 2009, p. 195.
99. Von Glahn, 'Monies of Account', pp. 463-505.
100. Ranabir Chakravarti, 'Early Medieval Bengal and the Trade in Horses: A Note', *Journal of the Economic and Social History of the Orient*, vol. 42-2, 1999, pp. 194-211. Also Syed Ejaz Hussain, 'Silver Flow and Horse Supply to Sultanate Bengal with Special Reference to Trans-Himalayan Horse Trade (13th-16th Centuries)', *Journal of the Economic and Social History of the Orient*, vol. 56, 2013, pp. 264-308.
101. Yunnan-India Road: Bin, *Between Wind and Clouds*, pp. 33-44, 45-9; Yunnan-Tibet Road, ibid., pp. 44-5. Yunnan-India horse trade:

ibid., pp. 49-54. For an overview, see idem., 'Rise and Fall of Cowrie Shells', pp. 326-9.

102. Chakravarti, 'Early Medieval Bengal', pp. 204-5. See also the *Ming Shu-Li,* for Yong-le Year 7, Month 10, Day 27 (3 December 1409): 'The envoy Xia-er-zhi-nei-mi-xu and others, a total of 59 persons who had been sent by Ai-ya-si-ding [Ghiyasuddin A'zam Shah], the king of the country of Bengal, and Zai-nu-li A-bi-ding Zainul Abidin], the king of the country of Samudera [Sumatra], offered tribute of horses and local products.' Record 697 of 3279, http://epress.nus.edu.sg/msl.
103. Yule, *The Book of Ser Marco Polo,* p. 201.
104. Ibid., pp. 235-41.
105. Najaf Haider, 'International Trade in Precious Metals and Monetary Systems of Medieval India: 1200-1500', *Proceedings of the Indian History Congress*, 59th Session, Patiala, 1998, pp. 244-6.
106. S. Goron and J.P. Goenka, *The Coins of the Indian Sultanates,* New Delhi: Munshiram Manoharlal, 2001, relevant geographic chapters.
107. William S. Atwell, 'Time, Money and the Weather: Ming China and the "Great Depression" of the Mid-Fifteenth Century', *The Journal of Asian Studies,* 61-1, 2002, p. 87.
108. Ibid., p. 90.
109. Malabar - all seven voyages; Aden - fourth through seventh voyages; Bengal - fifth through seventh voyages. J.V.G. Mills, 'Cheng Ho and his Expeditions', pt. 1 in Ma Huan, *Ying-yai sheng-lan*, pp. 5-33.
110. Haider, 'International trade', p. 239, citing Shihabuddin Abdullah Wassaf, *Tarikh-i-Wassaf,* Bombay, 1269 AH [AD 1852], vol. III, p. 300.
111. I wish to thank Kenneth Hall, Michael Aung-Thwin and John Whitmore for invaluable suggestions regarding this observation.

## BIBLIOGRAPHY

Abram, Nerilie J. et al., 'Seasonal Characteristics of the Indian Ocean Dipole during the Holocene Epoch' *Nature,* vol. 445, 18 January 2007, pp. 299-302.

———, 'Evolution of the Southern Annular Mode during the Past Millennium', *Nature Climate Change*, vol. 4, July 2014, pp. 564-9.

Attwell, William S., 'Time, Money, and the Weather: Ming China and the Great Depression of the Mid-Fifteenth Century', *The Journal of Asian Studies*, vol. 61-1, February 2002, pp. 83-113.

Bank of Canada, *Backgrounder: Money,* July 2012.

Beaujard, Philippe, *Les mondes de l'océan Indien*, Paris: Armand Colin, 2012.

Blanchard, Ian, 'The World of Islam: An Economic and Environmental Analysis', Ch. 3 in *Mining, Metallurgy and Minting,* Stuttgart: Steiner, 2001, pp. 37-102.

Bose, S.K. and Noman Nasir, *Early Coins of Bengal (c. 2nd Century BC-10th Century AD)*, Kolkata: Mira Bose, 2016.

Bouchon, Genevieve and Denys Lombard, 'The Indian Ocean in the Fifteenth Century', Ch. 3 in Ashin Das Gupta and Michael N. Pearson, *India and the Indian Ocean, 1500-1800*, Calcutta: Oxford University Press, 1987, pp. 46-70.

Chakravarti, Ranabir, *Exploring Early India up to c. AD 1300,* New Delhi: Macmillan, 2010.

———, 'Trade at Mandapikas in Early Medieval North India', in D.N. Jha (ed.), *Society and Ideology in India: Essays in Honour of Professor R.S. Sharma,* New Delhi: Munshiram Manoharlal, 2006. Reprinted in Ranabir Chakravarti, *Trade and Traders in Early Indian Society*, New Delhi: Manohar, 2002, rpt. 2007.

———, 'Early Medieval Bengal and the Trade in Horses: A Note', *Journal of the Economic and Social History of the Orient*, Leiden: Brill, vol. 42-2, 1999, pp. 194-211.

Chattopadhyay, Pranab K., 'In Search of Silver: Southeast Asian Sources for the Coinage of Bengal', in Gouriswar Bhattacharya et al., eds., *Kalhar: Studies in Art, Iconography, Architecture and Archaeology of India and Bangladesh*, Delhi: Kaveri Books, 2007, pp. 296-305.

Chattopadhyaya, B.D., 'Currency in Early Bengal', *Journal of Indian History,* vol. 55-5, 1977, pp. 41-60.

Chiu, Jonathon and Tsz-Nga Wong, 'On the Essentiality of E-Money', Bank of Canada Staff Working Paper 2015-43.

Cortesao, Armando, ed., *The Suma Oriental of Tome Pires*, London: Hakluyt Society, 1944, rpt., Delhi: AES, 1992.

Cribb, Joe, 'Money as Metaphor I (the Origins of Money and Coinage)', *Numismatic Chronicle,* vol. 165, pp. 417-38.

———,'The Origins of Money, Evidence from the Ancient Near East and Egypt', in Guido Crapanzano (ed.), *La Banca Premonitale*, Milan: 2004.

———, *The Indian Coinage Tradition: Origins, Continuity and Change.* Nashik: IIRNS Publications, 2005.

Cunningham, Alexander, *Coins of Medieval India*, London: Trubner & Co., 1894.

Dale, Gareth, '"Marketless Trading in Hammurabi's Time": A Re-appraisal', *Journal of the Economic and Social History of the Orient*, vol. 56, 2013, pp. 159-88.

Davies, Glyn, *A History of Money from Ancient Times to the Present Day*. Cardiff: University of Wales Press, 2006.

Deyell, John S., *Living Without Silver: The Monetary History of Early Medieval North India*, New Delhi: Oxford University Press, 1990; rpt. 1999

________, 'Monetary and Financial Webs: The Regional and International Influence of Pre-modern Bengali Coinage', in Rila Mukherjee (ed.), *Pelagic Passageways: The Northern Bay of Bengal World Before Colonialism*, New Delhi: Primus, 2011.

________, 'The China Connection: Problems of Silver Supply in Medieval Bengal', in John F. Richards (ed.), *Precious Metals in the Later Medieval and Early Modern Worlds*, Durham: Carolina Academic Press, 1983, pp. 207-27. Reprinted in Sanjay Subrahmanyam, ed., *Money and the Market in India 1100-1700*, New Delhi: Oxford University Press, 1994, pp. 112-36.

________, 'Cowries and Coins: The Dual Monetary System of the Bengal Sultanate', *Indian Economic and Social History Review*, Delhi, vol. 47-1, January-March 2010, pp. 63-106.

Eaton, Richard M., 'Multiple Lenses: Differing Perspectives of Fifteenth-Century Calicut', Ch. 3 in *Essays on Islam and Indian History*, New Delhi: Oxford University Press, 2001.

Faxien (Fa-Hsien), *A Record of Buddhistic Kingdoms*, James Legge, tr., Oxford: Clarendon Press, 1886.

________, *Record of the Buddhist Kingdoms*, Herbert A. Giles, tr., London: Trübner & Co., 1877.

Ferguson, Neill, *The Ascent of Money*, New York: Penguin, 2008.

Ferrand, Gabriel, tr., *Voyage du marchand arabe Sulaymân en Inde et en Chine, rédigé en 851, suivi de remarques par Abû Zayd Hasan (vers 916)*, Paris: Brossard, 1922.

Garg, Sanjay, 'Non-metallic Currencies of India in Indian Ocean Trade and Economies', in Himanshu Prabha Ray and Edward A. Alpers, eds., *Cross Currents and Community Networks: The History of the Indian Ocean World*, New Delhi: Oxford University Press, 2007, pp. 245-62.

George, Alain, 'Direct Sea Trade Between Early Islamic Iraq and Tang

China: From the Exchange of Goods to the Transmission of Ideas', *Journal of the Royal Asiatic Society*, Series 3, vol. 25-4, 2015, pp. 579-624.

Goitein, S.D. and M.A. Friedman, *India Traders of the Middle Ages: Documents from the Cairo Geniza*, Leiden: Brill, 2008, rpt. 2011.

Goron, S. and J.P. Goenka, *The Coins of the Indian Sultanates*, New Delhi: Munshiram Manoharlal, 2001.

Graeber, David, *Debt: The First 5,000 Years*. Brooklyn: Melville House, 2011.

Griffiths, Arlo, 'New Documents for the Early History of Pundravardhana: Copperplate Inscriptions from the Late Gupta and Early Post-Gupta Periods', *Pratna Samiksha: A Journal of Archaeology*, New Series, vol. 6, 2016.

Gupta, Parmeshwari Lal, *Coins*, New Delhi: National Book Trust, 1969 (numerous reprints to 2016).

Gupta, P.L. and T.R. Hardaker, *Punchmarked Coins of the Indian Subcontinent: Magadha-Mauryan Series*, revd. edn., Mumbai: IIRNS Publications, 2014.

Haider, Najaf, 'International Trade in Precious Metals and Monetary Systems of Medieval India: 1200-1500', *Proceedings of the Indian History Congress*, 59th Session, Patiala, 1998, pp. 237-54.

Hall, Kenneth, *Networks of Trade, Polity and Societal Integration in Chola-Era South India, c. 875-1400*, New Delhi: Primus, 2014.

———, 'Coinage Trade and Economy in Early South India and its Southeast Asian Neighbours', *Indian Economic and Social History Review*, vol. 36-4, 1999, pp. 431-59.

Hogendorn, Jan and Marion Johnson, *The Shell Money of the Slave Trade*, Cambridge: Cambridge University Press, 1986.

Husain, Mahdi, tr., *The Rehla of Ibn Batuta*. Baroda: Oriental Institute, 1976.

Hussain, Syed Ejaz, 'Silver Flow and Horse Supply to Sultanate Bengal with Special Reference to Trans-Himalayan Horse Trade (13th-16th Centuries)', *Journal of the Economic and Social History of the Orient*, vol. 56, 2013, pp. 264-308.

Kautilya, *Arthashastra*, tr. R. Shamasastry, Bangalore: Government Press, 1915.

Kosambi, D.D., 'On the Origin and Development of Silver Coinage in India', *Current Science*, no. 9, September 1941, pp. 395-400, reprinted in D.D. Kosambi, *Indian Numismatics*, New Delhi: Orient Longman, 1981, pp. 85-94.

Kulke, Hermann, K. Kesavapany and Vijay Sakhuja, *Nagapattinam to Suvarnadwipa: Reflections on the Chola Naval Expeditions to Southeast Asia*, New Delhi: Manohar, 2010.

Kurke, Leslie, *Coins, Bodies, Games and Gold: The Politics of Meaning in Archaic Greece*, Princeton: Princeton University Press, 1999.

Kuroda, Akinobu, 'The Eurasian Silver Century, 1276-1359 – Commensurability and Multiplicity', *Journal of Global History*, vol. 4, 2009, pp. 245-69.

Law, Randall, *Inter-Regional Interaction and Urbanism in the Ancient Indus Valley*, Kyoto: Research Institute for Humanity and Nature, 2011.

Li Chongyin, 'The Influence of the Indian Ocean Dipole on Atmospheric Circulation and Climate', *Advances in Atmospheric Sciences*, vol. 18-5, September 2001, pp. 831-43.

Ma Huan, *Ying-yai sheng-lan, 'The Overall Survey of the Ocean's Shores*, tr. J.V.G. Mills, Cambridge: Hakluyt Society, 1970.

Maheshwari, K.K., *Imitations in Continuity: Tracking the Silver Coinage of Early Medieval India*, Mumbai: IIRNS Publications, 2010.

Major, R.H., ed., 'The Travels of Nicolo Conti in the East in the Early Part of the Fifteenth Century', pt. 2 of *India in the Fifteenth Century, Being a Collection of Narratives of Voyages to India*, London: Hakluyt Society, 1858; rpt. Delhi: AES, 1992.

Major, R.H., ed., 'Narrative of the Journey of Abd-er-Razzak', pt. 1 of *India in the Fifteenth Century*.

________, Count Wielhorsky, 'The Travels of Athanasius Nikitin of Twer', pt. 3 of *India in the Fifteenth Century*.

________, 'Account of the Journey of Hieronimo di Santo Stefano', pt. 4 of *India in the Fifteenth Century*.

Majumdar, Susmita Basu and Sharmishtha Chatterjee, 'Cowries in Eastern India: Understanding Their Role as Ritual Objects and Money', *Journal of Bengal Art*, vol. 19, 2014, pp. 39-56.

Malekandathil, Pius, *Maritime India: Trade, Religion and Polity in the Indian Ocean*, New Delhi: Primus, 2010; rpt. 2013.

Mukherjee, B.N., *Coins and Currency Systems of Post-Gupta Bengal (c. AD 550-700)*, New Delhi: Munshiram Manoharlal, 1995.

———, *Coins and Currency System of Early Bengal up to c. 300 AD*, Calcutta: Progressive Publishers, 2000.

Nanda, Rajni, *The Early History of Gold in India*, New Delhi: Munshiram Manoharlal, 1992.

Pearson, Michael, *The Indian Ocean*, London: Routledge, 2003; rpt. 2010.

Qanungo, S.B., *A History of Chittagong*, vol. I, Chittagong: Signet Library, 1988.

Ray, S.C., 'Medium of Exchange in Ancient Kasmira: A Reflection of Contemporary Economic Life', *Journal of the Numismatic Society of India*, vol. XVIII, 1956, pp. 71-5.

Renaudot, Eusebius (tr.), *Ancient accounts of India and China*, London: Harding, 1733.

Rhodes, Nicholas G., 'Trade in Southeast Bengal in the First Millennium CE: The Numismatic Evidence', in Rila Mukherjee (ed.), *Pelagic Passageways: The Northern Bay of Bengal before Colonialism*, New Delhi: Primus Books, 2011, pp. 263-75.

Sahai, Bhagwant, 'The Nalanda Copper-Plate Inscription of Devapala', *The Inscriptions of Bihar*, Delhi: Ramanand Vidya Bhavan, 1983, p. 87.

Sargent, Thomas J. and François R. Velde, *The Big Problem of Small Change*, Princeton: Princeton University Press, 2002.

Sen, Tansen, *Buddhism, Diplomacy and Trade: The Realignment of Sino-Indian Relations 600-1400*, New Delhi: Manohar, 2003, rpt. 2004.

———, 'The Formation of Chinese Maritime Networks to Southern Asia, 1200-1450', *Journal of the Economic and Social History of the Orient*, vol. 49-4, 2006, p. 421-53.

Sharma, R.S., *Early Medieval Indian Society: A Study in Feudalism*, New Delhi: Orient Longman, 2003.

Sircar, D.C., 'Coins in the Inscriptions of the Pālas and Senas in Eastern India', *Journal of the Numismatic Society of India*, vol. 36, 1974, pp. 71-6.

Stein, Aurel (ed.), Kalhana's *Rājataranginī*, London: Constable, 1900.

Thapar, Romila , *Early India from the Origins to AD 1300*, Delhi: Penguin Books, 2003.

Tye, Robert ,'Gyges' Magic Ring? The Origin of Coinages and Open Societies', pamphlet published by the author, York, 2013. Available on www.academia.edu

von Glahn, Richard, *The Economic History of China: From Antiquity to the Nineteenth Century*, Cambridge: Cambridge University Press, 2016.

———, 'Monies of Account and Monetary Transition in China, twelfth-fourteenth Centuries', *Journal of the Economic and Social History of the Orient*, vol. 53, 2010, pp. 463-505.

———, 'Chinese Coin and Changes in Monetary Preferences in Maritime East Asia in the Fifteenth-Seventeenth Centuries', *Journal of the Economic and Social History of the Orient*, vol. 57, 2014, pp. 629-68.

_______, *Fountain of Fortune: Money and Monetary Policy in China, 1000-1700*, London: University of California, 1996.

von Mises, Ludwig, *The Theory of Money and Credit*, Indianapolis: Liberty Fund, 1980.

Wade, Geoff (tr. & ed.), *Ming Shu-Li*, http://epress.nus.edu.sg/msl.

Weatherford, Jack, *The History of Money*, New York: Crown Publishers, 1997.

Wicks, Robert S., *Money, Markets and Trade in Early Southeast Asia: The Development of Indigenous Monetary Systems to AD 1400*, Ithaca: Cornell University, 1992.

Yang, Bin, 'The Rise and Fall of Cowrie Shells: The Asian Story', *Journal of World History*, vol. 22-1, March 2011, pp. 1-26.

_______, 'The Bay of Bengal Connections to Yunnan', in Mukherjee, *Pelagic Passageways*, pp. 317-42.

_______, *Between Wind and Clouds: The Making of Yunnan (Second Century BCE to Twentieth Century CE)*, New York: Columbia University Press, 2009.

Yijing, *Da Tang Xiyu qiufa gaoseng zhuan*, tr. Latika Lahiri, *Chinese Monks in India: Biography of Eminent Monks Who Went to the Western World in Search of the Law during the Great Tang Dynasty*. Delhi: Motilal Banarsidass, 1986.

Yule, Henry (tr. & ed.), *The Book of Ser Marco Polo the Venetian, Concerning the Kingdoms and Marvels of the East*, vol. II, London: Murray, 1871.

# Contributors

JOHN DEYELL is an independent researcher originally from the University of Wisconsin, Madison. A former visiting Professor of the Centre for Historical Studies of the Jawaharlal Nehru University, New Delhi, he writes on the pre-modern monetary systems of the Indian Ocean world. His most recent book is *Treasure, Trade and Tradition: Post-Kidarite Coins of the Gangetic Plains and Punjab Hills* (2017).

SUCHANDRA GHOSH is Professor and former Head of the Department of Ancient Indian History and Culture at the University of Calcutta in Kolkata. She takes broad interest in the politico-cultural history of northwest India, early India's linkages with Southeast Asia, and the Indian Ocean Buddhist and trade network. She has co-edited a number of scholarly books, and her most recent is *From the Oxus to the Indus: A Political and Cultural Study, c. 300 BCE to c. 100 BCE* (2017).

RILA MUKHERJEE is Professor and former Head of the Department of History, School of Social Science, University of Hyderabad. The former Director of the Institut de Chandernagor, she is currently Chief Editor of the *Asian Review of World Histories*, and Series Editor of Cambridge's *Pasts and Futures*. She has edited an extensive corpus of scholarly books, most recently *Living with Water: Peoples, Lives, and Livelihoods in Asia and Beyond* (2017).

SAYANTANI PAL is Associate Professor of the Department of Ancient Indian History and Culture at the University of Calcutta, Kolkata. Her area of interest is early medieval Bengal, and she has published a number of articles on land grants.

M.N. RAJESH is Assistant Professor of the Department of History, University of Hyderabad. His special interests include medieval

Indian history, socio-religious movements in South India and the Deccan, and Tibetan history and culture.

Radhika Seshan is Professor and Head of the Department of History, Savitribai Phule University, Pune. The author of several scholarly books and numerous contributions to learned journals and anthologies, her most recent book, *Trade and Politics on the Coromandel Coast, Seventeenth and Early Eighteenth Centuries*, has recently been reissued in paperback.

Sutapa Sinha is Professor and Head of the Department of Islamic History and Culture, University of Calcutta, Kolkata. A Fellow of the Royal Numismatic Society, she is well-known for her numerous research notes on medieval Indian numismatics and coins. Her most recent book, *Coin Hoards of the Bengal Sultans 1205-1576* AD, was released in 2017.

Bin Yang is Associate Professor, Department of History, University of Macau. Formerly Associate Professor at the National University of Singapore, he authored a string of journal contributions exploring the interaction of economic and social factors in Southwest China. He has written extensively on Yunnan's connections with the Indian Ocean world, most notably his book *Between Wind and Clouds, the Making of Yunnan* (2008).

# Index

For Product Safety Concerns and Information please contact our EU representative GPSR@taylorandfrancis.com Taylor & Francis Verlag GmbH, Kaufingerstraße 24, 80331 München, Germany

Printed and bound by CPI Group (UK) Ltd, Croydon, CR0 4YY
08/05/2025
01864358-0001